D0073334

W. H. AUDEN

Juvenilia

W. H. AUDEN

———

Juvenilia

———

POEMS

1922–1928

EDITED BY

Katherine Bucknell

PRINCETON UNIVERSITY
PRESS

Library of Congress Cataloging-in-Publication Data
Auden, W. H. (Wystan Hugh), 1907–1973.
Juvenilia: poems, 1922–1928 / W. H. Auden; edited by
Katherine Bucknell
p. cm.
Includes bibliographical references and indexes.
ISBN 0-691-03415-X (alk. paper)
I. Bucknell, Katherine. II. Title.
PR6001.U4J88 1994
811'.52—dc20   93-35485

This book has been composed in Baskerville

Princeton University Press books are printed on
acid-free paper and meet the guidelines for permanence
and durability of the Committee on Production
Guidelines for Book Longevity of the
Council on Library Resources

Printed in the United States of America

2   4   6   8   10   9   7   5   3   1

CONTENTS

APPENDIX

INDEX

ACKNOWLEDGEMENTS

Individuals and libraries have generously allowed me to pore over poems and letters in their possession and to include them in this volume. I wish to thank Edward Mendelson and The Estate of W. H. Auden for allowing me to publish all material by Auden and for helping me gain access to it; the late John Auden for permission to publish letters in his possession and for ransacking his memory about days long past; Don Bachardy for his attentive welcome and for his permission to publish materials once belonging to Christopher Isherwood and now in his possession; the Henry W. and Albert A. Berg Collection of English and American Literature, the New York Public Library (Astor, Lenox, and Tilden Foundations), for permission to publish materials in its collection, and Stephen Crook and Philip Milito for their assistance; the Bodleian Library, Oxford, for permission to publish poems and letters in the Dodds Bequest; the British Library for permission to publish manuscripts and letters once belonging to Edward Upward and William McElwee, the staff at the Reading Room Enquiries Desk, especially Alison Bailey, Beverley Kemp, and Gillian Ridgely, for guiding me repeatedly to useful shelf-marks, Toni Everett of the Map Library, and Sally Brown, Curator of Modern Literary Manuscripts, for fishing uncatalogued materials out of skips so I could see them; the Poetry/Rare Books Collection, State University of New York at Buffalo, for permission to print a poem in its collection, and Robert J. Bertholf, Curator, for his help with the manuscript; the Governing Body of Christ Church, Oxford, for permission to publish poems and letters once belonging to A. S. T. Fisher, and J. Wing, Librarian, for his repeated assistance; the Literary Trustees of Walter de la Mare and the Society of Authors as their representative for permission to publish an extract from de la Mare's 'Sleepyhead'; Henry Holt and Company, Inc., for permission to reprint 'The Pasture' by Robert Frost; the Houghton Library, Harvard University, for permission to publish variants from a manuscript in its collection, and Jennie Rathbun for her help with this; the Library of King's College, Cambridge, for permission to quote from a letter in its collection, and Peter Jones, Librarian, for his generous help with other materials in the library; the College of St Mark and St John, Plymouth, for permission to publish poems in its collection, and D. S. Nicholson, Bursar, for his scrupulous attention to my enquiries; the Harry Ransom Humanities Research Center, University of Texas at Austin, for permission to publish poems in its possession, and Heather Moore, HRHRC Intern, for her dogged and careful research on my behalf; the late James Stern and Tania Stern for permission to quote from a letter in her possession; and Barbara Walters for permission to print variants from a poem once belonging to her father, David Ayerst, and now in her possession.

Numerous other people have also greeted my questions with gracious replies and furthered my research: Dr Ian Aitchison, Worcester College, Oxford; Sam Arnold-Forster; B. C. Bloomfield; Thomas Braun, Merton College, Oxford; Logie Bruce-Lockhart, former Headmaster, the Gresham's School, Holt; Humphrey Carpenter; Joyce Caruso; James Cummins, Curator, Elliston Poetry Collection, University of Cincinnati; Debbie Daniel; Peter Dickinson, Goldsmith's College, University of London; the Headmaster and staff of St Edmund's School, Hindhead, Surrey; H.R.H. Princess Sumaya el Hassan; A. R. A. Hobson; the Reverend Phillip Jefferies, St John's Church, Horninglow; Elizabeth Kennington; John Lanchester; David Luke, Christ Church, Oxford; Bobby Maguire; G. E. B. Maguire; J. R. Maguire; Robert Medley; Sir James Richards; Joel Silver, the Lilly Library, Indiana University; Janet Adam Smith; Edward Wilson, Worcester College, Oxford; and Robert A. Wilson. I am grateful to Columbia University and to Worcester College, Oxford, for fellowships which helped me start on this edition.

I would also like to thank Gabriel Carritt for showing me his Auden manuscripts and sharing his recollections; Sir Stephen Spender for his useful and important comments on a typescript of this book; and Edward Upward for his numerous extremely helpful letters and his delightful conversation. Others who helped generously by reading and commenting on the typescript or parts of it include Lucy Bucknell, Richard Davenport-Hines, Samuel Hynes, Mick Imlah, James Thackara, and John Whitehead. At Faber and Faber, John Bodley gave me sympathetic encouragement, and Christopher Reid and Stephen Stuart-Smith offered many constructive suggestions. At Princeton University Press, Robert Brown, Beth Gianfagna, and Jane Lincoln Taylor were diligent and sharp-eyed guides; Jan Lilly brought steady resourcefulness to designing the text. Anita Money has contributed enthusiastically to research for this volume, and I offer special thanks to her, to Rita Auden, and to Sheila Auden. For enabling me to shut my study door, I wish to thank Susan Wright, Karin Cooper, Felisbertha Rodrigues, Anne-Marie Butler, and especially Sally Mace and Sally Whitaker. My husband, Bob Maguire, has been ceaselessly patient and encouraging, and I am grateful for his wisdom, his good nature, and his sense of comedy.

The notes to this edition can barely suggest my indebtedness to the many poets and scholars who have edited and written about Auden's poetry before me, and to a few who are at it even as I write this. Three in particular have helped me so much and so often that no thanks I can offer here is adequate. John Fuller, Nicholas Jenkins, and Edward Mendelson have added immeasurably to the interest and satisfaction of working on Auden's earliest poems, and if the poems were mine to dedicate, I would dedicate this volume to them.

ABBREVIATIONS

WORKS BY AND EDITED BY AUDEN

CP   *Collected Poems*, ed. Edward Mendelson (London, 1991; New York, 1991).

DH   *The Dyer's Hand* (New York, 1962; London, 1963).

EA   *The English Auden: Poems, Essays, and Dramatic Writings, 1927–1939*, ed. Edward Mendelson (London, 1977; New York, 1978).

FA   *Forewords and Afterwords*, selected by Edward Mendelson (New York, 1973; London, 1973).

OBLV   *The Oxford Book of Light Verse*, ed. W. H. Auden (Oxford, 1938).

P(28)   *Poems* (London, 1928).

P(30)   *Poems* (London, 1930).

Plays   *Plays and Other Dramatic Writings, 1928–1938*, with Christopher Isherwood, ed. Edward Mendelson (Princeton, 1988; London, 1989).

MANUSCRIPT COLLECTIONS AND LOCATIONS

AA   Alan Ansen ledger notebook, Berg.

CAF   Constance Auden, loose folios, Bodleian, MS.Eng.Poet. c.68 (Dodds Bequest).

CAN   Constance Auden, notebook, Bodleian, MS.Eng.Poet. e.153 (Dodds Bequest).

CI   Christopher Isherwood, private collection, Santa Monica, Calif.

D   Michael Davidson, Fisher Collection, Christ Church Library, Oxford.

DL   Cecil Day-Lewis, HRHRC.

F   A. S. T. Fisher, Christ Church Library, Oxford.

M   William McElwee, British Library, Add.MS.59618.

P(B)   John Pudney, Berg.

P(M)   John Pudney, the College of St Mark and St John, Plymouth.

S   Stephen Spender, Berg.

U   Edward Upward, British Library.

DESCRIPTIONS OF CORRESPONDENCE

AL	Autograph Letter.
ALI	Autograph Letter Initialled.
ALS	Autograph Letter Signed.
AN	Autograph Note.
ANI	Autograph Note Initialled.
ANS	Autograph Note Signed.
AP	Autograph Postcard.
API	Autograph Postcard Initialled.
APS	Autograph Postcard Signed.
TL	Typed Letter.
TLS	Typed Letter Signed.

OTHER ABBREVIATIONS

AS1	*Auden Studies 1, 'The Map of All My Youth'*, ed. Katherine Bucknell and Nicholas Jenkins (Oxford, 1990).
'Auden's Juvenilia'	A. S. T. Fisher, 'Auden's Juvenilia', *Notes and Queries*, n.s. 21, no. 10 (October 1974): 370–73.
Berg	The Henry W. and Albert A. Berg Collection of English and American Literature, the New York Public Library (Astor, Lenox, and Tilden Foundations).
Bibliography	B. C. Bloomfield and Edward Mendelson, *W. H. Auden: A Bibliography, 1924–1969*, 2nd edn (Charlottesville, Va., 1972).
Bodleian	The Bodleian Library, Oxford.
Carpenter	Humphrey Carpenter, *W. H. Auden: A Biography* (London, 1981; New York, 1981).
Early Auden	Edward Mendelson, *Early Auden* (New York, 1981; London, 1981).
Fuller	John Fuller, *A Reader's Guide to W. H. Auden* (London, 1970; New York, 1970).
HRHRC	The Harry Ransom Humanities Research Center, University of Texas at Austin.
Lawlor	*W. H. Auden: Poems 1927–1929: A Photographic and Typographic Facsimile of the Original Notebook in the Berg Collection of English and American Literature in the New York Public Library*, ed. Patrick Lawlor (New York, 1985).
Lions and Shadows	Christopher Isherwood, *Lions and Shadows* (London, 1938).

Mackinnon   Lachlan Mackinnon, *Eliot, Auden, Lowell: Aspects of the
                   Baudelairean Inheritance* (London, 1983).
Medley   Robert Medley, *Drawn from the Life: A Memoir* (London,
                   1981).
'Some Notes on   Christopher Isherwood, 'Some Notes on Auden's Early
   Auden's Early   Poetry', *New Verse* 26–27 (November 1937): 4–8.
   Poetry'
Tribute   Stephen Spender, ed., *W. H. Auden: A Tribute* (London,
                   1974; New York, 1974).
The World,   Michael Davidson, *The World, the Flesh, and Myself* (Lon-
   the Flesh,   don, 1962).
   and Myself

INTRODUCTION

In 1922, as a fifteen-year-old schoolboy, W. H. Auden decided to become a poet. In 1928, recently graduated from university, he produced his first volume of verse. The 1928 volume *Poems*, hand-printed by his friend Stephen Spender, is the work of an accomplished, technically versatile poet whose lyricism is ballasted already by a weighty tone of authority. Auden was not yet twenty-two.

During the six years of his apprenticeship, from 1922 to 1928, Auden wrote more than two hundred poems. All of them that are known to survive are printed in this edition. He worked intensively at his writing, and his approach was from the outset both eclectic and disciplined. He looked for examples everywhere and imitated everything he liked. He ransacked the school library, his father's library, the Christ Church library; was given books by friends; borrowed books from friends; and became such a buyer of books that he went down from Oxford owing £50 at Blackwell's—by his own recollection his only debt.[1] His experiences usually served as the subject of his earliest work, but Auden was precociously interested in form and style, and occasionally he borrowed or faked the emotions about which he wrote; to the very young poet they sometimes seemed secondary to the fascination of perfecting the poem as a verbal object.

Auden's brilliance as an apprentice poet lay in his talent for imitation. He fell in love with his most important models and identified with them completely; indeed, for a time he effectively *became* the poet he was imitating, and shaped his young gift in the features of someone else's mature poetic personality. In later years, Auden was to draw on the terminology of psychoanalysis to describe this as acquiring a 'literary transference',[2] although he did not much notice that he did it over and over again. When, eventually, he moved on to a new model,

---

[1] 'As It Seemed to Us', review of Evelyn Waugh, *A Little Learning*, and Leonard Woolf, *Beginning Again*, *The New Yorker*, 3 April 1965, reprinted in *FA*, 516.

[2] See 'A Literary Transference', *The Southern Review* 6, no. 1 (Summer 1940): 78–86, reprinted in *Hardy: A Collection of Critical Essays*, ed. Albert Guerard (Englewood Cliffs, N.J., 1963), 135–42, and 'Making, Knowing, and Judging' (1956), where Auden says that the apprentice poet 'has to pretend to be somebody else; he has to get a literary transference upon some poet in particular'; *DH*, 37.

he took the old one with him as a permanent aspect of his creative imagination. Thus he developed by means of a series of obsessions that continually transformed and enlarged his poetic personality. The process enabled him to assimilate the resources of poetic tradition and prepared him to write as if he were giving new voice to the whole history of English literature. Throughout his adult career he was to draw on the writing of the past and of the present, continually discovering fresh aspects of the past and also of new contemporary writing. He did not confine himself to poetry for his models, but assimilated whatever he found to be the best and most useful in all kinds of writing, from fiction to philosophy, from psychology to the history of religion. In 1942 Auden wrote to Stephen Spender, 'You (at least I fancy so) can be jealous of someone else writing a good poem because it seems a rival strength. I'm not, because every good poem, of yours say, is a strength, which is put at my disposal'.[3] Other people's poetry was there for him to use; indeed, as a young man he apparently felt an obligation to use it. He told Spender that the differences in their attitudes arose because Spender was strong and he was weak; but Auden's was a fertile weakness.

It was not until the second half of 1926 that Auden came across T. S. Eliot's 1919 essay 'Tradition and the Individual Talent', but its argument must have struck him forcibly, for he had already begun to do by instinct what Eliot prescribes for all serious young poets. He had been labouring to acquire the historical sense which would enable him to write with a consciousness of tradition. After discovering Eliot's essay he redoubled his efforts with newly focused self-awareness. A year later he was still repeating Eliot's advice to others. In the summer of 1927 he wrote to his brother, John, 'In general I think you want to absorb a tradition . . . the only thing which can hold you up in expression is just a lack of the tradition',[4] and in another letter to John that year, 'I don't think it can be stressed too strongly, that a writer must undergo a strenuous discipline, and that he must cohere and continue in a tradition'.[5] The words are almost Eliot's own. By apprenticing himself to tradition, Auden was preparing to put it to his own use and thus to alter its future.

[3] 'Eleven Letters from Auden to Stephen Spender', ed. Nicholas Jenkins, *AS1*, 82.
[4] ALS, Hotel Esplanade, Zagreb, Croatia, [late July 1927].
[5] ALS, Christ Church, [June? or more likely December? 1927].

AUDEN might have known some of his first poetic models from his childhood reading and from his studies later at school. He seems to have come across many in anthologies. While at Gresham's he was given Walter de la Mare's *Come Hither!*,[6] and he also read in the school library several volumes of Edward Marsh's *Georgian Poetry*.[7] Thus, he tried his hand at Wordsworth, Keats, A.E., de la Mare, W. H. Davies, and others—perhaps on occasion as tasks set in the classroom. Many of his first poems uphold his later assertion that a beginner's efforts are 'an imitation of poetry-in-general,'[8] but in others a particular model is clearly recognizable. A few give the impression that he sat writing with a book of someone else's poems open in front of him. In fact, however, during this early period Auden usually took several months to absorb the work of a new poet before any stylistic influence appeared in his own poems. Poets such as Keats, de la Mare, and W. H. Davies, all of whom Auden was reading in 1922, are most clearly reflected in his work during 1923; and although he later recalled immersing himself in Hardy starting in the summer of 1923, Hardy's influence is most evident in poems Auden wrote during 1924. Auden discovered Edward Thomas in the autumn of 1924, yet Thomas shaped his work most tellingly in 1925.

But as Auden developed poetically, this process of assimilation

[6] See 'Making, Knowing, and Judging', *DH*, 36, where Auden says he received the book one Christmas. *Come Hither! A Collection of Rhymes and Poems for the Young of All Ages* was published in November 1923 by Constable and Co., so Auden would probably have received it for Christmas that year. By then, he had already discovered de la Mare's poetry himself (perhaps with the help of his friend Michael Davidson, who sent him numerous newly published books), for in October 1923, he wrote to his parents that he was sending them a volume of de la Mare with his favourite poems marked (ALS, Farfield, Holt, with CAF). De la Mare published a great many books in the early 1920s; possibly the volume Auden sent was *Songs of Childhood*, a selection that first appeared in 1902 and was reissued numerous times, including October 1923; otherwise it may have been *Down-ADown-Derry: A Book of Faery Poems* (1922); both volumes include many of the poems with which Auden appears to have been familiar. (A two-volume collected poems, *Poems 1901–1918*, appeared in 1920, but Auden's letter mentions only one volume.) Auden's sending his volume of de la Mare to his parents may have meant that he himself had begun to lose interest in it; the date when this occurred is important, as he later recalled that he had discovered Hardy in the summer of 1923 and read no other poetry for nearly a year. See below, p. xxxii.

[7] See W. H. Auden, 'A Poet of Honour', *The Mid-Century* 28 (July 1961): 3–9. *Georgian Poetry* appeared in five volumes covering the years 1913–22 and was published between 1915 and 1922. Auden appears to have been familiar with only some of the volumes.

[8] 'Making, Knowing, and Judging', *DH*, 36.

accelerated. Only weeks after he first read T. S. Eliot, signs of the encounter began to appear in Auden's work, and a full transformation followed in just a few months. His discovery in the spring of 1927 of the later Yeats—who had reinvented himself in the new style of the poems eventually collected in *The Tower* (1928)—brought even more rapid change. Nevertheless, the influence of these and other poets lingered long after Auden ceased to read and consciously imitate them.

One of the most striking features of Auden's juvenilia is the way in which the simple charm of his early pieces, many on natural themes, is repeatedly darkened by his apparent fear that his imaginative powers are somehow damaged or inadequate. He made technical progress with evident ease, yet the same poets he imitated and from whom he sought to learn his craft filled him with doubt about his worth as a poet. In the Wordsworthian 'California' the poet is too 'poor' to approach the moon which hangs invitingly at the end of an uphill track; in 'After Reading Keats' Ode' he fears to listen for the nightingale in case her song will not sound so beautiful to him as it did to Keats; in 'A Tale' he will not dance with a de-la-Mareish fairy because adult reason does not believe she exists, yet when the fairy weeps and abandons him he feels ashamed. The Romantic and post-Romantic poets on whom Auden first modelled his work seemed to him to have special powers enabling them to grasp the moon, to hear from the viewless wings of poesy the song of the nightingale, to see elves and fairies; Auden felt in himself the lack of their visionary imagination. At fifteen, he was already losing his faith in God; he was scientifically oriented and rational-minded, which should have made it easy for him to decide that magic, fairies, elves, and visionary experiences did not belong in his poetry. Indeed, he was to say years later that even as a child he had instinctively excluded magic from his games.[9] As an adolescent poet he was looking for some other theme.

Nevertheless, just as his abandoned Christian convictions continued to influence him throughout the 1920s and 1930s (until they began to re-emerge in about 1940), so too a hidden longing for poetic vision of the sort possessed by the Romantic and late-Romantic poets he professed to scorn played a significant part in the course of his

---

[9] See 'As It Seemed to Us', *FA*, 502.

development. In time, Auden quietly transformed the self-doubt of his first poems into the longed-for vision. In his 1933 poem 'Out on the lawn I lie in bed', he described what may have been a genuine visionary experience which he had one evening in June that year at the Downs School.[10] But it was not until 1964, in his introduction to *The Protestant Mystics,* that he called it a vision of agape (and even then he did so only indirectly, never openly claiming it as his own). Whether or not the experience seemed to him to be mystical at the time it occurred, or even shortly afterwards when he wrote the poem about it, certainly by 1964 Auden judged it to have been so. By the end of his life, Auden had begun to see aspects of his development as having been not unlike Wordsworth's; in 1972 he told a friend that he might write a long poem modelled on *The Prelude.*[11] As if he had finally overcome the uncertainty expressed in his juvenilia, by 1972 he aspired to be a visionary poet.

The long poem was never written, but the plan is revealing; indeed, it was not the first time Auden had privately expressed such a visionary aspiration. In 1942, when he was finishing his Christmas oratorio, *For the Time Being,* he told Elizabeth Mayer that he next wanted to write 'a sort of modern Vita Nuova.'[12] In the early stages of his relationship with Chester Kallman, Auden had had what he evidently came to believe was another visionary experience, and for a time planned to write a poem about it. But as with the poem modelled on *The Prelude,* he never did. In the end, his introduction to *The Protestant Mystics* is his most full-fledged public treatment of his private visionary ambitions. Written in late maturity, it illuminates the character and enduring significance of the anxieties first apparent in his juvenilia; it is Auden's answer, however equivocally stated, to the youthful inadequacy he felt when confronting the Romantic tradition, for it describes with the authority of personal testimony the visions of which he once doubted he was capable. In the 1964 essay, he anatomized four different kinds of visions; three of them are clearly based on his own experience (though with characteristic reticence he does not

---

[10] See Carpenter, 160–63, and *Early Auden,* 159–62.

[11] The friend was Emma Kann. See her reminiscence in *The W. H. Auden Society Newsletter* 10–11 (September 1993): 12. See also Edward Mendelson, 'Editing Auden', *New Statesman,* 17 September 1976, 376.

[12] ALS, Ann Arbor, postmarked 26 April 1942 (Berg).

say so outright). The visions are set in a hierarchy, the lowest described first, the highest, the Vision of God, last, and each level of the hierarchy is subtly associated with a stage in human development and so, indirectly, with a stage in Auden's own development.

At the bottom of the implied ladder is the Vision of Dame Kind, usually experienced in childhood, and of which the great exemplar is Wordsworth: 'The basic experience is an overwhelming conviction that the objects confronting him have a numinous significance and importance, that the existence of everything he is aware of is holy. And the basic emotion is one of innocent joy, though this joy can include, of course, a reverent dread.'[13] Auden's inaugural address as Professor of Poetry at Oxford (delivered on 11 June 1956, nearly ten years before the *Protestant Mystics* essay) described his early enthusiasm for lead-mining in similar terms. In that lecture he said that his childhood reading had to do with 'a private world of Sacred Objects', machines which created in him 'a passion of awe' which might, he explained, 'vary greatly in intensity and range in tone from joyous wonder to panic dread'.[14] In 'The Prolific and the Devourer' (1939), Auden described his boyhood obsession as 'a series of passionate love-affairs with pictures of, to me, particularly attractive water-turbines, winding-engines, roller-crushers, etc., and I was never so emotionally happy as when I was underground.'[15] But by 1956 his changed diction makes it clear that he had elevated passion to vision.[16] Like Wordsworth, Auden drew on these early numinous experiences throughout his career, but he warns in the *Protestant Mystics* essay against the danger of idolizing 'the experience itself as the *summum bonum*', for this might lead to a life spent regretting the loss of the vision or trying to recapture it. Even if it were possible to recapture the vision, it includes no other people except unimportant strangers, so 'continual indulgence in it could only lead to an increasing indifference towards the existence and needs of other human beings.'[17] These warnings offer a rebuke to Wordsworth, whose self-absorption and preoccupation with his childhood visionary experiences Auden criticized elsewhere.

[13] *FA*, 58.
[14] 'Making, Knowing, and Judging', *DH*, 34 and 55.
[15] *Antaeus* 42 (Summer 1981): 12. This work was unpublished in Auden's lifetime.
[16] See also 'As It Seemed to Us', *FA*, 502.
[17] *FA*, 62.

Above the Vision of Dame Kind, Auden placed the Vision of Eros, the revelation of 'the glory of a single human being' for which he offered Plato's *Symposium* and Dante's *Vita Nuova* as examples; in another essay written at about the same time, 'Shakespeare's Sonnets' (1964), he described the vision more fully, using the sonnets as an example. Again the vision is characterized by 'the feeling of awe and reverence', in this case in the presence of a sacred human being. But 'however great his desire, the lover feels unworthy of his beloved's notice'.[18] The Vision of Eros thrives on distance rather than intimacy; to embark on 'an actual sexual relation' spoils it, and it fades under the scrutiny of long-term intimacy.[19] This characterization is partly based on Auden's relationship with Chester Kallman, but some of the details derive from his earliest love affairs (as distinct from other, primarily sexual escapades) at school, at Oxford, and in Berlin, which drew their excitement and significance from unrequited longing. Auden alludes to these affairs in some of his earliest love poems and in his 1929 Berlin journal. The Vision of Eros contains an element of the adolescent hero-worship described in *The Orators*, and, as Auden describes it, it is frequently the vision of unrequited love.

The vision of maturity is the Vision of Agape, mutual love among equals. Auden's reasons for elevating the Vision of Agape above the Vision of Dame Kind and the Vision of Eros, and for excluding from his hierarchy any other mystical experiences, apart from the Vision of God, probably have as much to do with his personal intellectual and emotional needs as they do with the stature of brotherly love in the Christian church or with the attractiveness of the concept of agape as an ideal for modern society. The concept of agape freed him from the oppressive stereotypes of the conventional bonds of familial and sexual love which could never make him happy, and placed another, more suitable ideal in their place, an ideal he could share with the broad mass of humanity.[20] As it is presented in the essay, the Vision of Agape is a stage of illumination beyond Dame Kind or Eros, only one step short of the Vision of God. This last, to be pondered and perhaps longed for as he approaches the grave, Auden leaves to 'the pure in heart' and the Catholics, who are, he cannily says, less reticent than

---

[18] *FA*, 63.
[19] *FA*, 64.
[20] See Katherine Bucknell, 'Auden's "Writing" Essay', *ASI*, 26.

Anglicans like himself.[21] Still, nearly a decade later—in the year he died—he claimed a bit more in 'Profile' (1973):

> He has never seen God,
> but, once or twice, he believes
> he has heard Him.[22]

The introduction to *The Protestant Mystics* is in part Auden's mature response to the uncertainties he felt as an adolescent poet before the Romantic tradition. In the 1920s he felt excluded from the special vision of the Romantics as if he were somehow uniquely fallen. Wordsworth above all made him feel this, perhaps because Wordsworth's vision was not an especially magic or supernatural one but rather was convincingly grounded in reality and could not be brushed aside as imaginative fancy. As W. P. Ker—one of Auden's favourite critics in his undergraduate days—explained, Wordsworth's imaginative experiences as he presents them in his poems are merely 'extensions of ordinary experience'; they are heightened only by 'the intensifying of ordinary modes of perception', which accounts for the 'sense of security in Wordsworth's visionary moments, the sense of not being left to his own fantasy.'[23]

IN MANY of Auden's early poems, guilt emerges as a central theme, especially when the poet confronts the natural world; and the theme of guilt continues into his early published work. Where Wordsworth and other Romantic and Georgian poets have a privileged relation with nature, Auden is shut out. In 'To a Field-mouse' the poet cries out with shame far exceeding his apparent culpability at frightening the mouse. In 'The Old Lead-mine' he drops a stone down a disused mine shaft, the splash below fills him with dread, and he retreats as if he were one of the greedy men who the poem says have left the hillside scarred with shafts. In 'The Road's Your Place' he is turned back from a steep track to a mountain tarn by three threatening hills that voice the admonition of the poem's title and generally behave like the crag that pursues Wordsworth in his stolen boat on Lake Winder-

---

[21] *FA*, 71.

[22] *CP*, 777.

[23] 'Imagination and Judgement', in *Collected Essays*, ed. C. Whibley, 2 vols. (London, 1925), 2:286–87.

mere. In 'Who stands, the crux left of the watershed,' the landscape speaks again, saying 'Stranger, turn back'. But Auden's repeated failure to gain access to the natural world is self-imposed; his curiosity or desire regarding nature is frustrated by his own guilty fear that he is unworthy of it or that he might harm it.

One main source of these strong and reiterated patterns lies outside the poetic tradition, in Auden's early emotional experience. For instance, there are clear parallels between the attitude towards Mother Nature expressed in the poems and Auden's attitude towards his own mother. The poet himself recognized these parallels, if not at fifteen, certainly by the time he wrote the opening line of the prologue to *The Orators*: 'By landscape reminded once of his mother's figure'.[24] The conflicting desire and fear expressed towards nature in so many of his poems can be understood in part as the representation of a conflict he felt between desire for independence and fear of losing his mother's love; it can also be understood on a more primal (or, until after he had read Freud, unconscious) level as the representation of a conflict between incestuous sexual desire for his mother and fear of gratifying that desire. The experience of dropping the stone down the mine shaft, so suggestive in these respects, is one to which Auden would refer again in 'New Year Letter' (1940), where he would link it directly to a feminine principle, 'The deep *Urmutterfurcht* that drives / Us into knowledge all our lives.'[25] Like *The Prelude*, 'New Year Letter' has large autobiographical ambitions. To return, as in this passage from 'New Year Letter', to a seminal experience of childhood in order to reflect on its contribution to the growth of mature understanding is perhaps the most typically Wordsworthian of poetic procedures. And the passage includes among its many allusions several to Wordsworth. The 'boy of wish' returning to the landscape of Auden's youth recalls Wordsworth's boy of Winander, and the 'algebraic signs' that stand in 'New Year Letter' for all that man has lost and all that he seeks—techniques, achievements, beliefs—recall the stone and the shell shown to Wordsworth when he dreams about the Bedouin and the deluge. Both these passages are in book 5 of *The Prelude*, and Auden knew them well; he included the passage about the boy of

---

[24] *EA*, 61. Later he published the prologue under the revealing title 'Adolescence'.

[25] *CP*, 228. Auden borrowed 'Urmutterfurcht' from Wagner's *Siegfried*, 3.1; literally this means 'primitive mother fear'.

Winander in his 1950 anthology, *Poets of the English Language*, and he discussed at length the meaning of Wordsworth's dream of the stone and the shell in his 1949 Page-Barbour lectures entitled *The Enchafèd Flood*. When Auden's boy drops the pebbles down the well, the response is a sinister, frightening voice that tells him he no longer has his mother's love:

> There I dropped pebbles, listened, heard
> The reservoir of darkness stirred;
> *'O deine Mutter kehrt dir nicht*
> *Wieder. Du selbst bin ich, dein' Pflicht*
> *Und Liebe. Brach sie nun mein Bild.'*
> And I was conscious of my guilt.[26]

In the late 1960s in 'Marginalia', Auden restated, without the veil of allusion and foreign language in 'New Year Letter', the link between the loss of innocence and the child's first anxiety about being loved:

> Few can remember
> clearly when innocence came
> to a sudden end,
> the moment at which we ask
> for the first time: *Am I loved?*[27]

From the contemplation of his own and mankind's loss, and the recollection of his first recognition of his guilt before an overawing mother and an unyielding Mother Nature, Auden salvaged the creative impulse, the force that both drew and drove him on through life, as if all his poetic efforts were an attempt to recapture his mother's affection; or, as he put it for the innocent male of his 1948 poem 'In Praise of Limestone' (who never doubts 'That for all his faults he is loved'), as if his 'works are but / Extensions of his power to charm.'[28]

Auden's immense creative vitality throughout his career was also both fuelled and chastened by his fascination with death. The power and character of this fascination was again symbolized for him by the particular natural landscapes towards which he was drawn. In his 1971

---

[26] *CP*, 228; the German, bafflingly reworked from *Siegfried*, 3.2, says, literally: 'O thy mother returns not again to thee. Thou thyself am I, thy duty and love. Now that she has broken my picture,' but the last phrase may be Auden's attempt at a German equivalent of 'Now break my picture.' He apparently cared more for the rhyme than for the sense.

[27] *CP*, 786.

[28] *CP*, 540.

lecture 'Phantasy and Reality in Poetry', he observed an explicit connection between the compulsive allure for him of a limestone landscape filled with derelict lead-mines and of the mortal human body, and he noted that among the mines and machinery he had constructed in his childhood imaginative play he was by choice alone in a world abandoned by other living beings:

> Trying my hand at a little self-analysis, I note, firstly that, even aside from the man-made caverns of mines, a limestone cavity is full of natural caverns and underground streams. Then, looking at the cross-sectioned diagrams of mines in my books, I realise that they are like stylised pictures of the internal anatomy of the human body. As for my passion for lead-mines, I note, firstly that the word *lead* rhymes with *dead* and that lead is or was used for lining coffins: secondly that mining is the one human activity that is by nature mortal. Steam-engines may render stage-coaches obsolete, but this can't be foreseen. But when a mine is opened, everyone knows already, that however rich it may turn out to be, sooner or later it will become exhausted and be abandoned. Of this constructed world I was the only human inhabitant, although I equipped my mines with the most elaborate machinery, I never imagined any miners. Indeed, when I visited real mining areas, I preferred abandoned mines to working ones. Yet, whatever the unconscious relation between my sacred world and death may have been, [?this] I contemplated not with fear or grief but with intense joy and reverence.[29]

By the time he went up to Oxford, Auden's relationship with his mother, intimate and intense in childhood, had become turbulent and painful. His only known letter home from school, written in October 1923, when he was sixteen, still reflects a warm intimacy with both parents, especially his mother, and expresses his hope that they will soon visit him. But like any adolescent, he was struggling to establish his independence. In a 1942 letter he told his friend James Stern, 'You would be surprised how unpleasant too much parental love and interest can be, and what a torture of guilt it makes breaking away.'[30] During his last year at school or his first year at university, he wrote several elegies for apparently imaginary boys who died at about the age he

---

[29] Autograph manuscript, Berg, 17–18. The lecture was delivered at the Philadelphia Association for Psychoanalysis, 12 March 1971.

[30] ALS, the Maypole, Daylesford, Berwyn, Pa., 30 July 1942.

then was; he also wrote a series of poems on abandoned women ('The Dying House', 'Felo de se', 'Motherhood', and 'The Gipsy Girl'). Maurice Baring's 'In Memoriam, A. H.', printed in *Georgian Poetry 1916–1917*, was probably the model for at least one of the elegies, but the one beginning 'A wagtail splutters in the stream,' along with 'The Dying House' and 'The Gipsy Girl', have notably Wordsworthian features. Also, at about this time, or not long before, he presented to his mother a notebook of poems written out especially for her and sentimentally inscribed:

> *To Mother*
>   from her son, the author.
>
> You too, my mother read my rhymes
>   For love of unforgotten times
> 'And you may chance to hear once more
>   The little feet along the floor'.
>
>   R.L.S.[31]

After this, the stream of poems Auden had sent to his mother from school dwindled away to nothing.

Mrs Auden evidently suffered over these changes at least as much as her son did. What Auden describes in 'New Year Letter' as a loss of mother-love refers to the way he apparently felt during childhood (and perhaps again later) when she withdrew not her love but her approval. To Auden this may have seemed like the same thing. During his adolescence the situation was complicated by his discovery of his homosexuality and his (perhaps related) loss of faith. These were affronts to his mother, a devout Christian, and may have contributed to his sense, expressed in his poems at the time, that he was somehow an affront to nature. Several episodes make clear that his sexuality worried his parents. During 1923 and 1924, Auden accepted a chaste but intimate friendship with a journalist, Michael Davidson, who was homosexual; Davidson was in love with Auden, but Auden did not find him sexually attractive. When the friendship was discovered, it was forbidden by the school authorities, and Mrs Auden wrote to Davidson asking him not to see her son, although the meetings contin-

---

[31] The verse 'To My Mother' is slightly misquoted from Robert Louis Stevenson, *A Child's Garden of Verses* (London, 1885); it is not clear why Auden added the quotation marks around the last two lines.

ued clandestinely.[32] About the same period, Robert Medley visited the Audens over New Year 1923–1924, and Mrs Auden found on the floor of Auden's bedroom (which the boys innocently shared) what she felt was a suggestive poem about the school swimming pool. (This may have been 'Early Morning Bathing', though more likely the poem is now lost.) The boys were called into Dr Auden's study and questioned about the exact nature of their friendship. (Medley later recalled that the incident in fact precipitated Auden's first statement of his true feelings. These came as something of a surprise to Medley, but the two did not go to bed together until after Auden had arrived at Oxford.)[33] Somewhat later, during a holiday from Oxford, Auden at least twice took the son of the local Harborne grocer openly to the cinema. John Auden recalled that this was at a time when 'the classes in England kept to their aloof identities and stratifications, and Wystan's behaviour was evidently viewed with some dismay by our parents.'[34] Indeed, Auden's letter to his brother describing the episode says that their mother became suspicious about the cinema. On one occasion, when he set out to meet the boy there, she insisted that his father accompany him; the meeting with the boy had to be called off.

By then, relations with his mother had become so strained that Auden spent part of his first Christmas holiday from Oxford at the home of his new friend, A. S. T. Fisher. At Easter, he begged Fisher to return the visit, saying 'I know you can do wonders with my mother.'[35] Fisher apparently did his best; and after the visit he wrote to Mrs Auden, telling her among other things that her son was a 'genius', and saying 'the fact that he is naturally more self-sufficient than most people explains why he finds so little need for a personal God—or for a Mother.'[36] Fisher's condescension must have been annoying, but it goes to the nub, for at the root of the discord lay Mrs Auden's reluctance to accept her son's increasing independence and his need to establish his own identity as he grew older. In her reply she said: 'As regards our relationship to each other—he depended on me more than any of the others until lately—and twice in later years at school

---

[32] Many years later, Auden mentioned the friendship in 'As It Seemed to Us', saying of Davidson 'I owe him a great deal'; *FA*, 509.

[33] See Medley, 44.

[34] TLS, 43 Thurloe Square, 6 September 1982, to Edward Mendelson.

[35] ALS, Lordswood Road letterhead, [April 1926], F.

[36] Only the autograph draft of Fisher's letter survives in the Christ Church library.

I was able to come to his help in crises— . . . As a matter of fact he is as much his old self as possible when we are alone together. Nothing could have been happier than this last week—but when his friends are there he likes to assert his independence of me!'[37] Fisher did not mention Auden's homosexuality, but Mrs Auden was probably referring to it in her rather enigmatic statement, 'I do not know how much you know of his past life, but there has been much to cause both his father and me real anxiety.'

There is an underlying similarity between the pattern of Auden's changing relationship with his mother and the pattern of his changing attitude towards Romanticism. Although as a young man he sought to escape the power and intensity of his relationship with his mother, in later years he circled back to assume again his own version of the habits and convictions shared with her in childhood and cast off so painfully by him during adolescence. And just as he publicly derided Romanticism while at the same time privately aspiring to become a visionary poet, so he professed himself an atheist while at a deeper level he had begun to move slowly back towards the church and towards the spirituality of his mother almost as soon as he had rejected them. This circling back reflects not so much a change of heart as the eventual triumph of the obverse side of his own adolescent ambivalence. The choices he faced were difficult, and rejected alternatives haunted him with both the shadowy promise of untried opportunity and the grim threat of neglected obligation. At fifteen, he was already determined to be a poet, and he was prepared to pay a great price to satisfy his ambition, including the painful sacrifice of his parents' expectations for his future. He did not then want to be a Romantic or visionary poet; he needed a model who would help him find another way to write, and who would not make him feel inadequate as a poet. He found this model in Thomas Hardy.

IN THE summer of 1923, according to Auden's recollection in his 1940 essay 'A Literary Transference', Hardy struck for him 'the authentic poetic note'. Although Auden exaggerated when he wrote that 'for more than a year I read no one else',[38] Hardy awakened in

---

[37] ALS, 42 Lordswood Road, 20 April 1926, F.

[38] 'A Literary Transference', 136. See n. 6 above; Auden appears also to have been interested in de la Mare around this time, though his interest may have been waning. Probably at Christmas 1923 he received de la Mare's anthology *Come Hither!* and can hardly have ignored until the following summer all the poets represented there.

him an intense and long-lasting 'passion of imitation',[39] which, for the
first time, established the pattern of obsession and assimilation that
was to prove characteristic not only in his early development but
throughout his career. By early 1924, he was writing poems that
sounded like Hardy himself. As Auden explained, Hardy was not such
a good craftsman as to make Auden feel he could never equal his
achievements; on the contrary, Auden could easily see his faults: 'his
rhythmical clumsiness, his outlandish vocabulary were obvious even
to a schoolboy'. And, far more than Wordsworth might have done,
Hardy showed Auden the use of 'direct colloquial diction.'[40] Auden
said in his introduction to *The Oxford Book of Light Verse* that whenever
Wordsworth tried to write in 'the language really used by men' (as he
claimed in his preface to the 1800 *Lyrical Ballads*) he was not com-
pletely successful, and that in what Auden considered to be his best
work, the odes and *The Prelude*, 'his diction is poetic, and far removed
from the spoken word'.[41]

Auden called Hardy 'my poetical father';[42] he even said that Hardy
'looked like my father', and continued: 'that broad unpampered
moustache, bald forehead, and deeply lined sympathetic face be-
longed to the other world of feeling and sensation (for I, like my
mother, was a thinking-intuitive).[43] Here was a writer whose emotions,
if sometimes monotonous and sentimental in expression, would be
deeper and more faithful than my own, and whose attachment to the
earth would be more secure and observant.'[44] To a poet whose earliest
compositions show uncertainty before the natural world and ambiva-
lence about his attachment to the earth, Hardy offered a key to the
baffling maternal landscape. And Hardy's basic philosophical out-
look—of disillusioned modern scepticism—may also have seemed to
Auden like his father's. George Auden was essentially agnostic. He
was a medical doctor of broad classical learning complemented by
impressively catholic contemporary reading and attitudes. He took a
first in Natural Science in Cambridge in the 1890s, and was expert
in Greek and Latin as well as in several modern languages. In his
1965 essay 'As It Seemed to Us', Auden wrote 'one parent stood for

---

[39] 'A Literary Transference', 136.

[40] 'A Literary Transference', 141.

[41] *OBLV*, xiv.

[42] 'A Literary Transference', 142.

[43] Auden derived these categories from C.G. Jung, *Psychological Types*, trans. H. God-
win Baynes (London, 1923).

[44] 'A Literary Transference', 136–37.

stability, common sense, reality, the other stood for surprise, eccentricity, fantasy. In my case, it was Father who stood for the first, Mother for the second.'[45] But in the same essay he also wrote that when his father joined the Royal Army Medical Corps during the war, 'to some degree I lost him psychologically. I was seven—the age at which . . . a son begins to take serious notice of his father and needs him most'. He did not see his father again until he was twelve and a half: 'we never really came to know each other.'[46]

Auden's search for a poetic father, a figure who might balance the natural visionary power of Wordsworthian Romanticism and the emotional intensity apparently generated by his early relationship with his mother, did not end with Hardy. The search itself became part of the pattern of his general intellectual development and a theme of many of his poems. But Hardy served as his poetical father for nearly a year. In some of his poems Auden uses the voices of Hardy and Wordsworth together, like mingled parental voices, arguing with or balancing each other. Hardy was as unconvinced as the young Auden was by the Romantic vision of nature. He had already made the limitation of human insight a successful theme in his poems, and he provided a suitably ironic tone, free of self-pity, in which to write about it. He asked questions that could not be answered, and Auden began to do the same. The Hardyesque 'Allendale', for instance, is nothing but questions.

At the close of his 1956 lecture 'Making, Knowing, and Judging', Auden recited Hardy's poem 'Afterwards', calling it 'a rite of homage to sacred objects which are neither gods nor objects of desire.'[47] In part, he was paying tribute to Hardy's detachment, for the natural objects which the poem notices and lovingly, luminously describes are seen by Hardy as if after his own death. 'Afterwards' expresses the hope that the poet will be remembered because 'He was a man who used to notice such things'. Auden had apparently admired the poem for a long time. He included it in his 1935 anthology *The Poet's Tongue*, and he alluded to it as early as 1925 in his poem 'Frost'. In 'Frost' the observer in the poem is so excited by the pleasures of the scene before him that, he says, 'We do not notice every thing in our delight'. What 'we' overlook is evidence of suffering: 'The frozen buzzard caught upon the mill-hatch bars' and 'All who must walk the lanes of dark-

---

[45] *FA*, 499.

[46] *FA*, 500.

[47] The poem and Auden's remarks introducing it are not reprinted in *DH*, but see the 1956 publication of the lecture by the Clarendon Press (Oxford), 33.

ness blind to stars'. But despite the share of guilt he assigns to himself by using the pronoun 'we', the poet does notice these details because he includes them in his poem. For Auden, such evidence of suffering and death belonged among the sacred objects. 'Frost' and another early poem, 'Christmas Eve', contain the germ of his 1938 poem 'Musée des Beaux Arts', which describes the way suffering usually occurs: 'While someone else is eating or opening a window or just walking dully along.' The Old Masters noticed; Brueghel put into his *Icarus* the 'boy falling out of the sky' as well as 'the expensive delicate ship' that 'sailed calmly on.'[48] Auden first learned from Hardy the capacity exemplified in 'Afterwards' to feel passion for his subject, to notice its every feature, and yet to view it from a distance, with detachment.

In 'A Literary Transference' he wrote that what he valued most in Hardy 'was his hawk's vision, his way of looking at life from a very great height.' He went on to explain that 'from such a perspective the difference between the individual and society is so slight' that it appears as if 'reconciliation is possible.'[49] From the 1930s onwards, whenever Auden writes about Wordsworth, for instance in 'Letter to Lord Byron' (1936), the introduction to *The Oxford Book of Light Verse* (1938), or the introduction to *Poets of the English Language* (1950), he uses Wordsworth as the example of Romantic poets in general, who, as a result of the break-up of traditional communities at the time of the industrial revolution, 'turned away from the life of their time to the contemplation of their own emotions and the creation of imaginary worlds'.[50] The Romantic poet took himself as hero, which explained why 'the subject of the greatest long poem of this period, *The Prelude*, is . . . the Growth of a Poet's Mind.'[51] The hawk's vision reduced the rift between poet and society; it was a substitute for Romantic vision, replacing the advantages of intimacy with the advantages of distance, of intensity with panoramic perspective, of intuition with judgement.

THEN, in the autumn of 1924, Auden discovered Edward Thomas, and Hardy 'had to share his kingdom'.[52] Soon Auden's passion extended to Thomas's friend and mentor, Robert Frost. He was attracted

---

[48] *EA*, 237; *CP*, 179.

[49] 'A Literary Transference', 139, 140.

[50] *OBLV*, xv.

[51] Introduction to *Poets of the English Language*, ed. W. H. Auden and Norman Holmes Pearson, 5 vols. (New York, 1950), 4:xvi.

[52] 'A Literary Transference', 136.

to their gentle reticence and their down-to-earth natures perhaps more than anything else. In his 1936 introduction to Frost's poems, he was to say that Frost's 'qualities of irony and understatement, his mistrust of fine writing, are those of the practical man,' and he noted the similarity between Thomas and Frost, saying that Frost is not 'like Wordsworth, a poet who has had a vision in youth which he can spend the rest of his life in interpreting. His material is not given him in a rush at the beginning. What de la Mare wrote of Frost's friend, and to some extent pupil, Edward Thomas, applies equally to him. "These poems tell us, not so much of rare exalted chosen moments, of fleeting inexplicable intuitions, but of his daily and, one might say, common experience." '[53] Auden wrote about everyday experience by imitating Thomas and Frost. These models brought him back during 1925 to the natural themes of Wordsworth, and although he now dealt with such themes more confidently, his old ambivalence persisted. His descriptions of the natural world were calm, understated, even reticent, but images such as gates or mountains blocking his access to the landscape reappeared, now more overtly associated with his sexual nature. In 'The Hidden Lane (Near Selbrigg, March 1925)' he imagines at the end of the overgrown lane 'a lover like myself / Who tries to look this way, who knows?' but he does not venture past the gate he finds partway along the lane. In 'The Tarn' he sees two boys bathing together in a mountain lake, and he describes them as so 'splendid' that the sun seems to glow from within them, but the vision is brief and distant, and the poet is excluded from their laughter.

The conflicting emotions of fear and desire felt towards mother and Mother Nature, which emerged in so many of Auden's earliest poems, gradually evolved into a habitual attitude in his poems about love. The theme of unrequited love became a characteristic and, paradoxically, satisfying one, while the possibility that his love would be answered was at once longed for and dreaded. In his romantic friendships Auden often chose boys younger than himself, and he apparently preferred loving to being loved. Stephen Spender suggests that this simply reflects the conventional pattern of homosexual relations among upper- or middle-class young men of the period; the more intellectual and physically unattractive partner regarded himself as

---

[53] Robert Frost, *Selected Poems* (London, 1936), 12–13. De la Mare's observation (which Auden slightly misquotes) is in his foreword to Edward Thomas, *Collected Poems* (London, 1920), x.

the rejected lover. Spender recalls that Auden at the time considered himself ugly and therefore as typecast in this role.[54] During his school-days, his love for Robert Medley, two years older, and later for John Pudney, two years younger, remained chaste, though (in Medley's case anyway) not unanswered. Auden later went to bed with Medley in Oxford, but the romance was cut short because Medley met and fell in love with Rupert Doone almost immediately afterwards (Spender recalls that Auden was intensely jealous of Doone.)[55] But before that, at St Edmund's, Auden fell in love for the first time with a slightly older man, and the experience had distinctly religious overtones. In about 1943 he wrote in a notebook a list of everyone he had ever fallen in love with; the sixteen names on the list end with 'Chester' and begin with 'Mr Newman'.[56] Geoffrey Gunnel Newman was chap-lain and assistant master at St Edmund's during Auden's last few terms there. He had attended Charterhouse and took a B.A. from Keble College, Oxford, in 1913; afterwards he served as a chaplain in the army and navy during the war.[57] He arrived at St Edmund's near the start of 1920 and left in 1921. Auden's contemporary at the school, Harold Llewellyn Smith, later recalled: '[Auden's] attraction towards high church doctrines and practices was no doubt in the first place due to the influence of his mother; but in his last year at the school it was fortuitously strengthened by the advent on the school staff of the Rev. G. G. Newman, whom we boys believed, quite errone-ously, to be some sort of nephew of the cardinal. We duly went to confession—Wystan leading.'[58] Newman's religious stature apparently lent its own complications to the emotional and spiritual changes Auden was beginning to undergo in this period. Auden also placed him at the top of another list, that of the treacherous 'boon compan-ions' in his 1930 poem 'Get there if you can and see the land you once were proud to own': 'Newman, Ciddy, Plato, Fronny, Pascal, Bowdler,

---

[54] AN, 30 March 1992, to Katherine Bucknell.

[55] AN, 30 March 1992.

[56] The manuscript notebook is in the Lockwood Memorial Library, State University of New York at Buffalo. Auden apparently used it during 1942 and 1943 when he was working on 'The Sea and the Mirror'. See *Bibliography* J11, 245. The list has eight names from Auden's school and university years. In order the names are: Mr Newman, Robert [Medley], John Pudney, [illegible name], Tony Parker, William McElwee, Patrick McEl-wee, Gabriel Carritt.

[57] *St Edmund's School Chronicle* 7, no. 8 (June 1920): 116.

[58] 'At St Edmund's 1915–1920', *Tribute*, 36.

Baudelaire, / Doctor Frommer, Mrs Allom, Freud, the Baron, and Flaubert.' (Second in this list, Ciddy, is Cyril Morgan-Brown, head-master at St Edmund's and Christopher Isherwood's cousin.) The poem rather bitterly accuses its heroes of luring the poet's generation away from conventional virtue and happiness down a painful, neurotic road: 'When we asked the way to Heaven, these directed us ahead /To the padded room, the clinic and the hangman's little shed.'[59]

Auden may have become promiscuous during his first year in Ox-ford, but throughout his time at university he almost unfailingly fell in love with—as distinct from into bed with—heterosexual under-graduates younger than he who did not return his affection beyond admiring friendship. Among these, William McElwee and Gabriel Carritt became important subjects in Auden's 1928 volume *Poems*, and Carritt figured centrally in Auden's work as late as *The Orators.* For a time their school, Sedbergh, a Spartan northern establishment sur-rounded by barren fells, assumed mythological stature for Auden, who dreamed of the boys there and the harsh athletic life they led. He referred to Sedbergh in several poems. (According to Carritt, before he ever saw the school Auden once got as close to Sedbergh as Tebay, a railway junction fifteen miles away—he was apparently travelling from somewhere further north—and could not bear to go any closer to this place of fantasy.)[60] Spender recalls that Auden boasted at Ox-ford of his sexual conquests and in his rooms at Christ Church once remarked, 'Isn't it strange to think that in an hour's time I'll be in bed with Bill McElwee'.[61] But a letter to John Auden suggests that despite this remark (perhaps calculated to impress his younger friend), Auden may never have gone to bed with McElwee at all. During Easter

---

[59] *EA*, 48.

[60] Conversation with Katherine Bucknell, 2 November 1992.

[61] ALS, 14 November 1991, to Katherine Bucknell. On another occasion Auden shared a bed with Gabriel Carritt during a walking tour and, according to Spender, made advances. However, the episode with Carritt did not occur until 1931, long after Auden had left Oxford, and Spender says Carritt later reported that he was physically ill when he tried to respond (AN, 30 March 1992, to Katherine Bucknell). According to an unpublished poem Auden sent Carritt afterwards, the encounter resulted from a 'Shortage of blankets.' Auden may have regretted his attempt, for in the poem he describes himself as 'aware of the electric / Current between us, strength in my repen-tance.' The poem, beginning 'Gabriel, fully occupied in either,' was enclosed in a letter sent just before Carritt's final Honour School (his final examinations), which began on 11 June 1931; it is now in the Berg.

vacation 1927 Auden told his brother: 'I do sympathize very deeply with what you say [about] the degeneration to common lovers[.] I do believe it follows almost inevitably once physical relations start. Yet in heterosexual affairs at any rate I imagine, "Platonic" love is quite intolerable. William being heterosexual, makes sexual behaviour of course impossible. What saves the thing as far as I am concerned is that he is so fond of me as to make me convinced that if he were homosexual, the thing would be mutual.'[62]

Other contemporary letters suggest that for love of McElwee, Auden practised celibacy for a year or more, starting around Christmas 1926 when the two went to Austria together. He mentioned this jokingly to Isherwood soon after the trip: 'We had such a good time in Austria. Yes your smirk is almost justified, but I am vowed to celibacy for two years.'[63] Later he told John Auden that he had kept this vow for a year: 'As you may imagine, I shall not enjoy asceticism, even if I achieve it, I have anyway for the last year.'[64] In the letter to his brother, Auden made it clear that he associated his asceticism with his duty to his role as an artist. This is the letter in which he preached, in earnest, highbrow tones, Eliot's doctrine of discipline and tradition, and he went on to proclaim:

> As to sex I am becoming convinced that for myself, asceticism is the only thing. As a bugger, there are only three courses open to one in afterlife.
> 1) Middle-aged sentimentalism. The education of youth. Schoolmasters etc.
>> The hand on the shoulder.
>> You have the glorious gift of youth.
> 2) The London bugger. Sucking off policemen in public lavatories.
>> The doors shut. We're all buggers here.
> 3) Asceticism. The pursed mouth.
> I have seen too much of the first two classes to wish to find myself among them. Secondly, qua writer, I think celibacy's indicated.

---

[62] ALS, 'Wildboarclough, Staffs. [sic]'; apparently Auden was in Wildboar Clough, Derbyshire, the county next to Staffordshire.

[63] ALS, Lordswood Road letterhead, [early January 1927].

[64] ALS, Christ Church, [June? or more likely December? 1927].

Thus it appears certain that Auden was not privately so lighthearted about sex as his publicly professed enthusiasm suggests. One friend, David Ayerst, sensed that he felt guilty about his homosexuality but never admitted it; in July 1927, he told another friend, V. M. Allom, 'There still lingers in my mind the idea of something indecent in a mutual homosexual relation.'[65]

Through his reading of Freud, Jung, and probably a few others, Auden had begun to find ways of thinking about his psychological make-up. In his 1927 poem 'Narcissus' he suggests that his liking for solitude has cut him off from the boys mentioned in the poem, leaving him alone with his poetic ambitions and his self-love; a letter to McElwee written while he was at work on the poem suggests there may already have been a link in his mind, as there is in Freud's work, between the idea of Narcissus and melancholia.[66] According to Spender, Auden thought 'that homosexuality was a neurosis—though one that he accepted, just as he later considered it a sin—though he sinned.'[67] However, it seems clear that far from accepting it, Auden tried in the 1920s and possibly again later to 'cure' himself of his homosexuality. In 1928, he briefly underwent psychoanalysis, telling his brother John beforehand 'I wish to improve my inferiority complex and to develop heterosexual traits.'[68] Afterwards he wrote breezily to Isherwood, 'Had a most pleasant week with my analyst. Libido, it is proved, is towards women. The trouble is incest.'[69] This makes it sound as if his examination of his Oedipus complex had been essentially a holiday, but perhaps his lightness of tone concealed disappointment. Deeper psychological self-understanding did not begin to emerge in Auden's writings for another year. In Berlin in 1929, he kept a journal in which he took notes on his reading of Freud and other psychologists, and in which he minutely examined his homosexuality. He noted, among other things, that romance, for him, was more exciting before it was consummated than afterwards; he had already hinted at this in his letter to John Auden describing the relationship with McElwee. In the

[65] Carpenter, 47–49.

[66] For this letter, written 15 April 1927, see note to 'Narcissus'.

[67] AN, 30 March 1992, to Katherine Bucknell.

[68] ALS, Hotel Esplanade, Zagreb, Croatia, [late July 1927].

[69] ALI, on Lordswood Road letterhead and attached to a draft poem beginning 'In your house came a voice' (eventually revised as 'The spring will come'), [March–April 1928].

1929 journal he also observed that he associated reciprocal love with despair, that guilt about his homosexuality drove him continually in search of new partners, and that part of the attraction, for him, of homosexuality was what he called 'its difficulty and torments.'[70]

He drew on some of these discoveries in characterizing the Vision of Eros some years later, and when he wrote poems about his relationship with Chester Kallman he sometimes seemed still to be conforming to or referring to the attitudes towards love first expressed in his adolescent work. In his 1939 poem 'The Prophets' he described a close link, as if of predestination, between his early love of machinery and lead-mines—expressed in Hardyesque poems such as 'The Traction-engine' and 'The Pumping Engine, Cashwell' or the Edward Thomas–like 'The Old Colliery'—and his then new-found love for Kallman. 'Those beautiful machines that never talked / But let the small boy worship them' had offered him no response to his love, nor had they complained when he withdrew it: 'all the landscape round them pointed to / The calm with which they took complete desertion'.[71] When Kallman proved unfaithful, Auden was first jealous, then disillusioned, and eventually resigned. In the end, he responded by offering to Kallman's challenge an increase in his own affection. Thus, in 'The More Loving One' (1957), he wrote, 'If equal affection cannot be, / Let the more loving one be me.'[72] Gradually, the idea of loving without equal return of love became generalized into a model for God's love, and Auden continued to associate it, as he had throughout adolescence, with the landscapes he had first loved in boyhood. In 1948 he wrote:

> when I try to imagine a faultless love
> Or the life to come, what I hear is the murmur
> Of underground streams, what I see is a limestone landscape.[73]

Later, in his notably Hardyesque poem 'Amor Loci' (1965), Auden found the same analogy in the peculiarly austere and forbidding quality of his favourite northern lead-mining landscape, long associated for him with unrequited and unrequitable longing:

---

[70] The journal is in the Berg. Some passages have been printed in *EA*, 297–301.
[71] *CP*, 255–56.
[72] *CP*, 584.
[73] 'In Praise of Limestone', *CP*, 542.

To me, though, much: a vision,
not (as perhaps at
twelve I thought it) of Eden,
still less of a New
Jerusalem but, for one,
convinced he will die,
more comely, more credible
than either day-dream.

How but with some real focus
of desolation
could I, by analogy,
imagine a Love
that, however often smeared,
shrugged at, abandoned
by a frivolous worldling,
does not abandon?[74]

WHEN Auden went up to Christ Church in October 1925, his search for poetic models continued, but the search now became more eclectic and less personal and he no longer needed his poetic forebears to resemble his own father. He decided to change schools, and he read Philosophy, Politics, and Economics during the spring of 1926 while he completed, as required, the first year of Natural Science; by the autumn of 1926 he settled on English. His wide academic reading, as well as the discovery of many new poets, is reflected in his work. He read and imitated Housman, Sassoon, Gordon Bottomley, Emily Dickinson, and others, but not until he discovered T. S. Eliot, in about May 1926, did he reach another great watershed. His tutor, Nevill Coghill, recalled that Auden once arrived for his tutorial claiming to have torn up all his poems 'because they were no good. Based on Wordsworth.' He told Coghill, 'I've been reading Eliot. I now see the way I want to write.'[75] Within a few months everything Auden had achieved until then seemed to be lost in the self-conscious sacrifice of his poetic personality to a version of Eliot's tradition. He filled his

---

[74] *CP*, 780.

[75] See Nevil Coghill, 'Sweeney Agonistes (An Anecdote or Two)' in *T. S. Eliot: A Symposium*, ed. Richard March and Tambimuttu (London, 1948), 82. Coghill is vague on the date when Auden said this, 'towards 1926–7', and he may be mistaken. Auden apparently did not go to him for tutorials until the autumn of 1926, but he had discovered Eliot the previous May, and he had begun to imitate him, in moderation at first, within

work with arcane allusions, used the most difficult and awkward-sounding words he could think of, added epigraphs and footnotes, and splintered his verse into syntactically discrete shards. He still borrowed from texts he had long known well, like Shakespeare and the Bible, and he also expanded his idea of tradition to include many of Eliot's own favourite writers—Catullus, Dante, Marvell, Donne, Webster, Tourneur, Dryden, and others. He read up on mythology in *The Golden Bough*, and he began, with far more originality, to draw on the Middle English and Anglo-Saxon works prescribed in the Oxford English syllabus as well as on the Icelandic sagas he had known since childhood. In Eliot, Auden admired both classical learning and apparent modernity, and he added to his version of Eliot some attributes borrowed from his own father, so that Auden himself seemed for a time to be part scientist, part doctor, and part poet. Isherwood later wrote in *Lions and Shadows* that 'Hugh Weston' in his Eliot phase insisted that it was the poet's duty to be 'clinically minded'; 'Weston' put into his poems 'oddments of scientific, medical, and psycho-analytical jargon,' and handled themes such as love with 'a pair of rubber surgical gloves.' 'Weston' also insisted that poetry must be 'austere' until Isherwood grew sick of hearing the word.[76]

All this perhaps reflects Auden's determination to write a kind of poetry that could not be described, like the poetry of the Romantics, as in any way self-indulgent. Now that he had given up the formal study of Natural Science, Auden resolved to take a scientific approach to poetry. His family had a strong tradition of academic achievement and public service. Both his grandfathers had been clergymen; his learned father was a doctor; his mother had been a nurse (she also had a university degree, then extremely rare among women); his academically gifted elder brother, John, was preparing to be a scientist. Moreover, in the Auden household, great emphasis was placed on personal sacrifice. When Mrs Auden wrote to Fisher in the spring of 1926 about the loss of harmony between herself and her youngest son, one of her chief complaints was his greed and selfishness. He gobbled food whenever he saw it, was demanding more money to spend as he chose, and altogether appeared to scorn what she called

---

weeks. Auden probably dramatized his announcement to impress Coghill. Nevertheless, it makes an important point—that his new style of writing came as a decisive, relatively sudden change.

[76] *Lions and Shadows*, 191.

the 'high ideals' of 'self-sacrifice, self-discipline (self-control even).'[77]
In his memoir, John Pudney recalls that when Auden threw his poems
into the school pond at Gresham's, he then pronounced that 'he had
got poetry out of his system once and for all and that the human race
would be saved by science.'[78] He and Pudney rescued the poems that
evening. At Oxford, after Auden changed from reading Natural Sci-
ence to reading English, he still worked harder at his poetry than at
his academic work, but he fretted about his academic future. As he
began to prepare for his final exams he wrote with comic bravado to
William McElwee, 'I have one foot in the grave which swallowed [illeg-
ible] and Burns; schools are becoming a nightmare; I have even less
character or intellect than I thought; and I shall start blood-spitting
next week.'[79] He recalled many years later that the guilt he suffered
over his neglected academic career made his time in Oxford the most
miserable of his life: 'I was more unhappy than I have ever been be-
fore or since. I might or might not be wasting my time—only the fu-
ture would show—I was certainly wasting my parents' money.'[80] In
another essay, he suggested how urgently, during the Oxford years,
he had felt the need to succeed in order to vindicate his choice of
profession: 'I was always conscious of a dull, persistent, gnawing anxi-
ety. To begin with, I felt guilty at being so idle. . . . I knew very well
what sort of degree I was going to get and what a bitter disappoint-
ment this was going to be to my parents. More important than guilt,
however, was ambition. . . . I had been quite certain since the age of
fifteen of what I wanted to do.'[81] Even as he prepared to return to
Oxford in 1956 wearing a mantle of acclaim as Professor of Poetry, the
old fears assaulted him again: 'I have been discovering surprising
things about myself in relation to England and Oxford in particular
while working on my inaugural lecture. Fits of real blind sweating
panic during which a printed sentence makes no sense and I do not
take in what people say to me.'[82] Despite the remarkable success that
came early and stayed late, Auden was never complacent about the
choice he made in adolescence; guilt over neglected possibilities—

---

[77] ALS, 42 Lordswood Road, 20 April 1926.
[78] *Home and Away: An Autobiographical Gambit* (London, 1960), 47.
[79] ALS, Lordswood Road letterhead, [Easter vacation 1928].
[80] 'Making, Knowing, and Judging', *DH*, 42.
[81] 'As It Seemed to Us', *FA*, 513.
[82] ALS, 'Forio, May 8th', to Stephen Spender, Berg.

the other perhaps more self-sacrificing or more self-effacing contributions he might have made—clung to him like a shadow and shaped his poetry throughout his career.

Auden's obsession with Eliot, like his obsession with Hardy, lasted about a year. During this period, he drew not only on Eliot, but also on the work of other modernists, such as Gertrude Stein, Virginia Woolf, Ezra Pound, and especially Edith Sitwell, whose influence on his work during 1926 is not easy to distinguish from that of Eliot. He also discovered Gerard Manley Hopkins, Wilfred Owen, and Katherine Mansfield, and he read Joyce, D. H. Lawrence, Kafka, and Thomas Mann. Then in the late spring of 1927 he read, apparently at the suggestion of his friend Cecil Day-Lewis, some of the recent work of Yeats. He wrote to Isherwood that of the modern poets he was reading that summer term, 'the later Yeats alone seems to me to be $a+$.'[83] Soon after this he wrote again asking, 'Have you seen Yeats' poem in the June *Criterion*[?] It is very good.'[84] The poem was 'The Tower', and it brought about a revolution in Auden's work. His 1927 poem beginning 'I chose this lean country' is modelled on the third part of 'The Tower'—Auden especially liked this section of Yeats's poem and later printed it on its own in his 1935 anthology, *The Poet's Tongue*. In 'I chose this lean country' Auden once again took up the old theme of the unhappy lover confronting an unyielding landscape, and in it he made clear for the first time, as he was much later to do in poems such as 'In Praise of Limestone' and especially 'Amor Loci', that this was the landscape of his choice, satisfying to him precisely because of its austerity. He wrote 'I chose this lean country' during a visit to Appletreewick or immediately upon his return; Appletreewick is the village in the Yorkshire dales where he had spent a happy holiday with Medley in the summer of 1923, and about which he had already written some of his most vivid early poems. He returned there with Day-Lewis to write the preface to *Oxford Poetry 1927*, which he told Isherwood 'should be as important as the preface to the Lyrical Ballads.'[85] The

[83] ALS, [Christ Church, May 1927], enclosing drafts of 'Narcissus', 'Aware', 'Bach and the Lady', and 'The Seekers' (later entitled 'Extract').

[84] ALS, attached to a draft poem entitled 'Letter to a Friend upon His Weekend Visit to His Home' (beginning 'Out of sight assuredly, not out of mind'), [late May 1927].

[85] ALS, Hotel Elephant, Ljubljana, Croatia, [?late July 1927], private American collection. He told Allom the same thing; see Carpenter, 70.

preface draws on the ideas of T. S. Eliot and I. A. Richards in order to challenge the Wordsworthian definition of poetry as 'emotion recollected in tranquillity' with the claim that emotional and intellectual apprehension should be simultaneous. However, 'I chose this lean country' marks Auden's first move away from the cerebral, multi-layered, artificial Eliot productions of his middle Oxford years towards the simpler, tougher, more reticent, and essentially English plain style that he had first begun to learn as a schoolboy under the influence of Hardy, and later Thomas and Frost. Yeats's influence was tempered in the poem by the sinewy strains of Robert Graves, another student of Hardy whom Auden had first read at school in *Georgian Poetry 1918–1919* and had recently rediscovered. And the Old English poetry in which Auden had been immersed partly for academic reasons now added to his new, shorter lines a bold, haunting drive that lingered through *Poems* (1928) and after.

Auden passionately admired Yeats's mastery of language, but this mastery was married in his view to an eccentric vision. He felt profoundly ambivalent towards the vision which seemed to him far more subjective and esoteric than Wordsworth's. He was sceptical of its truth, but longed to share its power. Only after Yeats's death was Auden able to articulate this ambivalence. In 'The Public v. the Late Mr William Butler Yeats' (1939), he put Yeats on trial with the accusation: 'In 1900 he believed in fairies; that was bad enough; but in 1930 we are confronted with the pitiful, the deplorable spectacle of a grown man occupied with the mumbo-jumbo of magic and the nonsense of India. . . . The plain fact remains that he made it the centre of his work.'[86] Yet by offering in his essay the cases both for the prosecution and for the defence, Auden embodied his own equivocal attitude. In the end, the argument for the defence sets aside Yeats's beliefs on the ground that poets should not be judged for their ability to solve the problems of their generation, 'for art is a product of history, not a cause.'[87] This defence derives from I. A. Richards's assertion in *Science and Poetry* that 'it is *not* the poet's business to make true statements'; Richards argued that 'poetry conclusively shows that even the most important among our attitudes can be aroused and maintained without any belief entering in at all.'[88] Auden had read Richards in

---

[86] *EA*, 391.
[87] *EA*, 393.
[88] *Science and Poetry* (London, 1926), 56 and 61.

about 1927, and even paraphrased his ideas in a letter to John Auden: 'Art exists to produce emotion. . . . it is immaterial if the ideas induced by a poem seem true or false; All ideas in poetry are Richards' pseudo-statements. If the ideas can be reached, the poem is successful. Begin with the stimulus that gave you the ideas, and the ideas will follow in the reader.'[89]

Auden's 1939 defence of Yeats underpins the all-important turn from political to private poet that he was then about to make in his own career. He was again using Yeats as a model, a poetical father of sorts; now it was by identifying Yeats's inadequacies, as he had once as a schoolboy identified Hardy's quite different inadequacies, that Auden at last prepared to set Yeats aside. His essay makes clear his tremendous admiration for what he calls 'the excitement out of which his poems arose' and for Yeats's diction, which shows, in contrast to Wordsworth's, 'a continual evolution towards what one might call the true democratic style.'[90] But the content of Yeats's vision was less important. Thus Auden arrived at a tenable position for himself: on the one hand there was poetry, on the other hand there was belief; they were separate worlds. When Auden wrote his 1964 introduction to *The Protestant Mystics*, he never mentioned Yeats. By then he had no need to, for he did not regard Yeats's vision as a genuine mystical experience, such as Wordsworth's, but rather as an artifice devised for the purpose of writing poetry. It offered no challenge to Auden's own poetic power, nor did it offer a strength on which he could draw. Nevertheless, the introduction to *The Protestant Mystics* suggests that what was true for Yeats—that the content of his vision was unimportant—was not necessarily true for other poets, such as Wordsworth, Plato, and Dante. Indeed, it seems unlikely that Auden ever thought there was an absolute divide between poetry and belief, however useful or attractive he sometimes found this idea. His 1964 essay 'Writing' features a characteristic wobble between the notions of belief and deep emotional involvement: 'a poet is constantly tempted to make use of an idea or a belief, not because he believes it to be true, but because he sees it has interesting poetic possibilities. It may not, perhaps, be absolutely necessary that he *believe* it, but it is certainly necessary that his emotions be deeply involved, and this they can never be

---

[89] AL, partly missing, on letterhead of George A. Auden, City of Birmingham Education Committee, Medical Department, [1927].

[90] *EA*, 392–93.

unless, as a man, he takes it more seriously than as a mere poetic convenience.'[91]

In 1927, when Auden first became obsessed with Yeats, his own work was, in any case, about to enter a new phase. During that spring, Auden had assembled a long poem in parts which he called, for a time, 'The Megalopsych', and which eventually became the first poem sequence in his 1928 *Poems*. This was the final fruit of his Eliot period: a series of fragments presented as a single work. With Isherwood as his critic, Auden had established the habit of culling the best lines from his earlier work and reusing them in new poems; for 'The Megalopsych' he salvaged whole poems and parts of poems that he wished to preserve. Perhaps he thought them his best or his most characteristic work; certainly some parts of the poem refer to moments of emotional significance in his personal life. Around the time that he was assembling 'The Megalopsych' Auden also decided to collect some of his work and send it to T. S. Eliot. Thus, a prolonged period of sifting and revising brought him to a new understanding of himself as a poet. 'The Megalopsych' stands in relation to Auden's earliest work as *Poems* stands to his juvenilia as a whole: it is the culmination of his work until then and the point of departure for the rest of his career.

The many influences and obsessions of Auden's earliest period finally began to coalesce into an apparently unified poetic voice during the summer of 1927 when he went to Yugoslavia with his father for about a month, roughly from 21 July to 19 August. When he mentioned it over half a decade later in a slick and joky travel piece in the Downs School magazine, he wrote, 'I once went to Yugoslavia with father and wished I was dead'; the piece makes clear that his father was an enthusiastic tourist and he was not.[92] Stephen Spender recalls that Yugoslavia was exceptionally hot and that as a young man Auden found heat unbearable, although, says Spender, Auden found 'the young Yugoslavs exceedingly beautiful.'[93] Auden sent Isherwood an impressionistic letter, reminiscent in places of Eliot's 'Gerontion', suggesting that his new circumstances reminded him intensely of his school-days and of earlier trips abroad, possibly with his father to Germany in the summer of 1925 or to Austria with William McElwee in the winter of 1926–27:

[91] *DH*, 19.
[92] 'In Search of Dracula', *The Badger* [2], no. 4 (Autumn 1934): 22.
[93] AN, 30 March 1992, to Katherine Bucknell.

We walked into the school chapel and held hands. The sensible barriers crumbled. There was Winder too of course. 'You haven't told me' I whined. Now the cooled brain in an irreverent hour. When the thunder began Plato looked up into the sky, Aristotle put up his umbrella.

'We went out into the Hofgarten,' sugar in rectangles again, cognac, and the Blue Danube waltzes under undistinguished trees. Bezahlen bitte. Jesus wept.

No, I didn't go to Iceland after all, but came to Yugo-Slavia, and am writing in the heat of the day, while Memory drones on like a Satirist reciting in the Dog Days. The recrudescence of Atmosphere is too much for me, hence the opening paragraph, a description of my spiritual progress. The girls have ham legs and ham eyes, the boys speak strange tongues, but the message is the same.[94]

Auden's father was a figure of liberation and of cure, from mother, from home, from religion, from psychological paralysis. Yet when Auden looked to his father, and to the scientific techniques and modern attitudes associated with his father, for a solution to his own psychological and sexual unhappiness, none was forthcoming. Indeed, Auden apparently understood his father to be the source of what he regarded as inherited weakness in himself. Two poems written near the end of the Yugoslavia trip and immediately following his return, 'Truly our fathers had the gout' and 'We, knowing the family history', take up this theme of paternally inherited illness; the poems were abandoned, but the theme was to recur during the Berlin period and afterwards in poems such as 'On Sunday Walks', 'The Silly Fool', 'Under boughs between our tentative endearments', and again, centrally, in *The Orators*. Many years later Auden said that he admired his father's gentleness and learning, but he also found him weak: 'as a husband he was often henpecked.'[95] In 1929, Auden recorded several scenes in his Berlin journal demonstrating his father's reluctance to engage in conflict of any kind, such as accepting stamps in an amount he did not want in order to avoid troubling the girl who was selling them to change them, or quelling a family argument with the plea, 'For God's sake don't say anything.' Apparently what Auden took for

[94] ALS, Hotel Elephant, Ljubljana, Croatia, [July 1927], private American collection.
[95] 'As It Seemed to Us', *FA*, 501.

weakness in his father brought about in him at the time feelings of physical revulsion; he noted that he could not bear to light his father's cigarette with the match he had used to light his own. Yet in 1942 he told his friend James Stern: 'When I was 15 I was on a walking tour with my father, and we were sharing a bed: I suddenly had a most violent longing to be fucked by him. (Not being a novelist, I have to confess that he didn't).'[96]

In *The Orators* the search for a leader recapitulates and expands Auden's restless adolescent search for poetic models and intellectual mentors, and Auden's handling of the theme reveals an underlying link between his relation with his father and his tendency to fall in love with young, heterosexual, athletic types such as Gabriel Carritt. Auden borrowed a few details for *The Orators* from Freud's 'Mourning and Melancholia' (he had taken careful notes from Freud's essay in his 1929 Berlin journal). He used some of these details to present the narcissistic wound in 'Letter to a Wound' as, in part, a psychological symptom of the speaker's melancholia. Among other things, the wound represents one possible response to the psychological loss Auden had experienced many years earlier when his father left for the war in 1917. Try as he might to replace his father with other 'masculine' types, he had become obsessed, like the speaker of 'Letter to a Wound', with his own psychological symptoms. Longing for direct contact with a masculine figure persisted, but as the habit of mind reflected in Auden's earliest love poems and other poems suggests, this longing continued unrequited, and apparently at the time Auden preferred it that way.

Whether the trip to Yugoslavia briefly satisfied Auden's need for contact with his father or whether it gave him a renewed sense of their shared inadequacies—probably both are true—it certainly made him all the more determined to reinvent himself as a poet. As Auden mentioned to his brother John before undergoing psychoanalysis in 1928, he felt he had an 'inferiority complex'; he was apparently borrowing the terminology from Adler, who describes the usual response to feelings of inferiority as compensation, in other words, the increase of effort.[97] In the 1942 letter to Stephen Spender in which Auden de-

---

[96] ALS, the Maypole, Daylesford, Berwyn, Pa., 30 July 1942.

[97] See Alfred Adler, *The Neurotic Constitution: Outlines of a Comparative Individualistic Psychology and Psychotherapy*, trans. Bernard Glueck and John E. Lind (New York, 1917; London, 1921).

scribed his weakness as a poet and contrasted it with Spender's strength, he did not hint at the ruthless self-discipline required to transform all the available writing of other people into his own work of art; on the surface of this effort, visible to the world, is the famous routine of hours spent writing, but only private and mysterious labour produces a new poem. In 1942, just as in 1927, Auden was thinking of his weakness as something for which he must compensate with rigorous self-criticism; he set about shaping his poetic identity according to a self-conscious plan and he prepared to remake himself as a poet by revising much of his work for the book that his publisher titled *The Collected Poetry of W. H. Auden*, which eventually appeared in 1945. He wrote his letter to Spender in April; in May he wrote to Louise Bogan: 'Now and then I look through my books and is my face red. . . . I sometimes toy with re-writing the whole lot when I'm senile, like George Moore.'[98] The timing of this is suggestive, because 1942 also was overshadowed by continual, fertile musings on his relationship with his father; the July letter to James Stern in which he described his sexual longing at fifteen for him was one of a series of revealing recollections of his father in letters to Stern that summer.

Only a few days after his return from Yugoslavia in 1927, Auden wrote the now famous poem beginning 'Who stands, the crux left of the watershed,' in which Edward Mendelson has suggested he first discovered his own poetic voice.[99] The journey abroad and the prolonged contact with his father triggered an important change in his writing; other, more important changes were to come after he left Oxford for good. Auden wrote many years later in 'As It Seemed to Us': 'At nineteen, I was self-critical enough to know that the poems I was writing were still merely derivative, that I had not yet found my own voice, and I felt certain that in Oxford I should never find it, that as long as I remained there, I should remain a child.'[100] Although he preserved in some collections of his adult work a few of the poems written in Oxford when he was twenty and twenty-one and printed in *Poems* (1928), it was not until after Auden arrived in Berlin that he began steadily to produce mature, publishable work. Visiting home briefly in February 1929, he sent a copy of *Poems* to E. R. Dodds (he apparently gave copies to a number of friends at this time) with a

---

[98] Quoted in Jenkins, 'Eleven Letters from Auden to Stephen Spender', 80 n. 8.
[99] *Early Auden*, 32ff.
[100] *FA*, 513–14.

letter saying that the second poem in the volume, the one beginning
'I chose this lean country', 'is now completely rewritten as it is far too
Yeatsian at present.'[101] He meant that he had already reworked it into
a different poem beginning 'From scars where kestrels hover'. He had
expunged the most obvious echoes of Yeats and added in his manu-
script notebook 'Berlin. Jan 1929' at the foot.[102] He had also revised
and redated several other contemporary pieces. Fully aware that he
had still been in the grip of his useful obsession with Yeats when he
composed 'I chose this lean country', he was determined to progress
towards something new. Alone in Berlin, cut off from family, friends,
and familiar institutions, he had started to come to terms with the gift
of his own weakness. The student began to transform himself into
a master.

[101] ALS, Lordswood Road letterhead, [February 1929], with Dodds's copy of *P(28)*,
Bodleian.
[102] AA, 165.

TEXTUAL NOTE

The Contents of This Book

This volume includes all the known surviving poems that Auden wrote between March 1922, when he decided to become a poet, and October 1928, when he left England to live in Berlin. Auden was a schoolboy at the Gresham's School, Holt, from September 1920 until June 1925; he went up to Christ Church, Oxford, in October 1925 and sat for his final Honour School in June 1928. By the time he left for Berlin the following autumn, he had prepared for publication his first volume, *Poems* (1928), which was both the culmination of his youthful poetic development and the point of departure for his mature career. The poems from *Poems* (1928) are reprinted here along with Auden's schoolboy and other undergraduate poems in roughly chronological order. It should be borne in mind that for Auden's earliest poems, only a few dates can be fixed with any certainty. Auden's artistic development and his early intellectual life were rich and animated; I have included in the notes to the poems as much as I could find out about the experiences, ideas, and literary interests they reflect. Also, I have pointed out many of the revealing connections between his first writing and his mature public work.

Manuscripts and Letters

Throughout his adolescence Auden sent or gave copies of his poems first to his mother and later to his close friends. As identified in the notes to this edition, the collections of manuscripts and typescripts are, for the most part, named after the person to whom Auden first sent or gave them. They are described below in chronological order. All unpublished letters referred to in this edition are in the possession of their recipients or the heirs of their recipients unless another owner is named.

The Constance Auden collection, originally belonging to Auden's mother, Constance Rosalie Bicknell Auden, is the earliest and the second-largest group of Auden's unpublished work. Now in the Department of Western Manuscripts, Bodleian Library, Oxford, it includes a large number of loose folios (MS.Eng.Poet.c.68) and a notebook

(MS.Eng.Poet.e.153). Many of the loose folios are lined sheets of vary-ing sizes, often with two or three poems on one folio, and often with writing on both sides. They appear to have been sent home from school either as they were written or in bunches. They have been bound and numbered by the Bodleian, one number to each recto, and for convenience I refer to these numbers in my notes, but the numbers bear no relation to any original ordering of the poems. The notebook is a presentation copy, written out for Auden's mother and inscribed to her (see Introduction, p. xxx). It has stiff covers wrapped in blue marbled paper and measures 6½ inches by 8 inches (46½ cm by 20 cm), with a total of sixty-nine folios, of which the last twenty-two folios are blank. The folios are lined on both sides and numbered in pencil, rather eccentrically, apparently partly by Dodds. All folio sides bearing poems or parts of poems are numbered, but blank folios oc-curring within the sequence of poems are not numbered, so that sometimes recto and verso of the same folio have sequential numbers and sometimes they do not, depending on whether there is writing on the verso. For the blank folios in the back of the notebook, the system of numbering changes, and each folio is assigned one number, on the rectos, as in the loose folios. This part of the sequence was probably completed by a librarian. Again, I refer to these numbers in my notes for convenience.

It seems likely, from ink and handwriting, that Auden copied poems into the notebook from time to time, singly and in groups; the last poem in the notebook, 'Stone Walls', was written in February 1925, and may well have been added to the book after it was pre-sented.[1] There is evidence, too, that Auden revised a few of the poems some time after they were written out, and perhaps even after he pre-sented the notebook. It is unclear when he began to write in the note-book, and the poems are not written out in chronological order, al-though they sometimes approximate it. Many poems appear both among the loose folios and in the notebook; also, the loose folios and the notebook include poems not in the other part of the collection. Some of the loose folios' poems predate the notebook, while others post-date it. Apparently Auden was sending or giving poems to his

---

[1] Auden wrote a different poem called 'Stone Walls' in 1923 or 1924, and the 1925 'Stone Walls' exists in several versions. In the notebook, the 1925 'Stone Walls' begins 'The hills are used to walls about them', but in this edition I have printed the version beginning 'One almost takes a hedge for granted'.

mother (or perhaps to his parents together, as his only known letter home from school, kept with the collection, is addressed to them both) before he began to prepare the notebook, and he continued to do so both while he was preparing the notebook and afterwards. Thus only some of the poems in the notebook are fair copies of the loose folios, though it seems likely that poems appearing in both parts of the collection might have been his or his mother's favourites.

The collection as a whole dates from 1922 to 1925 and includes a few pieces that were also published in schoolboy publications. A note with the collection says: 'These early poems of Wystan are not to be destroyed—nor given to him—They can be entrusted to a librarian— C. R. Auden 1st July 1940.' Mrs Auden gave the collection to E. R. Dodds in July 1940, and he deposited it in the Bodleian; it is has often been wrongly referred to as the Dodds collection, though in fact it forms only part of the collection of Dodds's papers in the Bodleian. Some annotations made by Dodds appear on the loose folios.

In 1922 or 1923, Auden became friendly with Michael Davidson, a journalist, whom he met through the Gresham's music master, Walter Greatorex. Davidson, about ten years older than Auden, then lived in Norwich, where he worked for *The Eastern Daily Press*. The two exchanged frequent letters, Auden enclosing his poems and Davidson sending recently published volumes of verse that he learned about through his work at the newspaper. Davidson later recalled meeting Auden in about 1922, but he also said that Auden was sixteen years old, which would not have been until 1923. The friendship remained close for about two years, until Davidson moved to London in 1924.[2] Even then, however, the two remained in touch for a time, as evidenced by a postcard in the Davidson collection addressed to Davidson at a London address and postmarked 13 May 1925. The card bears only a revision to one of Auden's recent poems and nothing else, so their correspondence must still have been frequent enough to make salutations or explanatory preambles unnecessary. In addition to this postcard, one letter, a small collection of typescripts (possibly prepared by Davidson from manuscripts Auden gave or sent him), and one autograph poem survive from this friendship. Of the nineteen typescript poems, thirteen are numbered at the top in a series of numbers ranging up to thirty-nine; clearly many poems are missing.

[2] *The World, the Flesh, and Myself*, 67, 126.

Probably it was Davidson who typed and made carbons of a number of the poems in this collection (some of them are typed in purple), and he appears to have suggested changes. Revisions on some of the type-scripts are in a graceful, mature hand that may be Davidson's writing. Auden sometimes accepted these suggestions, sometimes not. For instance, in the case of 'Stone Walls' ('One almost takes a hedge for granted') he wrote out the poem again in the new version incorporating the changes marked on the typescript, and then later reverted to an earlier version closer to what appears to have been his own first draft. A few of the typescripts and carbons in the Davidson collection exactly match their counterparts in the Isherwood collection, right down to the typographical errors, corrections, and revisions (although some such duplicates in the Isherwood collection were later altered again), which makes clear that Auden sometime gave out carbon copies of the same typescripts. Of the six unnumbered typescripts in the Davidson collection, five do not exist in any other collection and one exists only in an earlier collection; these may have been deliberately excluded from the numbered sequence Auden and Davidson were assembling, perhaps because they were too obviously influenced by Hardy.

In 1927 these typescripts, manuscript, and pieces of correspondence were given by Davidson to A. S. T. Fisher, a contemporary of Auden whose rooms were on Auden's staircase during their first term in Christ Church. Fisher eventually deposited the Davidson collection in the Christ Church Library along with his own collection of autograph poems and transcriptions, and the collection as a whole became known as the Fisher collection. Fisher obtained his part of the collection in a variety of ways. Some poems and fragments were given to him by Auden; others he took down from Auden's recitation; one he apparently copied when he stayed with the Audens in April 1926 from the notebook Auden had given to his mother; still others he copied from undergraduate magazines. Among all the collections of Auden's surviving juvenilia, the Fisher collection appears to be the least reliable textually, and some items are wrongly dated, probably from faulty recollections years after they were written. Still, I have relied on Fisher's transcriptions for the few poems that do not exist in any other collection (there is little doubt that these poems are by Auden), and I have also recorded substantive variants from some of his other texts, despite the likelihood that Fisher introduced them himself, because there is at least a possibility that Auden recited the poems to Fisher in texts different from those he wrote down. Fisher's handwriting appears to have changed rather dramatically towards a formal italic hand in later years, so it is usually possible to distinguish contemporary from subsequent transcriptions, and I have not recorded variants from any transcriptions made after the 1920s, nor from transcriptions made during the 1920s where these are obviously copied from undergraduate publications. One poem from the Davidson collection, 'He Revisits the Spot', has been lost, along with another poem, 'California', transcribed by Fisher from Mrs Auden's notebook. Fisher apparently still possessed these in the late 1960s when he wrote an article, 'Auden's Juvenilia' (eventually published in *Notes and Queries* in October 1974), based on his collection. I have relied on transcriptions made by B. C. Bloomfield in the early 1960s for the text of both these poems. A further mystery associated with the Davidson and Fisher collections is that Fisher once lent Geoffrey Tillotson four typescripts, 'Buzzards', 'Farglow', 'The crocus stars the border', and 'He Revisits the Spot', and Tillotson made a note, later seen by Edward Mendelson, of the numbers assigned to the poems as, respectively, 16, 17, 28, and 29, but these numbers do not correspond to the numbers of the same poems in the collections. Either Tillotson's note is wrong, or there were four *more* typescripts, numbered differently, and now lost.

The Isherwood collection, still privately held in California, is the largest surviving group of Auden's unpublished early poems. Auden began sending his work to Isherwood for criticism soon after Christmas 1925 when they met through Fisher and renewed their preparatory school friendship. Some of the first manuscripts Auden sent to Isherwood were written well before their meeting, and later he sent Isherwood nearly everything he wrote during his undergraduate years and for a time thereafter, along with many letters discussing his progress. The poems are on various sizes and kinds of paper, in typescript, manuscript, and carbon. Isherwood typed some of the poems himself at Auden's request. He acquired a typewriter in August 1925 when he became secretary to André Mangeot's string quartet, and a letter from Auden says, 'Here are two more poems for you. If you could possibly type some of the untyped ones for me I should be most grateful.'[3] Isherwood was a more fastidious writer than Auden and probably made some corrections, particularly to Auden's punctuation (see pp. lxvii–lxviii). In any case, he may have kept carbons of the poems he typed, or, if Auden was having poems typed by someone else, Auden may have sent the carbons to Isherwood. Isherwood was a severe and generous critic—severe in his judgements, generous with his time—and he offered copious advice which appears to have helped Auden progress, especially through his worst fads and absurdities. Isherwood's greatest contribution was perhaps more general than particular, in providing a serious and attentive audience whom Auden was determined to please. Some time after he gave Isherwood the poems, Auden added pencilled dates to many of them. This may have been between mid-March and mid-April 1936, when Auden visited Isherwood in Portugal to work on *The Ascent of F 6*; Isherwood apparently showed Auden the manuscripts and typescripts he had saved throughout the 1920s, perhaps in preparation for writing 'Some Notes on Auden's Early Poetry', which appeared in the *New Verse* Auden Double Number in November 1937, or in preparation for writing *Lions and Shadows*, begun in October 1936 and published in 1938.[4] A few lines from the early work and the letters Isherwood saved with it reappear in 'Underneath the abject willow', written in March 1936, around the time of the Portugal trip.[5] It is somewhat remarkable that after a decade Auden could still recall the months as well as the years in which he had written these early poems, but it is not impossible. Still, he may have dated the poems on some earlier occasion. For the most part, these pencilled dates seem to be reliable, apart from a few clear misrememberings that I have mentioned in the notes. Also, in some of the dates, Auden wrote the numerals '3' and '5' in a style that makes them all but indistinguishable from one another. Other evidence suggests that Auden may not have sent Isherwood *any* poems written before 1924, but for a number of poems probably written in 1925, I have used square brackets around the last numeral, '192[5]', to register the possibility that Auden may have written '1923'. The pencilled dates appear to stop with the last of Auden's poems written at Gresham's, as if he were marking only those poems which predated

---

[3] AL, signed 'Dodo', probably written during the first half of 1926.

[4] When he dated the poems, Auden may have revised some of them as well. See 'Revisions and Variants', below, p. lxix.

[5] See 'I chose this lean country' and note.

the renewal of his friendship with Isherwood; Isherwood himself would presumably have remembered when the later poems were written. Possibly this means that other undated poems from the earlier part of the collection were written in the summer or autumn of 1925.

Isherwood introduced Auden to Edward Upward in a Soho restaurant in 1927, but they had exchanged letters before this, and Auden had sent Upward some of his poems nearly a year earlier. Upward recalls, 'I was tutoring in Cornwall in 1926 at the time of the General Strike. . . . I think it was after the Strike that Auden first wrote to me—in Cornwall—and sent me some early poems.'[6] The General Strike was in early May 1926, and most of the poems that Auden sent Upward were written before that (some as early as 1924), the rest within the following month. Of these a small number of typescripts, one manuscript, and one fragment survive with a few letters among Upward's papers in the British Library.

Also in the British Library are two manuscripts that were apparently enclosed in letters Auden sent to his Oxford friend William McElwee around the same period; the letters and poems are kept together (Add.MS.59618).

John Pudney, a friend from Gresham's, was the recipient during Auden's Oxford years of a number of manuscripts and typescripts; those that have survived are divided between the library of the College of St Mark and St John in Plymouth, Devon (where they were presented by Pudney and Janet Adam Smith in memory of her husband and Pudney's friend, Michael Roberts), and the Berg Collection of the New York Public Library. (Four poems in the Berg Collection which, based on watermarks and other internal and external evidence, I have included among those originally given to Pudney, belonged to Michael Roberts before reaching the Berg, but it is almost certain that Pudney, and not Auden himself, gave the poems to Roberts some years after they were written.) In his memoir, Pudney recalls a 'thick sheaf' of poems written at Gresham's, but only a few poems have survived, and none of these was written at Gresham's.[7] All the known Pudney poems are clearly from the Oxford period.

In the summer of 1927 Auden sent a small batch of new poems to

---

[6] ALS, Sandown, Isle of Wight, 13 November 1989, to Katherine Bucknell. See also Upward, 'Remembering the Earlier Auden', *Adam International Review* (1973–74): 17–18.

[7] *Home and Away*, 46.

Cecil Day-Lewis, with whom he co-edited *Oxford Poetry 1927;* these are now in the Harry Ransom Humanities Research Center at the University of Texas at Austin. Two poems which Auden wrote on the endpapers of books he possessed are also in Austin, where some of Auden's library is now held.

Stephen Spender preserved some of the copy, mostly typescript, for the 1928 *Poems* and also an earlier manuscript poem; these are now in the Berg with many of Auden's letters to him.

A few further individual manuscripts are held privately and by libraries; these are mentioned in the notes to the relevant poems.

Although friends like Medley, Pudney, Davidson, and Tom Driberg tell of or are associated with tales of countless poems given to them by Auden and somehow lost or destroyed, I have found specific references to only a handful of poems that have not survived to be included in this edition. Those recipients who did save Auden's poems were very careful with them, and it is clear that Auden often sent the same poems to more than one person. I believe that there were not a great many more; his output as represented in this volume is already enormous.

In 1927 Auden began to use a ledger notebook, which appears to be the earliest surviving example of work written out for himself rather than for someone else; nonetheless, on Christmas Eve 1949 this, too, was given to a friend, Auden's student and secretary, Alan Ansen. Although it lacks many pages, the notebook contains work written from late May or early June 1927 until March 1929, including much of the material for *Poems* (1928) and *Paid on Both Sides* almost entirely in chronological order, most with dates and places of composition at the foot, and a few with Auden's own annotations. The Ansen notebook shows a watermark throughout: 'H. P. Pope Ltd / Stationers Printers / Birmingham'; this watermark is also on some of the loose lined sheets in the Isherwood collection. However, the notebook folios and the loose folios are not exactly the same size, nor do the lines on them appear to match (it has not been possible to examine the folios side by side). The notebook is now in the Berg Collection, and has been reproduced in a photographic facsimile with a physical description, transcriptions, and annotations by Patrick Lawlor. For the convenience of readers, the page references in my notes are to this facsimile.[8]

---

[8] For a description of his pagination, see Lawlor, 125.

Early Publications

Many of Auden's earliest poems were published in schoolboy and un-
dergraduate publications and in his first collection, *Poems* (1928),
printed by hand by Stephen Spender and dedicated to Isherwood.
The schoolboy and undergraduate publications are now difficult to
find, even in copyright libraries. Roughly thirty copies of *Poems* were
originally printed, although the book itself says 'About 45 copies'.
Spender recalls that when he asked the Holywell Press to complete
the printing for him after he broke his hand-press, he requested forty-
five, but the press discarded some of the printing he had already done
and completed only about thirty bound copies.[9] The volume is de-
scribed in Bloomfield and Mendelson's *Bibliography*,[10] although the
list of copies and their owners traced has grown since the publication
of the *Bibliography*: no. 2, Isherwood, now in a private American collec-
tion; no. 4, Cecil Day-Lewis, now in a private American collection; no.
9, Edward Upward, now in the British Library; no. 10, D. van Lennep
(later owned by John Hayward), now in a private English collection;
no. 11, A. H. Campbell, now in the Edinburgh University Library; no.
12, Winifred [Paine],[11] now in the collection of the late John Johnson;
no. 15, E. R. Dodds, now in the Bodleian; no. 16, John Layard, now in
a private collection; no. 17, Stephen Spender, now in the University of
Cincinnati Library;[12] no. 18, Gabriel Carritt/Sidney Newman, now in
the Berg Collection; no. 19, Gabriel Carritt, now in the Houghton
Library, Harvard University; no. 24, Sheilah Richardson (briefly
Auden's fiancée), now in the Durham University Library; 'No. 24-
About', D. G. O. Ayerst, now in a private American collection; un-
numbered, William Plomer, now at the Columbia University Library;
unnumbered, Stephen Spender, originally inscribed by Auden to
Spender and later inscribed by both Auden and Spender to Cyril Con-
nolly, now in the McFarlin Library, University of Oklahoma, Tulsa;[13]
unnumbered, George Rylands, now in the Library of King's College,

---

[9] Conversation with Katherine Bucknell, 17 November 1992.

[10] Pp. 1–3.

[11] Winifred Paine was a companion to Spender and his sister Christine after their
parents died. She is called 'Caroline' in Spender's memoir *World within World* (London,
1951).

[12] Spender, ALS, 4 July 1991, to Katherine Bucknell.

[13] Spender, ALS, 4 July 1991.

Cambridge; unnumbered, Father Martin D'Arcy, now in the Pierpont
Morgan Library; unnumbered, now in the Lilly Library, Indiana Uni-
versity, Bloomington. George Auden's copy disappeared after his
death. Louis MacNeice's copy is lost, but a typed transcript made by
Ruthven Todd in 1937 is now in the Poetry/Rare Books Collection at
the State University of New York at Buffalo. The transcript does not
copy Auden's inscription (if any) to MacNeice, nor does it record the
number of the printed copy. A. L. Rowse also received a copy, which
he lent to a friend who was killed in the Second World War; this copy
is now lost. Another lost copy belonged to E. H. Jacob.

For the text in this volume, I have used the Isherwood copy, which
bears the inscription 'To Christopher with love from the Author
"Dura virum nutrix" ' in Auden's autograph, and has Auden's and
Spender's autograph corrections throughout. (The phrase 'Harsh
nurse of men' perhaps refers to Isherwood's nurturing role as Au-
den's critic.) I have collated this with six other copies: the Upward
copy, the Dodds copy, the Carritt/Newman copy, a microfilm-photo-
copy of the Winifred Paine copy,[14] a facsimile reproduction of the
Spender/ Cincinnati copy,[15] and a facsimile reproduction of the Shei-
lah Richardson copy.[16] The Upward copy is signed in ink by Auden
and in pencil by Upward. In 'W. H. Auden's *Poems* of 1928', Joanna
Leevers has said that the Upward copy 'has manuscript corrections by
Auden himself,' but many of them are by Spender.[17] The Dodds copy
has an inscription to Dodds in Auden's hand, but almost all of the
corrections are in Spender's hand. The Carritt/Newman copy is
signed 'G. Carritt' in ink and 'Sidney Newman' in pencil. Carritt
signed both his copies in the same way. He recalls that he and Auden
and Newman were close friends at the time the book was printed, and
that he may have given one of his copies to Newman or simply asked
Newman to sign it.[18] The microfilm-photocopy of the Winifred Paine
copy has the pages assembled with rectos and versos reversed; this
does not alter the numbering but it makes the preliminary material
look odd. The Spender/Cincinnati copy is not inscribed, and it bears

[14] Produced by University Microfilms (Ann Arbor, Mich., 1961).
[15] Printed by the George Ellison Collection of Twentieth-Century Poetry, University
of Cincinnati, 1964.
[16] Printed for sale at the Ilkley Festival of Literature, 1973.
[17] *The British Library Journal* 14, no. 2 (Autumn 1988): 204.
[18] ALS, 11 September 1991, to Katherine Bucknell.

revisions and numerous cancellations in Auden's and Spender's hands; these are identified in a list at the front of the facsimile edition. The Richardson copy has 'S. M. Richardson 26.2.29', probably in her hand, and crossed out, on the recto of the front free endpaper, but no inscription. Auden may have given out a number of copies of the volume when he visited home from Berlin in February 1929.

It is not an aim of this edition to record the fortunes of *Poems* after it was printed. Rather, I wish to emphasize how Auden's work developed towards the publication of his first volume. Therefore, I have not printed individual variants from all the copies of *Poems* listed above. Almost all the differences among these volumes arose because they were corrected by hand by more than one person over a period of time. The differences are not always trivial, but it is for the most part easy to detect Auden's intention by focusing on the similarities rather than the differences among the copies. I have therefore emended the Isherwood text only where the other copies, taken as a group, tend to show that another reading is closer to Auden's final intention. I have listed such emendations with the draft variants, though it should be clear from their respective names which are which. I have recorded as many draft variants as possible because they tell a great deal about Auden's development; these are discussed further in 'Variants and Revisions' below. (I have not recorded variants in punctuation except where these happen to appear among other recorded variants.) Often the most interesting differences among those copies of *Poems* that I have been able to examine are not variations in the text but variations in who made corrections to the text. In general, the earlier in the numbered sequence, the more likely that at least some corrections were made by Auden. But in all the copies, there are some changes that were made only by Spender, and this accords with Spender's recollection that he made the revisions himself from a corrected proof or typescript supplied to him by Auden.[19] Many of these were to improve badly inked letters (such alterations cease at the start of the professionally printed pages); others are more substantive, however, and it seems clear that Spender or a typist who gave him copy misread Auden's handwriting. Still others, and only a few, might be revisions that Auden wished to

[19] See Spender's '*Poems* (1928) by W. H. Auden printed by S.H.S.', an autograph manuscript written 13 June 1974, King's College Library, Cambridge, Misc. 25, fos. 7–10.

make to the printed text, and he seems to have persuaded Spender to write these out for him, although Auden wrote them into some copies himself. They both overlooked a few misprints, which I have emended according to the manuscripts and typescripts. Considering the amateur nature of the printing of the book, the corrections that I have been able to see are relatively consistent, although, again, the copies earlier in the sequence seem to have a few more corrections. The Carritt/Newman copy oddly has almost no emendations at all, but as Carritt was given two, Auden or Spender might not have taken the trouble to correct both. The Spender/Cincinnati copy also stands out from the pattern. Many poems and parts of poems are cancelled and the notation 'PTO' appears at the bottom of many pages, but the markings do not correspond to any later edition of Auden's work. This copy was clearly prepared for a unique purpose now forgotten.

CHRONOLOGY

Dates given for the poems in this volume are intended to indicate the earliest date at which a poem was regarded by Auden as finished, even if he subsequently decided to revise it. I have done this according to Auden's own habit, established from the Ansen notebook. In the notebook, Auden placed dates at the bottom of his poems apparently as he first completed writing them out; this seems clear because he occasionally made a note of the date at which he subsequently revised a poem if the revision was substantial. Substantial revisions of this sort, in the Ansen notebook and for earlier work, are mentioned in the notes, with additional dates where possible.

I have largely relied on Auden's own dates for his poems. For undated poems I have looked for clues in letters, recollections, publication history, subject matter, and style, and as I have indicated by enclosing them in square brackets, many of these dates are conjectural only. The earliest poems, in particular those in the Constance Auden collection, can only be grouped in roughly chronological clusters. It is relatively clear from the way the poems have survived that the Constance Auden collection includes Auden's earliest work, the Davidson and Fisher collections his next work, the Isherwood collection the next, and so on. But there is a great deal of overlap among these groups, and there are some very early poems that Auden saved and sent repeatedly to different friends years after they were written. I have used the shape of the collections only as a guide.

Within the Constance Auden collection, neither the notebook nor the folios offer a chronological order; still, in some instances it is clear that poems that appear in close sequence in the notebook or on the same folio among the loose folios were written at about the same time. I have followed the order Auden gave the poems in the notebook, although I have altered it where there is clear evidence to do so. Thus poems with definite early dates are moved to the front, where they are known to belong, and poems appearing in the loose folios on the same folio as a poem also appearing in the notebook are added into the sequence just before, just after, or as close as possible to the poem with which they share a loose folio. Poems which do not appear in the notebook, which do not share a folio with any other poem, and for which there is no other clear evidence of date, fall towards the end of the sequence. A drawback to this arrangement is that, among the very early poems on loose folios, there are certainly some which may be placed too late in the sequence simply because there is no certain evidence on which to move them forward. However, other possible arrangements seem to offer worse drawbacks.

It appears that Isherwood arranged part of his collection in chronological order, in so far as he knew what this was, but the arrangement is not complete, and it has been somewhat disturbed. As the sequence of Auden's work progresses into the Oxford period, the external evidence becomes more plentiful and stylistic changes become somewhat more clear-cut, so that even conjectural dates are more likely to be accurate; for later poems I have more confidently interleaved dated and undated work, though even in the mid-1920s some poems are placed at the end of the year in which they were probably written. An apparent slowing in Auden's output during the first half of 1927 may have come about because some poems written during this period were revised and recycled for 'The Megalopsych', and it is no longer possible to establish earlier texts or dates of composition. Auden arranged the contents of his 1928 *Poems* in chronological order, except for poems 3 through 8, which appeared slightly out of sequence. In the present edition, the contents of *Poems* are printed in strictly chronological order and interleaved with other contemporary compositions not included in the 1928 volume. The original order for *Poems* may easily be established from the poem numbers included in the notes.

EMENDATIONS

Published and unpublished work appears side by side in this volume because, in one sense, all of Auden's adolescent work is work in progress, a preparation for his mature work. In this period he was continually revising and re-revising his work, often after it was published, and frequently he cannibalized poems so thoroughly that distinctions between individual pieces are vague. This makes the conventional notion of final intention difficult to apply. For published poems, I have usually used the published text, and where more than one of these exists, I have usually used the latest published text. But a published text may deviate for any number of reasons from what appears to have been Auden's latest intention; Auden probably did not see or have the opportunity to alter proofs for most of his work that appeared in schoolboy and undergraduate publications, though he sometimes corrected friends' copies of his work. Where it is possible to establish that some other text better represents his final intention, I have preferred it. Evidence for such decisions is usually described in the notes. For unpublished poems, where more than one copy of the poem exists, I have only sometimes been able to distinguish Auden's latest draft or fair copy with any certainty. Even then, problems arise; for instance, frequently the latest fair copy will have been executed quickly and, while perhaps offering a crucial revision of a word or phrase, will omit punctuation carefully worked out in an earlier draft. Because Auden was young and still learning when he wrote these poems, there is a temptation to preserve his best intention rather than his latest one, but I have tried to let his own youthful judgements stand and allow readers to see his work as nearly as possible as he left it. In almost all cases, for published and unpublished texts, I have not amalgamated texts (except in the case of *Poems*, discussed above); rather, I have made a firm choice of one text or another, on whatever evidence or intuition that offered itself, and I have recorded substantive variants in the notes. A few exceptions to this practice occur near the end of this edition, where Auden's many dated drafts, together with the printed text of *Poems* and the handwritten corrections, make it possible to establish clearly how his intentions evolved. (Again, I have not recorded any details of punctuation among the variants, unless a punctuation mark happens to fall among other, more significant variants, which is not often, or unless I have made what seemed a significant emendation to the punctuation; see below for more on punctuation.) Where I have made an emendation, it is described in the notes or represented among the variants, although obvious typographical errors and misprints have been silently corrected. For the small number of words that I could not decipher, I have offered my best conjecture in square brackets preceded by a question mark. Also, I have added an open square ( ) at the foot of the page where a break between stanzas or verse paragraphs might not otherwise be apparent. Untitled poems are headed by three open squares.

I have made a few other silent changes in the text. The margins of Auden's first poems are ragged at best, and I have regularized these according to the simplest scheme apparent on the page, bearing in mind rhyme and other indications of underlying pattern. I have regularized the forms of titles throughout, and I have sometimes regularized the use of upper- and lower-case to achieve internal consistency within individual poems or titles. When young, Auden frequently capitalized words like 'Summer' or 'Autumn' to apostrophize or anthropomorphize; where such an intention is clear, I have usually tried to carry it out through a whole poem. He also habitually, though not always, capitalized some apparently random words, such as 'joy' and 'cuckoo'. Where this habit perhaps hints at special significance I have not altered it; Auden often wrote the letter 'j' as a capital when it came at the start of a word, and most of these I have made lower-case. Also, I have normalized spelling and accidentals throughout. The hyphen offers something of a problem in a neologist like Auden; I have regularized it where a clear norm exists, but I have tried not to alter any apparent attempts to create a new double-barrelled word.

In his earliest poems, Auden did not seem to pay much attention to punctuation, and although he frequently got it wrong (for instance, he usually reversed the colon and the semicolon), I have nearly always reproduced his punctuation as he left it. Some of the poems printed here have almost no punctuation at all. I have added or changed punctuation only where the text threatened otherwise to be confusing, and I have recorded such emendations where they seem significant. It is worth noting that some of the punctuation in Auden's typescripts was probably not added by Auden but by the typist. Davidson, Fisher, and Isherwood all served as typists at some time (Fisher supplied some of the copy to Spender for *Poems*),[20] although there were almost certainly others as well. All three were more meticulous writers than Auden, but there is evidence that Auden at least sometimes saw and approved or disapproved typescripts prepared by them. Since Auden so often followed Isherwood's advice in revising his early work, there is little harm in accepting Isherwood's punctuation where it is not possible to tell precisely what is his and what is Auden's, but I have tried to avoid accepting what is obviously not Auden's decision. Among the earlier manuscript transcriptions made by A. S. T. Fisher, during 1925 and 1926, the punctuation is less reliable than any later typescripts because Fisher took the poems down primarily from recitation and probably punctuated as he saw fit. But where Fisher's is the only surviving copy of a poem, I have retained his punctuation. The typewriter used for the Upward typescripts was worn in such a way that the colon and semicolon are sometimes indistinguishable, which compounds the problem of Auden's general misuse of these two marks, and I have had to surmise his intention from syntax and from punctuation in the other copies.

REVISIONS AND VARIANTS

This edition is intended to give a sense of Auden's development, so I have tried to print as much material as possible. Thus, a handful of poems are printed twice, showing in some cases only minor revisions, because it is clear that at one point Auden regarded them as complete and that at a later moment he rewrote them or, in the case of 'The Megalopsych', used them in a sequence, or rearranged the whole sequence, thereby creating a new work. Where Auden physically cancelled part of a poem, I have usually not printed it, except in the case of some whole lines or stanzas and a few relatively complete poems (all are described as cancelled in the notes) or in the case of a cancellation apparently having been made long after a poem was complete.

[20] *Bibliography*, 2.

On the other hand, I have printed poems and parts of poems which are clearly superseded by a later draft but which Auden never scored out or destroyed; most of these appear in the notes. Because of this practice, the poems that appeared in the 1928 *Poems* are presented, rather unconventionally, with numerous abandoned variants detailed in the notes. I found it impossible to distinguish, in the work preceding *Poems*, between drafts and variants, and to introduce such a distinction partway through the edition seemed confusing; more importantly, it promised less information to the reader.

The end date for this volume is October 1928, and revisions made after this date to any of the poems included here are not incorporated into the text, nor are they listed among the variants. However, for unpublished poems, and occasionally even for published ones, the question of when in time a revision might have been made is difficult to answer (sometimes Auden dated revisions or described them in his dated letters to Isherwood). When Auden added pencilled dates to the poems Isherwood had saved throughout the 1920s, he almost certainly revised a few of the poems as well. This may have been in the mid-1930s, but it is not possible to say for certain which revisions are from the 1920s and which, if any, from the 1930s, so I have incorporated all of them into the text as being roughly contemporary with the time of composition, and I have only occasionally remarked in the notes on the possible time lapse.

The date at which Auden made the last revisions to *Poems* is uncertain. His latest known letter discussing the proposed contents of the volume instructs Spender which poems may be left out if space runs short, and these poems ('Deemed this an outpost, I', 'The houses rolled into the sun', and 'The weeks of blizzard over') were indeed dropped. This letter is on paper watermarked 'H. P. Pope / Stationers Printers / Birmingham',[21] and has on the reverse the poem beginning 'Out of sight assuredly, not out of mind' written in May or June 1927 and heavily revised sometime during the following year. It seems likely that the letter was sent from Birmingham, but it may have been sent from Spa, Belgium, where Auden apparently spent three weeks in August 1928, or from Tapscott, where he went to stay with William McElwee in September; it seems less likely that it was sent from Berlin,

---

[21] ALS, Berg.

in October or later. Spender printed *Poems* during the long summer
vacation,[22] and he recalled later that he took the work to be finished
by the Holywell Press,[23] in Oxford, at the end of the summer vaca-
tion,[24] in early to mid-October, when he returned there for the start of
Michaelmas term. This was roughly the same time that Auden left for
Germany. (Auden's instruction that Spender could drop three poems
if necessary might even have been a response to a plea from Spender
after the project had been started and was proving too much for Spen-
der's small printing set.) In his 1974 essay on the project, Spender
recalls that he sent Auden proofs, but he does not say where or when
he sent them, or whether they were for all or part of the book.

In any case, it is almost certain that Auden did not see a copy of
Poems, and perhaps not even proofs or the partial text completed by
Spender on his own, until after he arrived in Berlin. Two letters from
Berlin suggest that Spender probably forwarded at least some finished
copies to him there. In one letter Auden wrote: 'The books have not
yet arrived. As one parcel sent me was returned I am anxious. I give
you my new address, to which please send them',[25] followed by the
address of his lodging in the Nikolassee, the Berlin suburb where he
lived from October or November until about New Year 1929. The
second, probably later, letter refers to an exchange apparently about
the misprints in *Poems*, implying that by late November or early De-
cember Auden had seen at least one copy of the book and perhaps
asked Spender to make corrections: 'Please don't think I was cross
with you about the books. It was jolly nice of you to do it at all and I
know what my script is like.'[26] Spender could have begun making cor-
rections to the volume at almost any time in Auden's absence during
the autumn. It seems unlikely that any corrections were made before
Auden left for Berlin, although it is possible that on the basis of proofs
or partial proofs he had already given instructions for them.

---

[22] *World within World*, 116.

[23] *Bibliography*, 3.

[24] See '*Poems* (1928) by W. H. Auden printed by S.H.S.', King's College Library, Cam-
bridge, Misc. 25, fos. 7–10.

[25] ALI, on paper watermarked 'WHS' (probably W. H. Smith), Berg.

[26] ALS, on paper watermarked 'WHS', Berg. This letter can be dated to November
or December 1928 because it also says, 'that awful poem of mine in O.P[.] was taken
without permission and against my express wishes.' This refers to 'In Due Season',
published in *The Oxford Outlook* in 1926 and republished in *Oxford Poetry 1928*; *Oxford
Poetry 1928* appeared 9 November 1928 and must have been sent to Auden in Berlin.

I have used *Poems* (1928) as the final text for the poems in that volume, and I have incorporated into that text the alterations made by hand by both Auden and Spender in the Isherwood copy (as representative of the copies Auden gave to his closest friends) because the majority of these are corrections rather than revisions to the text. For a few well-known poems (those that reappeared in the 1930 *Poems*, including those incorporated into the second version of *Paid on Both Sides*), the texts printed here differ from the texts established by Edward Mendelson in the *The English Auden* and the *Plays*, and show Auden's work at an earlier moment of its development. I have not used or recorded any variants from the first version of *Paid on Both Sides*, even though it was completed before Auden left for Berlin, because that text was thoroughly rewritten before it was published, and it seems confusing to give to the interim version—incorporating only a few lyrics—greater authority than *Poems* (1928), and also, perhaps most importantly, because Auden did not make the same revisions to the text of *Poems*.

Notes to the Poems

The first section of each note lists the known texts for each poem in order from the most representative of Auden's final intention to the least; the copy text heads the list. Usually, this results in the texts being listed in reverse chronological order, and any printed version of the text appearing first, but neither of these is always the case. Each text is identified either by the name of the publication in which it appeared or, if unpublished, by the name of the person to whom Auden sent or gave it. Where one collection offers two or more variants of the same text, they are numbered in parentheses. Other page, item, or folio numbers refer to any assigned in the manuscript collection or publication in question. (As mentioned above, page numbers for the Ansen notebook refer to the published facsimile.) For unnumbered manuscripts, such as those in the Fisher and Isherwood collections, I have listed other poems and correspondence which appear on the same folio, or which were clearly posted together in the same envelope.

The list of texts gives some physical description, such as autograph or typescript, ink or pencil. It mentions revisions only where made by a different method (such as pencil over ink, or autograph over typescript). It mentions paper only where a watermark or letterhead clearly identifies it. Watermarks and letterheads are useful in dating some of the poems, but Auden sometimes took paper with him from one place to another, and he tended to write randomly on whatever paper he could find, so these cannot be relied on. Wherever possible the list of texts also mentions a date and sometimes a place of composition, and identifies the hand in which these are written.

Next is a list of variants, including titles, epigraphs, and dedications, and showing substantive emendations. (In general I have not annotated cancelled or variant readings.) The variants are followed by details of the first publication or the first few publications of the poem after the publication of *Poems* (1928). For example, some of Auden's earliest poems appeared in *Lions and Shadows*, in Humphrey Carpenter's biography, and elsewhere; others appeared in Auden's own subsequent books. The Bloomfield and Mendelson *Bibliography* gives further details for subsequent publication in Auden's own books, and anyone wishing to know the full publication history of individual poems must look there and in Mendelson's 'W. H. Auden: A Bibliographical Supplement'.[27] I have tried to supply details of publication of Auden's earliest poems in books by others, especially for books appearing after the *Bibliography*, as the 'Supplement' deliberately does not include these. However, unless the entire poem was printed, I have not recorded it.

[27] *ASI*, 203–36.

POEMS

California

The twinkling lamps stream up the hill
Past the farm and past the mill
Right at the top of the road one sees
A round moon like a Stilton cheese

A man could walk along that track
Fetch the moon and bring it back
Or gather stars up in his hand
Like strawberries on English land.

'But how should I, a poor man dare
To meet so close the full moon's stare?'   10
For this I stopped and stood quite still
Then turned with quick steps down that hill.

[*March? 1922*]

CAN, 17, ink autograph; F, Fisher's autograph transcription, now lost, transcribed by
B. C. Bloomfield in the early 1960s. Variants: TITLE California] 'California (Birming-
ham)' *F.* 1. stream] streamed *F.* 7. Or . . . stars up] And . . . up stars *F.* 11. For this]
And so *F.* 12. quick . . . that] slow . . . the *F.* Printed in 'Auden's Juvenilia', 371, and
Carpenter, 29.

In the late 1960s, Fisher recalled: 'I secured a few manuscripts, took down others
from his recitation, and copied what his mother showed me as his first poem, when I
stayed at his home in April 1926; 'Auden's Juvenilia', 370. Apparently this first poem
was 'California', although it seems technically more accomplished than some of
Auden's other earliest pieces. On his copy, Fisher wrote '16 years', but if this was
Auden's first poem, or among his first, it would have been written when he was fifteen.
Auden himself recalled that his first poem had been a Wordsworthian sonnet on Blea
Tarn in the Lake District. No such poem is known to survive, but Auden quoted the last
line and a half in his foreword to B. C. Bloomfield's *W. H. Auden: A Bibliography: The
Early Years through 1955* (Charlottesville, Va., 1964), ix: 'and in the quiet / Oblivion of
thy waters let them stay'. Auden may possibly have visited Blea Tarn with his brother
John and their father when the three stayed at Derwentfolds Farm twelve to fifteen
miles north of it during an August 1922 holiday. But if this August visit inspired the
sonnet, the poem is not likely to have been Auden's first, as he later recalled that he
decided in March to become a poet (see 'Letter to Lord Byron', *EA*, 194; *CP*, 109–10).
Perhaps he had forgotten about other earlier poems, or perhaps the Blea Tarn sonnet
was his first poem and had another, previous inspiration. In any case, 'California' may
have been the first poem that Auden sent home or presented to his mother.

Fisher thought the 'California' of the title was the small village near Birmingham,
and he was probably told that by Mrs Auden. But also there is a house at Gresham's that
was then called 'California'. It was purchased by the school in 1945 and renamed
'Applegarth'; C. L. S. Linnell and A. B. Douglas, *Gresham's School History and Register,
1555–1954* (Holt, Norfolk, 1955). For a time it was used as a house for the senior school

and afterwards as a staff house. It is a small flint house, in the traditional Norfolk style, and stands at a crossroads but not near a hill.

As Carlos Baker has noted, the last stanza of 'California' closely echoes the closing lines of Wordsworth's 'The Solitary Reaper'; *The Echoing Green* (Princeton, 1984), 320.

A Moment

Behold the sky
That once was one great glowing sapphire
Begins to die,
And now is but a glinting opal fire,
Smould'ring to a faded scarlet,
O'er the embers of the sunset.

And lo, a soft gossamer-like cloud,
That round the crescent moon, enveils
Its vap'rous shroud,
And passing on its way, reveals   10
Her, trembling, silvery, rainbow-clad
Silent, frailly sad.

March or April 1922

The Gresham 9, no. 10 (8 April 1922): 147, unsigned but probably by Auden (see below), with an editor's note: 'We publish this in spite of technical errors. Considering the age of the author it shows great promise'. Reprinted in *The W. H. Auden Society Newsletter* 4 (October 1990): 1.

This appears to be Auden's first published poem, printed shortly after he began writing poetry in March 1922; see 'Letter to Lord Byron' (*EA*, 194; *CP*, 109–10) and Medley, 38. However, no manuscript is known to survive, nor is there any evidence that Auden or his family preserved a printed copy. The poem's final line is used again in two later adolescent poems, 'The Dark Fiddler', where it again appears in the final line, and 'Humpty Dumpty', where it appears in l. 84. This type of quarrying is characteristic of Auden throughout his earliest period.

Like several other early poems ('Dawn', 'Everest', 'Nightfall'), 'A Moment' is apparently influenced by the Irish poet A.E. (George William Russell). See, for instance, A.E.'s 'By the Margin of the Great Deep' and 'The Great Breath,' which both appeared in *The Oxford Book of English Verse*, ed. Arthur Quiller-Couch (Oxford, 1922).

Another early poem of Auden's, 'Sunset from Primrose Hill', about fourteen lines long, was published probably in the autumn of 1922 or early in 1923 in the first number of an amateur literary magazine edited by James M. Richards and Raymond Rivière, contemporaries of Auden's at Gresham's. Richards recalled in 1989 that the magazine was produced by cutting and pasting contributions in the authors' own handwriting and then copying them by machine (although this seems an unlikely method of reproduction in 1922); he also recalls that the magazine ran to three numbers, of which about six copies were printed and circulated among the editors' friends. All copies are now lost. (3 ALS, 22 May 1989, 27 May 1989, 14 Sept. 1989, to Katherine Bucknell.) In an earlier published account Richards recalls, slightly differently, that the editors copied out the contributions in their own handwriting (this would have made it possible to reproduce the magazine by cyclostyle), and that the magazine ran only to two numbers, not three; see *Memoirs of an Unjust Fella* (London, 1980), 36.

The Blind Lead the Blind

Gas lamps flared yellow in the muddy street
Fog on the houses crept apace
When Beauty passing on her naked feet
Saw Tawdriness with painted face

Standing surrounded by an eager throng.
Stopping to listen, she heard her say
'Come! I am Beauty, worship with a song'

— — — —

Then Beauty sighed and went her lonely way.

[*1922*]

CAN, 1, ink autograph.

Pardon

They brought her to the place where Christ stood by
A woman taken in adultery:
'We must stone her, Moses said,
Such as these were better dead'

Christ made no answer, with his hand
He drew strange figures in the sand
What he wrote then we cannot tell
But teeth were gnashed that day in Hell.

[*1922*]

CAN, 2, ink autograph.
   Auden focuses on an enigmatic sentence in the biblical narrative (see John 8.1–11), 'But Jesus stooped down, and with his finger wrote on the ground, as though he heard them not.'

Dawn

Far into the vast the mists grow dim,
　　A deep and holy silence broods around,
Fire burns beyond the vaporous rim,
　　And crystal-like the dew bestrews the ground.

The last laggard star has fled the glowing sky,
　　Comes a quiet stirring and a gentle light,
A vast pulsating music, throbbing harmony,
　　Behold the Sun delivered from the gloom of night!

Before 16 December 1922

The Gresham 10, no. 2 (16 December 1922): 23, unsigned; CAF, fo. 20r, ink autograph.
Variants: 2. A . . . holy] Deep Holy *CAF.* 3. beyond . . . vaporous] upon the shadowy
CAF. 4. And . . . bestrews] Dew, our Mother's tears, glimmers on *CAF.* 5. last . . . glow-
ing] starry host fades dimmer in the *CAF.* 6. Comes . . . and] There comes a whispering
CAF. Reprinted in John Fuller, 'W. H. Auden's First Published Poems', *Notes and Queries*,
n.s. 20, no. 9 (September 1973): 333.
　　Like several early poems, 'Dawn' shows the apparent influence of the Irish poet A. E.;
see note to 'A Moment'.

On Seeing Some Dutch Pictures

Centuries of life have passed
Since first you learned to paint
And yet no knave or saint
Though knowledge has gone on so fast
Can show a home as you could do
Or make a jug look half so blue

So when I pass your pictures by
And see the people there, I sigh
For how I wish that modern men
Were just as simple now as then.　　　　10

[Late autumn 1922]

CAF, fo. 12r, pencil autograph.
　　In *The Gresham* 10, no. 4 (31 March 1923): 56, the Society of Arts records 'a lecture
given at the end of last term by C. R. O. Medley on "The Dutch School of Painting"'; this

would have been December 1922, before Auden's friend left for art school. Auden was in the Society of Arts with him and may well have shared an interest in Medley's topic. Auden's paper on folklore was read to the society at the start of the next term.

Joy

Joy comes
Not to the sound of beaten drums
But swift on silent wings
She comes in little things
A laugh or look maybe
Or else perhaps a tree
Or scarlet poppy flower
Flaming in a drowsy hour.
Who can foretell or know
When Joy will come—or go?   10

[*1922*]

CAN, 11, ink autograph; CAF, fo. 12v, pencil autograph. Variants: 8. drowsy] drowsing *CAF*. Four additional lines following 8: She came to-day upon a hill / And made my heart stand quiet and still / But then alas she went away / To what sweet place I cannot say *CAF*.

Envoi

You go
Now you are glad
And I am sad
We know not why
It's so

And I
Will wish you well
Through heaven or hell
Come! Lets shake hands
Good-bye!   10

[*November or December 1922*]

CAN, 6, ink autograph.
   This was probably written for Robert Medley; see note to 'Envoi No. 2'.

Envoi No. 2

You go
And you are glad
And I am sad
I know not why
    It's so

You'll paint
What will be good
I never understood
The reason why
    I mayn't   10

You'll die
The world may you forget
But you'll linger yet
With me, no matter why
    Or why?

[*November or December 1922*]

CAF, fo. 11r, ink autograph.
    Auden's friend Robert Medley left Gresham's at the end of the autumn term in 1922
to study painting at the Byam Shaw School of Art and later at the Slade (Medley, 41–42);
both 'Envoi' and 'Envoi No. 2' were almost certainly written for him. Auden later wrote
two further envois, the first beginning 'Take up your load and go, lad' and the second
beginning 'From the red chimneys smoke climbs slow and straight,' which may also
have an association with Medley.

The Circus

When I lie within my little room,
Through the evening's pleasant gloom,
I hear the rhythmic thudding in the field
Of roundabouts from sight by window ledge concealed
But when I lie upon my little bed
They cast a flickering shadow overhead
    And this is what they said.

'O come to the fair O come to the fair
There lights and music, songs and beer

Drink and in your careless joy forget   10
What the world has been and the world is yet
For those who think must ever live in Hell.
For sin and sorrow are more than you can tell
O ye who for one hour would fain be free of care
O Drink ye! drink and come ye to the fair.'

[*1922*]

CAF, fo. 11v, ink autograph. Auden used a full stop at the end of l. 2.

Everest

Far up into the amethystine vapours
    Towers the ridge in white immensity
Gazing at the stars that burn like tapers
    Deep in the sky that is Eternity

A world above a world you lie
    Wet weeping clouds do hide thee from our sight
In vain to reach thy head we try
    O gaunt eventual limit of our light

You see the fall of the Gods of yesterday
    And the fall of the Gods of the morrow   10
Yet never a sigh or regret you say
    For the infinite ocean of sorrow

O triumph of the Moulder's hand!
    There in the blue twilight, unsought, unknown
There in that crystal-vestured land
    Silence and Beauty sit enthroned, alone!

[*December 1922*]

CAF, fo. 17v, ink autograph.
   Auden probably attended George Leigh-Mallory's lecture at Gresham's on the first
Everest expedition. The expedition ended in June 1922 when, on the third attempt to
reach the summit, seven porters were killed in an avalanche. When Mallory visited
Gresham's in late 1922, the lecture hall was filled to capacity. The reporter for *The
Gresham* found the talk, with maps and pictures, thrilling: 'he took us from point to
point of that journey, by dazzling towers of ice, over heartbreaking rocks, up dizzy
ascents, over abysmal crevasses'; *The Gresham* 10, no. 2 (16 December 1922): 22. The

poem looks forward to the theme of the Lords of Limit in 'The Witnesses' and to *The Ascent of F 6*, and it apparently borrows its heightened tone and its grandiose imagery of absolutes from Shelley's 'Mont Blanc'.

A Dream

Desperately my spirit willed me
    Out of Sleep's timeless vast
    And through grey nothingness I passed
And by a still Eternity.

Then in the dim room I heard you breathing
    Ghost-like I stood beside your bed
    Softly I touched your dreaming head
You smiled and lay there never stirring.

And then I knew that you had seen
    And that you knew that I was there   10

————

And you were glad that I had been

[*Late 1922 or early 1923*]

CAF(1), fo. 23r, ink autograph; CAF(2), fo. 17r, ink autograph. Variants: CAF(2) has no title and it offers two additional stanzas following the first:

And girt about with unknown powers
    I saw the pictures in your well-loved room
    And through the quiet listening gloom
I heard the clock tick out the silent hours

While looking in through latticed bars
    The moon your tumbled hair reveals
    While o'er your face a flame there steals
The firelight of a myriad stars.

A February Dawn

The hail is shot from heavy skies
And dashed against the blackened pane
And lashed the tilèd roofs with rain
While morning opens sleep-rheumed eyes

Now far and wide the twigs are blown
And frozen every iron hill
And hung with icicles the mill
That waves wild arms with creaky moan

Now in the houses dark we see
The hour is waking other folk   10
And from the chimneys now the smoke
Heralds another day to be.

[February? 1923]

CAF, fo. 15r, ink autograph.

A Rainy Afternoon

Ceaselessly from grey skies fell the rain
    A dull and leaden shower
While stillborn thoughts within the brain
    Whirled formless without power.

Then suddenly they cleared; I saw
    Beside the petty griefs of men
How Nature's griefs were infinitely more
    And I felt humbler then.

[1922 or 1923]

CAF, fo. 15v, ink autograph.

The Coming of Love

I bid Love come; but lo
Love smiled and went her way
Love came; I did not know
Love when she came to-day.
And now I bid Love go
But Love has come to stay.

[*1922 or 1923*]

CAF, fo. 15v, ink autograph.

Nightfall

Cool whisper of the trees,
And odorous gloom,
The silent falling of the dew,
Sweet unforgettable ecstasy of sound
Of leaves drinking the young dew.
Bluer—dimmer—stiller—
The night is come.

Before 9 June 1923

The Gresham 10, no. 5 (9 June 1923): 65, unsigned; CAN, 3, ink autograph; CAF(1), fo. 15v, ink autograph; CAF(2), fo. 6r, ink autograph. Variants: TITLE Nightfall] A Prose Poem *CAF(2)*. 2–3. And . . . / The . . . the] An . . . / The . . . the *CAN*, An . . . / Deep silences brimming over / And noiseless falling *CAF(2)*. 5–6. drinking . . . young / Bluer] eagerly sipping the cold / Soft caresses of the evening wind / Bluer *CAF(2)*. Reprinted in John Fuller, 'W. H. Auden's First Published Poems', *Notes and Queries*, n.s. 20, no. 9 (September 1973): 333–34.

Like 'A Moment', 'Dawn', and 'Everest', this poem may reflect Auden's admiration for the Irish poet A.E. (see note to 'A Moment'), and the image of leaves drinking is borrowed from W. H. Davies' 'The Rain', which begins 'I hear leaves drinking Rain' (included in Davies' 1916 *Collected Poems*).

Envoi

Take up your load and go, lad
   And leave your friends behind
Whistle a song and be glad
   For now their thoughts are kind

Do not pause to reason why
   You sin, as sin you must
There's no time before you die
   Live—ere you are only dust.

Turn you not to left or right
   Bear your sorrows well   10
Though the road be blackest night
   And the last end but Hell.

Go! This ugly world to rouse
   And, for your mother's sake
Make for yourself the youthful vows
   Which you are bound to break.

[1922 or 1923]

CAF, fo. 6v, ink autograph.

   This 'Envoi' may have been addressed to Robert Medley (see note to 'Envoi No. 2'), or, if addressed to the poet himself, it may refer to the difficulties beginning to arise in Auden's relationship with his mother—possibly his loss of faith or his homosexuality. It has the ring of A. E. Housman; for instance, from *A Shropshire Lad*, 60:

        Now hollow fires burn out to black,
           And lights are guttering low:
        Square your shoulders, lift your pack,
           And leave your friends and go.

        Oh never fear, man, nought's to dread,
           Look not left nor right:
        In all the endless road you tread
           There's nothing but the night.

To a Toadstool

O Scarlet Beauty with thy milk-white eyes
See! I have plucked thee up thou lovely thing.
For he, I know, who eats thee shall be wise
And see the fairies dancing in a ring
Shall learn to read the willow's lonely sighs
And share the passion of the nightingale.
But I have read too oft men's tales and lies
So now with hand pressed close to lip, I quail.

[*1922 or 1923*]

CAN, 4, ink autograph; CAF(1), fo. 29r, ink autograph; CAF(2), fo. 26v, ink autograph.
Variants: 3. know, who *CAF(2)*] know who *CAN, CAF(1)*. 5. willow's . . . sighs] willow's
sighs *CAF(1), CAF(2)*. 7. read] heard *CAF(1), CAF(2)*. Printed in Carpenter, 33.
   The poetic language and fairy atmosphere probably reflect the influence of Walter
de la Mare and perhaps Keats; see note to 'A Tale'.

To a Field-mouse

I stood amid the new-mown hay
Its sweet fresh smell had filled my head
When there I saw a pair of round brown eyes
Gleaming between the stalks so homely wise;
They stared a second, turned and fled
And waving grasses marked their way.

'I meant no harm! Come back again!' I said
   My cry was born adown the breeze
I was ashamed because you were afraid.
   I asked your pardon on my knees.   10

[*1922 or 1923*]

CAF, fo. 29r, ink autograph.
   Perhaps the theme of this poem was suggested to Auden by de la Mare's 'The Hare',
included in *Songs of Childhood* and *Poems 1901 to 1918*. The image of the startled animal
reappeared in Auden's 1927 poem beginning 'Who stands, the crux left of the water-
shed,' printed in *P(28)*.

To a Small Buddha

Downward you cast your eyes
A half-smile hovers on your lips
A knowing of things unseen
    A Comprehension
    A Deep Peace
A silent silent laughter.
When I die shall I know all these things
When I die shall I also be a buddha?

[*1922 or 1923*]

CAN, 5, ink autograph; CAF, fo. 29r, ink autograph. Variants: 8. buddha? *this edn*]
buddha *CAN, CAF.*

On a Greek Tomb Relief

    Death sent
To fetch you, but you had no idle care.
You paused one moment more to dress your hair
    And went.

[*1922 or 1923*]

CAN, 5, ink autograph.

After Reading Keats' Ode

Quietly I lay awake upon my bed
As night was sweeping down the vale
A whisper came to me that said,
'O listen to the nightingale!'
But I remembered thy immortal ode
The matchless glories of thy poesy.
What if her song that rode
The night should not so beauteous be

As thou didst hear it. So I be bereft
Thy wondrous vision of the divine bird.   10
So closing fearful eyes I turned and slept
And somewhere the nightingale sang on unheard.

[*1922 or 1923*]

CAF, fo. 26r, ink autograph. Variants: Title Keats' Ode *this edn*] Keats Ode *CAF.* 8.
night *this edn*] night. *CAF.* 9. bereft *this edn*] bereft. *CAF.*

Belief

We do not know
If there be fairies now
   Or no.
But why should we ourselves involve
In questions which we cannot solve.
   O let's pretend it's so
And then perhaps if we are good
Some day we'll see them in the wood.

[*1922 or 1923*]

CAN, 7, ink autograph; CAF, fo. 25v, ink autograph. Variants: Title Belief] Faith *CAF.*
1. We] I *CAF.* 4. should . . . ourselves] in pain yourself *CAF.* 5. In . . . we] With . . . you
CAF.
   Another poem, 'A Tale', also takes up the question of whether or not fairies exist;
both poems are influenced by Walter de la Mare (see note to 'A Tale').

Sonnet

'Lay not up for yourselves treasure on Earth . . .'

This world is full of lovely things.
Who would not wish to tread this earth
When Spring gives trees and creatures birth
And every bird at mating sings?
Its beauty always now about us clings
We hope that we shall not forget

I do not wonder men are scared of Death
What angel has a thrush's wings?

And so I only ask three things;
Flowers beneath my dancing feet   10
And overhead a bird that sings
And last not least, a friend to meet.
In these, in these my heaven is
But God perhaps will alter this.

[1922 or 1923]

CAF, fo. 25r, ink autograph.
    The epigraph is slightly misquoted from Matthew 6.19.

A Tale

A fairy came to my window last night
As I was lying open-eyed awake

'O come outside' she said
'And dance with me under the lovely trees
          To the music of the nightingale
Come down to the cool calm pond
Where the weed gleams like silver
And soft wingèd night moths flutter
          Silently Silently.'

But Reason said within me   10
There are no fairies now.
You are a fool; best stay in bed

  But the fairy wept
Because I would not go out
So because it grieved me to hear her weep
    I went to the window and said;

'I must not go out
And if they saw me go

They would not believe
That I had been dancing with a fairy'   20
———But still the fairy wept.———
    Was it faithlessness?
    Was it cowardice?

I went back to my bed heavy-hearted
And tonight I went again to the window
    And called my fairy

But she would not come
And I am ashamed.

[*1923*]

CAF, fo. 27r–v, ink autograph with an autograph note, 'I wonder what you will think of this. It is an experiment.' Variants: 23. Was it *this edn*] Wast it *CAF*.

'A Tale' is closely modelled on de la Mare's 'Sleepyhead', the first poem in his *Songs of Childhood* (1902, where it is titled 'The Gnomies') and also in his two-volume collection *Poems 1901 to 1918* (London, 1920); it was the eleventh poem in his *Down-ADown-Derry* (1922); see Introduction, p. xxi and n. 6. The following text is from *Poems 1901 to 1918*:

As I lay awake in the white moonlight,
I heard a faint singing in the wood,
'Out of bed,
    Sleepyhead,
Put your whitefoot, now;
    Here are we
    Beneath the tree
Singing round the root now.'

I looked out of window, in the white moonlight,
The leaves were like snow in the wood—

De la Mare's fairy sings again; then 'Sleepyhead' concludes:

But, as soon as I stooped in the dim moonlight
    To put on my stocking and my shoe,
The sweet shrill singing echoed faintly away,
    And the grey of the morning peeped through,
And instead of the gnomies there came a red robin
    To sing of the buttercups and dew.

As a schoolboy Auden also knew some of de la Mare's many other poems on magic, fairies, changelings, and elves, such as 'Bluebells', 'The Faeries Dancing', 'The Honey Robbers', and 'The Mocking Faery' (the last of these he later included in his 1963 volume *A Choice of de la Mare's Verse*).

Early Morning Bathing

What! are you still asleep in bed
The sky is such a brilliant blue
And dappled sunlight overhead
Throws down its dancing beams on you

What colours there are in the wood
Green hues I cannot count; and birds
Are busy singing in that wood
Too full of happiness for words

Hullo! so you are also here
O did you see; that dive was fine—   10
Lord! how the sun shines over there
You blasted fool! That towel is mine!

The bell sends forth its welcome chimes
Five minutes more to food I see
This world is far too good sometimes
For foolish folk like you and me.

[*Spring or summer 1923*]

CAN, 8–9, ink autograph.

    Robert Medley recalls a poem 'about the swimming pool at Gresham's' which Auden read to him one night when Medley was visiting the Auden household over New Year 1923–24. To Medley the poem seemed 'just another poem', but when Mrs Auden found it on the bedroom floor, the boys were called into Dr Auden's study and asked how close their friendship had become. According to Medley, they easily persuaded Dr Auden 'that our relationship had never been sexual,' and the poem was burnt (Medley, 44). It seems unlikely that 'Early Morning Bathing' would have aroused much concern in Auden's parents, and Auden certainly would not have included it in the notebook he presented to his mother if it had brought about such an embarrassing confrontation; there must have been another poem on the same theme. See also 'The Tarn', a more suggestive poem of related interest.

Woods in Rain

It is a lovely sight and good
To see rain falling in a wood.
The birds are silent, drunk with sound
Of raindrops kissing the green ground,
They sit with head tucked under wing
Too full of joy to dare to sing.
Flowers open mouths as wide I say
As baby blackbirds do in May;
While trees shake hands as grave and slow
As two old men I used to know,   10
And hold out smiling boughs to find
Whence comes this sweetest breath of wind.
But now the sun has come again
And he has chased away the rain.
The rain has gone beyond the hill,
But leaves are talking of it still.

[*Spring or summer 1923*]

Public School Verse: An Anthology, vol. 4, *1923–1924*, ed. Martin Gilkes, Richard Hughes, and P. H. B. Lyon (London, 1924), 18, with Auden's name misspelled as 'Arden'; CAN, 10, ink autograph; CAF, fo. 30r, ink autograph. Variants: 7. flowers] the flowers *CAF*. 13–14. not in *CAN*. 15. The rain] Now Rain *CAN*. 16. it] him *CAN*.

Michael Davidson recalls that he submitted a poem of Auden's to *Public School Verse* 'without saying anything to him' and that 'I had the additional joy, when the book appeared, of reviewing it in the *Eastern Daily Press* and devoting the whole review to Auden. But he was furious and I, in consequence, chagrined' (*The World, the Flesh, and Myself*, 130). Davidson's unsigned review, probably the first of Auden's work, quoted ten lines of the poem, praising it for its simplicity and comparing it to John Clare (*Eastern Daily Press*, 26 September 1924, 6). If Auden was angry with Davidson, he was also pleased, though shy, about having his work published. He wrote to his parents in October 1923, 'I also have a little surprise for you; I have had some things accepted for the 1924 volume of Public School Verse; so I shall make my first appearance in print so to speak next year. Don't tell anybody this will you, not even the family' (ALS, Farfield, Holt, with CAF). Of course, Auden had already had several poems published in *The Gresham* by the time he wrote this letter. The letter can be dated by its statement that 'Confirmation takes place next Monday week'. According to *The Gresham*, confirmation was on 5 November that year, which places the letter within a week or ten days before Monday, 29 October, and possibly on Sunday, 21 October, as other evidence suggests Auden may regularly have written home on Sundays. The poem was almost certainly written well before this. A request for submissions to volume 4 of *Public School Verse* appeared in *The Gresham* on 9 June 1923, asking that poems be submitted by 30 November. Auden knew a month *before* this deadline that his piece had been accepted, so it may have been submitted early. Moreover, it may not have been newly written when

Davidson submitted it, as Davidson recalls 'choosing what I thought the best from my stock' (*The World, the Flesh, and Myself*, 130).

In an interview with Horst Bienek for German radio (Deutschlandfunk, 9 September 1965), Auden described 'Woods in Rain' as 'eine Pastiche von einem englischen Dichter W. H. Davies'; in theme and imagery the poem recalls for instance 'The Rain' by Davies, on which Auden drew for his earlier poem 'Nightfall'. 'Woods in Rain' may also be compared to Wordsworth's 'A Whirl-Blast from behind the Hill'.

Appletreewick

Fair land where all is brave and kind
Thy face is often in my mind
Where heather may be always seen
And there is grass that's really green
Where trees remember how to dance
And squirrels peep through every branch.
The birds will sit on nests they've made
Still as you pass all unafraid.
Where all the flowers have mossy thrones
And streams play hide and seek with stones   10
Or make each mill a spinning top
Blowing big bubbles as they drop.
Clouds chase each other in blue skies
And throw their shadows in our eyes
Where one can walk for miles and miles
And meet with neither gate nor stiles
Where cottages are small and white
Their windows shine like stars at night.
And there are inns where one can go
And meet the finest men I know.   20
There one can sit by blazing fires
Can smoke and talk for hours and hours
Of harvesting, of sheep, of carts,
To men with simple lovely hearts.
Fare well. I hear in my day-dreams
The laughter of thy woods and streams.
Thy hills must now be white with snow
But whiter is thy heart, I know.

[*Autumn or winter 1923*]

CAN, 12–13, ink autograph.

In August 1923, Auden spent a week with Robert Medley and his family in Appletree-wick in the Yorkshire dales. Probably this poem was written the following winter, per-haps around the time Medley visited the Audens in Harborne for New Year's; this was the first time the two friends had seen each other since the August holiday. There was a lead-mine at Appletreewick which is mentioned in one of Auden's favourite boyhood books—Westgarth Forster, *A Treatise on a Section of the Strata from Newcastle-upon-Tyne to Crossfell*, 3rd edn, revised by W. Nall (Newcastle-upon-Tyne, 1883)—but the poem makes no mention of this usually obsessive interest.

The Sower

The sun had stained the roofs with blood
Wearied and sick at heart was I
Till all at once there came a flood
Of song from a small wren nearby

He stood beside the open pane
Opening his beak so sharp and thin
Methought he brought a golden grain
To my sad heart and dropped it in.

Which grew and blossomed more and more
With flowers richer far than words   10
And in the upper branches bore
A flock of happy singing birds.

[*1922 or 1923*]

CAN, 14, ink autograph.

The Lost Secret

Gone is the wind
Where? Where?
For yesterday
I heard him say
I'll tell you a secret
That nobody knows
    Come near

I'll whisper it
Soft, in your ear
He spake so low   10
I could not hear
Gone is the wind
Where? Where?

[*1922 or 1923*]

CAF, fo. 10r, ink autograph; CAN, 15, ink autograph.
  Auden may have modelled this poem on Walter de la Mare's 'The Song of the Se-
cret', which begins 'Where is beauty? / Gone, gone:' and which appeared in his *Poems
1901 to 1918* (London, 1920).

Prayer

Give me the thing I need the most
The childish heart that cannot boast

The child who never turns his back
On Beauty's silent quiet attack

Feels upon his lips her kiss
Knows no other joy than this

Hears her slow insistent voice
And all unlearnèd must rejoice

Makes all things happy where he's been
Calls nothing common nor unclean.   10

Bears innocent his mind on tireless wings
Sees the eternal loveliness of things

[*1922 or 1923*]

CAN, 28, ink autograph; CAF, fo. 10r, ink autograph. Variants: TITLE Prayer] A Prayer
CAF. 3. child] heart *CAN*. 8. unlearnèd] unlearned *CAN*. 9–10. not in CAF. Printed
in Mackinnon, 53.
  Auden may have modelled this poem on W. H. Davies' 'The Happy Child'; Davies
used a similar form in several other poems as well—'Leisure', 'Charms', and 'The White
Cascade'—all included in his 1916 *Collected Poems*. The theme is pervasive, but it is worth
noting that it figured in some of the hymns that Auden probably sang at school—for

instance, in Charles Wesley's hymn beginning 'O for a heart to praise my God', no. 357 in *The Public School Hymn Book*, which appeared for the first time in 1920, edited by a committee of the Headmasters' Conference that included Walter Greatorex, Auden's teacher and friend, and two other masters from Gresham's. John Keble's hymn beginning 'Blessed are the pure in heart', no. 270 in the hymnal, is on the same theme.

Autumn

Autumn is come, dear kindly dame
With love that puts us men to shame
We cannot stir outside the house
Some hare will cross our path or mouse
Apples like ruby gems are set
Deep in long grass that's green and wet
And when along the lanes we go
Red berries wink on each hedgerow
Burdock keeps clinging to our coats
And 'Old Man's Beard' drapes all the roads   10
And if we seek the wood, we there
Find wealth to take away all care
Our hour is scarce a minute old
But leaves will pelt us with leaf-gold
Leaves dance along the woodland way
Like town children at their play
They form soft cradles where at ease
May grow the roots of baby trees
And there are toadstools red and black
And squirrels along every track   20
The oak has emptied all his cups
The pig upon his acorns sups
Spiders stand tiptoe on the gate
Ready to launch on their unknown fate
The sycamore throws feathers here
And thistledown sails on the air
The stubble fields are black with birds
Chattering and saying farewell words
Cattle are lowing home to farms
To lie asleep in strawy barns   30
Slowly through the darkening haze

Comes the Sun's old wandering gaze
Now night has come and very soon
We'll see the face of Lady Moon
Hundreds of falling stars one sees
Star fruit falling from starry trees

— — — —

Rich days that teach our foolish mind
To know Death's Face, that it is kind

[*Autumn? 1922 or 1923*]

CAF, fo. 10v, ink autograph.
   Ll. 34–36 recall Auden's poem 'California'; see especially ll. 7–8. Like 'Woods in Rain', this poem is a pastiche of Davies; it may be compared, for instance, to Davies' 'Autumn'. It also suggests the influence of de la Mare, and the 'stubble fields' (27) perhaps allude to Keats's 'stubble-plains' in his ode 'To Autumn' (26).

The Dragon-fly

Thine is a painted face, for all thy wings
Like two bright rainbows. Lo thou art
Greedy and cruel more than kings,
A husk with but a stone for heart

Full of black thoughts to wound and kill
Like a false queen upon her throne.
All this is true but thou art still
One of the loveliest creatures known.

[*1922 or 1923*]

CAN, 16, ink autograph.

To a Child in Tears

Weep not sweet child, for now thy tears
Make all this beauteous garden sad
The grass a look of sorrow wears
Even the sun cannot be glad

But needs must hide his face in cloud
The flowers that held their heads so proud
Droop trembling for they fain would weep
Disconsolate the thrushes cheep.
Weep not sweet child, weep not, for see
How all this earth must weep with thee!   10

Lo when thy smile breaks through thy tears
A whoop of joy flies all along.
The sun in brilliant gold appears
And birds burst laughing into song
The flowers have lost all trace of care
But toss their silky heads in air.
A beetle as he scurries by
Winks up at thee with roguish eye.
Smile then sweet child, again, again.
And let thy lovely smile remain.   20

[*1922 or 1923*]

CAN, 18–19, ink autograph.
   The theme of this poem may have been suggested to Auden by W. H. Davies' 'The
Weeping Child'.

November at Weybourne

The starlings gather on the eaves
      And shiver stiff with cold
The elms still bear bewildered leaves
      That dare not lose their hold
Yon willow stoops as one who grieves
      For a Spring that is old.

The starlings fly but there are these
      To speak to us instead
The surge of wind through writhing trees
      The huddled clouds of lead   10
The waste of cold dark-featured seas
      And the men that are dead.

[*February 1924; revised 1924 or 1925?*]

CAN(1), 21–22, 20, ink autograph; CI, ink autograph with ink and pencil autograph revisions, wrongly dated 'February 1923' in Auden's hand (see below for date); CAN(2), 21–22, ink autograph with stanzas 2 and 3 cancelled. Variants: TITLE Weybourne] Salthouse *CI.* 1. gather] twitter *CI.* 3. elms ... bear] elm ... bears *CI.* 4. That] Which *CI.* 7. The starlings fly but there are these] Small matter that? Are there not these *CI.* Between stanzas 1 and 2, CI has a further, middle stanza:

> 'We'll come again' the starlings cry—
> Upon the winter air
> The flowers will burst through grass, the sky
> That robe of blue will wear
> Institched with cloud dead winters fly
> Whene'er April is here.

The cancelled stanzas of CAN(2) read:

> 'He'll not forget' the starlings cry
> Have no fear, have no fear
> The flowers will burst through grass, the sky
> That robe of blue will wear
> Stitched with pearl clouds, winter will fly
> Before the young sun's stare
>
> But there is nought now that one sees
> But joy that has fled
> The surge of the wind through the trees
> And the skies like lead
> And the frozen blackened seas
> And the men that are dead.

Apparently Auden first wrote out the three-stanza version of this poem, CAN(2), probably late in 1923 or early in 1924. Sometime during the following year or later, he wrote out the revised three-stanza version which he eventually sent to Isherwood, probably early in 1926. After he had completed this second three-stanza version, though not necessarily as late as 1926, Auden returned to the notebook, cancelled the last two stanzas of his earlier notebook version, and combined them into the new second (and final) stanza, which he wrote out on the verso of the preceding page. The Isherwood copy also has pencil alterations which may have been made after the final notebook draft—possibly a number of years after, when Auden dated the poems for Isherwood (see Textual Note, p. lviii).

Auden dated Isherwood's copy of the poem (entitled 'November at Salthouse') 'February 1923', having scored out a false start, 'November 192'. But February 1923 is almost certainly too early, even for the first version of the poem, as the poem borrows a phrase from the letter Auden sent to his parents from Gresham's in October 1923: 'It is a singularly lovely Autumn this year, in fact I do not remember a lovelier one. Some of the trees still bear bewildered leaves as if they did not dare to lose their hold on life. It is all very thrilling. The moons have been wonderful too.' (For details of this letter and date, see note to 'Woods in Rain'.) Auden often incorporated phrases from his letters into his poems, but I know of no instance where he did the reverse (unless making a specific reference). Possibly the poem's title suggested to him the November date and he recalled that the autumn which had apparently inspired the poem was the autumn of 1923; then, when he corrected the time of the actual composition of the poem to February, he neglected to write 1924. It may be that he wrote the poem in November 1923 and revised it in February 1924, later putting the date of revision on Isherwood's copy even though Isherwood's was not the revised text. He may have done the same when dating Isherwood's copy of 'The Old Lead-mine', revised in a similar way. Auden eventually reused the phrase 'bewildered leaves' in his 1926 poem 'Thomas Epilogizes'.

Weybourne is on the seacoast, a few miles north of Gresham's, Holt. Auden habitually took long solitary walks from school, and Medley recalls him being found at Weybourne by the school naturalist, R. P. Bagnall-Oakley, looking at the sea alone (*Tribute*, 41). Salthouse (in the Isherwood title) is also on the coast two or three miles north of Holt. It is occasionally mentioned in reports of the school Natural History Society as a place where various bird species have been sighted, and Auden included it in his rambles. Some years later he still vividly recalled once seeing a snowstorm approach from the sea over the marshes there; see note to 'The Mill (Hempstead)'.

Finis

Fear not
That nobody knows
The Back of Beyond.
What shall befall
    After

Grieve not
All things lovely pass
Soon, soon to their place
E'en lovelier
    Must come.   10

    Not yet
A little longer
Only a little
Till the Father
    Cries Home!

    And then
Go, with no word said
Into the darkness
We know not of
The night.   20

[*1923 or 1924*]

CAN, fo. 23, ink autograph; CAF, fo. 14v, ink autograph.

    The CAF version has an autograph note in the margin, 'So sorry I forgot to send this last Sunday. Here it is.'

Bawbee

I know a very lonely lane
    And a red brick wall
With a hole in it that's round and
    Very very small.

When we were children we would go
    Jonathan and I
With stones in hand to fill the hole
    As we passed it by.

And always on the other side
    A little green man   10
Was waiting there to catch the stones
    In a silver can.

It's ever so long ago now
    Since we passed that wall.
But that little man is waiting
    For the stones to fall.

He's wondering; for he can't
    Make it out at all
Why no more stones go tumbling
    Through that red brick wall.   20

[1923 or 1924]

CAN, fo. 24–25, ink autograph; CAF, fo. 9v, ink autograph. Variants: 20. that] the *CAF*.
Bawbee is dialect for a halfpenny, and has come to be used as slang for money or cash.

The Old Lead-mine

This is the place where Man has laid his hand
To tear from these dark hills his gold
He found it not, they say, but left his brand
Of greed upon the spot for all men to behold.

I peered a moment down the open shaft
Gloomy and black; I dropped a stone;

A distant splash, a whispering, a laugh
The icy hands of fear weighed heavy on the bone

I turned and travelled quickly down the track
Which grass will cover by and by   10
Down the lonely valley; once I looked back
And saw a waste of stones against an angry sky.

[*February 1924*]

CI, ink autograph, dated 'Feb. 1924' in Auden's hand; CAN, 27, ink autograph; D, blue TS (carbon), with title corrected in Auden's hand, numbered '14' in [Davidson's] hand. Variants: 8. weighed] weigh *CAN.* 10. Which] That *CAN.* 12. stones] stone *D.* Printed in Mackinnon, 55.

This poem apparently refers to an experience Auden had at Rookhope, probably in the summer of 1922; this date is suggested by the title of another poem 'Rookhope (Weardale, Summer 1922)'. He rewrote 'The Old Lead-mine' within a year or two (printed separately below as 'The Old Mine'), and it is possible that the date on the Isherwood version refers to the time at which he revised the poem even though he did not give Isherwood the revised version; see note to 'November at Weybourne'.

Auden was to draw several times in later work on the experience described in 'The Old Lead-mine'. In the 1930 poem beginning 'Get there if you can and see the land you once were proud to own' he wrote 'Head-gears gaunt on grass-grown pit-banks, seams abandoned years ago; / Drop a stone and listen for its splash in flooded dark below' (*EA*, 48). And in 'New Year Letter' he described it as the seminal moment of his life as a civilized human being and as an artist:

> There
> In ROOKHOPE I was first aware
> Of Self and Not-self, Death and Dread:
> Adits were entrances which led
> Down to the Outlawed, to the Others,
> The Terrible, the Merciful, the Mothers;
> Alone in the hot day I knelt
> Upon the edge of shafts and felt
> The deep *Urmutterfurcht* that drives
> Us into knowledge all our lives,
> The far interior of our fate
> To civilise and to create,
> *Das Weibliche* that bids us come
> To find what we're escaping from.
> There I dropped pebbles, listened, heard
> The reservoir of darkness stirred;
> '*O deine Mutter kehrt dir nicht*
> *Wieder. Du selbst bin ich, dein' Pflicht*
> *Und Liebe. Brach sie nun mein Bild.*'
> And I was conscious of my guilt.   (*CP*, 228)

The Old Mine

The whole hillside is scribbled on, but men
Found little here for all their pains
Broke the silence in the valley and then
Sought wealth in other places, but the scar remains

Chance walkers hurry quickly down the track
Which grass will cover by and by
Down the lonely valley; once they look back
And see a waste of stones against an angry sky.

[*Revised 1924 or 1925*]

CAN, 26, ink autograph. Printed in Mackinnon, 55–56.

   Like the two-stanza version of 'November at Weybourne', this shortened version of 'The Old Lead-mine' was added to the notebook probably after the notebook was assembled and perhaps even after it was presented. The handwriting is more mature, the pen softer, and the ink more watery than in other entries. In this instance, though, Auden did not score out the earlier version of the poem, but left two distinct compositions. The later, two-stanza version, 'The Old Mine', suppresses the seminal experience of dropping the stone down the shaft and the dramatic response that ensues (see note to 'The Old Lead-mine').

March Song

The Frogs are croaking in every pond
The Thrushes sing in the woods beyond
Dormice are uncurling their furry backs
And the Snail is leaving his silver tracks
The Violets are foaming among the dead leaves
And Daffodils are dancing in golden sheaves
The Marigold raises his yellow glazed cup
And Merry Old Sun soon fills it up

The Piper of Hamelin is back in the town
He's brought all those long-lost children down   10
Old Pan is drawing his notes again
And his song is no longer a song of pain.
The Prince has awakened the Princess at last

The castle starts up from the sleep that's past.
And why? What ails it with thee and me
Here love! Here's a kiss for thee.

[March? 1923 or 1924]

CAN, 33, ink autograph. Printed in Mackinnon, 54.
    This poem shows the influence of Davies and de la Mare. Auden apparently invented the happy sequel to the traditional tale of the Pied Piper.

Alston Moor

April, fair maid, is come with laughter in her eyes
    And everywhere she weaves her lovely spells
On plain and hill; I know that now the South Wind cries
    Her name upon the long slow curvings of the fells.
    Sheep are walking the roads again
They fill the dales with aching calls
And stonechats build their nests in climbing walls.

Lo! You have poured your richest gifts upon my mind
    Your rain has sealed his kiss upon my lip.
Lo! You have given me your love, and I shall find   10
    Within your loneliness companionship,
    Your weariness a sweet content
Your barrenness bright flowers and birds
Your coldness tenderest warmth, your dumbness words.

[April? 1923 or 1924]

CAN, 29, ink autograph; CAF, fo. 14r, ink autograph. Variants: TITLE Alston Moor] The Fells Alston *CAF.* 3. South] north *CAF.* 7. And] While *CAF.* I have interpolated some punctuation from the CAF version.
    Alston Moor, lying on the borders of Cumbria, Northumberland, and Durham, is at the heart of Auden's beloved lead-mining district; the Pennine Way scrambles over it at an altitude of several thousand feet.

Skyreholme Mill

I. By Day

The humble lichens dye with gold these grey stone walls
The sparrows build and quarrel too beneath this roof
Yonder a cool-voiced maid her cows to milking calls
Horses in meadows print the grass with joyous hoof.

A shining summer morn; all now is busy in the mill
The stream will try to race the clouds he loves the best
The shouting mill-wheel longs to roll on down the hill
And play at racing down the valley like the rest

II. By Night

Night falls; the moon sails up the hill
She ploughs through cloudy seas and stormy bars
All sound within these walls is still
The wheel lifts rigid arms towards the stars.

White gleams the long road up the fells
Stranger than thought or dream; a waking sheep
Stirs; his trembling cry upswells
     Silence—We sleep.

[1923 or 1924]

CAN, 31–32, ink autograph.

   The poem is cancelled with a diagonal line across each page. A new poem on the same subject and with the same title is added on the verso of the preceding folio, 30; this is printed separately below, p. 80. Like 'November at Weybourne' and 'The Old Lead-mine', this poem appears to have been rewritten at a much later date, perhaps after Auden presented the notebook to his mother. Skyreholme is in North Yorkshire, one mile east of the village of Appletreewick where Auden spent a holiday with Robert Medley in the summer of 1923; see note to 'Appletreewick'.

September

I see men in a barley field
They are reaping the last ripe square
A gun in either hand they wield
And wait the last run of the hare.

The guns scream out and soon then lie
A dozen either killed or maimed
I watch them fall with undimmed eye

— — — —

O soul sleep on lest thou be shamed.

[September? 1923 or 1924]

CAN, 32, ink autograph.

The Plane Tree

Thou hast no birds upon thy boughs
Who build their cosy nests and sing
No fields of grass with sheep and cows
Who shout for joy when it is Spring
No flowers, no brooks, no lovely skies
No stars at eve ope laughing eyes.

Thy home is in the roaring street
Thy only songs are made by trams
The little tap of wearied feet
For sound of measures danced by lambs   10
The skies wear drab and sooted hues
Instead of dappled whites and blues.

Yet art thou richer, humble tree
Than fifty thousand oaks or elms.
Tired men walk miles at sight of thee
So thy poor beauty overwhelms

I know in Heaven's streets, yes, there
—Thou wilt be planted everywhere.

Thou makest the child forget his tears
Babes in their mothers' arms will leap   20
Thou calmest suicides' despairs
And makest youthful harlots weep
And those who dwell within this place
They wake and bless thy dear green face.

[1923 or 1924]

CAN, 34–35, ink autograph. Variants: 14. fifty *this edn*] fivety *CAN.* 15. thee *this edn*]
thee. *CAN.* 17. streets, yes, there *this edn*] streets yes there *CAN.*

Speech

The gift of speech is a very terrible thing O Man
Keep watch over thy tongue lest it betray thee
Try how thou wilt
Thou canst not hide thyself
No word of thine but reveals some corner of thy heart
No phrase but lays bare some secret place.

Keep watch
Thou dost not know thy power
Though thou hadst never imagined it
It may be that someone hangs upon thy slightest word   10
One chance word and the whole course of his life is made beautiful
Another, and all the devils of hell enter into his soul.

Keep watch
Make thyself clean and true
That as thou goest through life
Tired men may hear thy words and find strength in them
And though they knew it not
They shall bless thee in their hearts.

[1923 or 1924]

CAN, 36–37, ink autograph. Variants: 14. true *this edn*] true. *CAN.*

Dawn

On the cold waterfall, the flush of dawn gleams bright
As the wind shouts by his mighty laughter voicing.
The sun rolls back the gorgeous fabric of the night
And the stars go down behind the hills rejoicing.

Awake, Awake O heart! Clean-limbed and sun-kissed stand
Purged of each paltry thing that makes thee less
Than thy true self; Doth it not welcome thee? This land?
With all its splendid men, its loveliness?

[*1924*]

CAN, 41, ink autograph; CAF, fo. 28v, ink autograph; D, blue TS (carbon), numbered
'10' and with revisions in [Davidson's] hand. Variants: 1. cold waterfall] foaming water-
falls *D.* 2. As the wind] as wind *D.* 4. And the stars] And stars *D.* 8. loveliness? *D*]
loveliness *CAN, CAF.*

In his essay on Auden's early poems, Fisher compares this poem to Housman
('Auden's Juvenilia', 372), but it echoes Robert Bridges' 'Awake, My Heart'.

Song

Past all your knowing
I shall be going
To far-away kingdoms
    Soon, Soon
Where walks no moon.

Not a stream falls there,
Not a bird calls there,
Only wild silences,
    A night
No candles light.   10

Where e'en Earth's seeming
Is past my dreaming
And none in the darkness,
    Save I
For company.

[*1924*]

CAF, fo. 28r, ink autograph.

This poem bears comparison with two other early pieces, 'The Lost Secret' and 'Stone Walls' (beginning 'Where do they travel to'), influenced by de la Mare and by Hardy.

March Winds

Three weeks ago they came, leaping over
The hills and sowing the glittering rains.
Now they have passed and none know whence they go;
We who are left behind, we only see
This English Spring is lovelier than we
Remembered it; only know a thing has
Touched us we are too small to understand.

[*March? 1924*]

CAF, fo. 28v, ink autograph.

Auden used a slightly revised version of this poem in the fourth stanza of his 'Elegy' beginning 'Why was it that you gave us no warning.'

The Mill

O there is peace here! There scarcely lifts a sound
Save for the creaking of the mill, and that drowned
By the murmur of the weir; the pool is crowned
With lilies; surely a lovelier ground
    Could not
    Be found?

Yet in the black trees against the evening sky
And the tossing mill-wheel's weary creaking sigh
And the long drone from the rushing weir nearby
There trembles a sullen questioning cry   10
    We are—
    But why?

[*1924*]

CAF, fo. 4r, ink autograph.

This poem draws closely on Thomas's 'The Mill-Water', yet it is haunted by the echo of Hardy that is audible also in Auden's 'The Last Time', 'By the Fire', and other poems.

Two Triolets

I

What need has man of heavenly things
When earth is lovely past belief?
E'en now the youngest blackbird sings
What need has man of heavenly things
A snowdrop nods, a catkin swings,
Dew shines on the wild strawberry-leaf
What need has man of heavenly things
When earth is lovely past belief?

II

Come Love! We'll play; just you and I
Without one thought of the Hereafter
On yonder bubbling hill we'll lie
Come Love, we'll play. Just you and I
We'll watch the bees go droning by
And make the daisies fill with laughter
Come Love! We'll play; just you and I
Without one thought of the Hereafter.

[*1923 or 1924*]

CAF, fo. 4v, ink autograph.

The Last Time

Last time we met
It was a summer day; the walls
Were splashed with streaks of black and gold.
From every tree the thrushes' calls
The ageless mating story told
Last time we met.

She will not come
The thrushes call both long and loud
Drowsy sunlight still is staining

The walls; the sky scarce shows a cloud   1 0
But it might as well be raining
    She will not come.

[*1923 or 1924*]

CAF, fo. 5r, ink autograph.
  Like 'The Mill', 'By the Fire', and many other poems, this shows the influence of
Hardy.

By the Fire

Dying embers glowed in the grate
The room was dark, the hour was late
A sudden flame shot up and sent
A flicker through the shrouding gloom
A dancing shadow round the room
    Came and went.

  'Was it her shadow
  Was she there
  I do not know
  I do not care   1 0
  If it was or no.'

[*1923 or 1924*]

CAF, fo. 5v, ink autograph.

The North

O the North is a wild land, a splendid and a fair;
They've deep shadowed grassy dales and wide brown fell tops there.
All day within my aching head insistent voices go;—
'Friend of our lovely hills, why come you not, why tarry so?'

There's many a white flower, many a windy place
Many a brown hill water and many a lovely face
The stone walls ramble up and down the fells and climb about,
The air is clean and wholesome and the pine trees shout.

You may follow the sheep all day over the springing turf
While the leaping waterfall drones in your ears like the surf   10
The rain is there; you may watch it sweeping across the hills
Till every burn is singing and every peat pool fills.

They've little scattered houses there, and cosy whitewashed inns
Where you may turn to rest and talk when the starlight begins.
Calm eyes and fearless have the simple dwellers in that land,
And there is peace and healing there for all who understand.

Though my soul is sick with longing the great time is not yet
I am counting every day to it for I shall not forget.
And when the poplar tree has burst his buds to flame, I'll start
With a song upon my lips and a shouting in my heart.   20

[*1923 or 1924*]

CAF, fo. 7v, ink autograph. Variants: 13. They've *this edn*] There *CAF*.
    This poem recalls both in sound and sentiment Yeats's much-anthologized 'The Lake
Isle of Innisfree', but the first line echoes the first line of Robert Graves's 'Rocky Acres':
'This is a wild land, country of my choice', and Graves's poem may be an influence.
Auden would have read it in *Georgian Poetry 1918–1919*. The fruitful influences of Yeats
and Graves were to converge again a few years later in 1927 when Auden wrote the
poem beginning 'I chose this lean country', drawing once more on 'Rocky Acres' and
on Yeats's 'The Tower'.

We Sat

We sat in the shaded lamplight
Talking far on into the night
        As many have sat

We planned what things should come to be
The great things future years would see
        As many have planned

And thinking thereupon our eyes
Shone radiant with an glad surmise
        As many have shone

The days slipped by, year followed year   10
We found we built upon the air
    As many have found.

                                    [*1923 or 1924*]

CAF, fo. 8r, ink autograph.
    Like so many poems from this period, this shows the influence of Hardy.

My Lady of the Wood

Deep in a woodland dell
Only the leaves may tell
The cottage roof where dwell
        My love and I
Seldom a stranger's face
Comes to that lonely place
Seldom do strange feet trace
        The path nearby.

There we watch dawn and eve.
Snails on the blackberry leaf   10
Wonders beyond belief
        Daily we view
'Oft have I seen her set
Early to know if yet
Bloomed the first violet
        Mantled in blue.

Lo in the path she walks
Jays cease their chattering talks
Mice drop their barley stalks
        Ants turn to stare   20
Hawks let their prey go free
Hares they forget to flee
Flowers crane their necks to see
        Her passing there.

O she is lovelier far
Than yond bright morning star

Purer than moondrops are
    Guileless as they
Eyes like the stories told
Of the green elves of old   30
While in the firelight gold
    The listeners lay

Dearer to me than all
To see the laughter fall
Upon her when I call
    Hourly her name
To know the tenderness
Hid in each lock and tress
All the deep lovingness
    I can inflame.   40

And when she is not there
I have no need to fear
She will forget me where
    She dwells the while
Out of the hills and trees
Where stirs a passing breeze
Or running water is
    Breaks her warm smile

[*1923 or 1924*]

CAF, fo. 8v, ink autograph.
   This theme derives from Wordsworth's Lucy poems, though it is common enough
that Auden may have found it in one of the late Romantic or Georgian poets that he
liked.

March

Thou comest now impulsive gusty March
Setting thy rusty crowns upon the larch
We smile to see once more thy boyish face
And waving tangled hair in every place

The fields are green but in the hedge's shadow
Like pools of frozen milk still lingers snow

The sky is Spring's own blue but pranked with white
Where cloudlets frisk in the fresh Spring sunlight

The gurgling brooks are now so wondrous clear
That rows of tiny coloured pebbles peer   10
Between the tresses of the water weed
On which fat snails with shells like fine pearls feed

The birds now chase each other two by two
And paired are even timid hedgehogs too
Pools of blue rain now sparkle in the grass
And throw your face back as you pass

The high wind tugs me on to see the wares
For sale in this, the best of Nature's Fairs
And every thing of blue and every thing of green
I vow that it's the loveliest I've seen   20

[*March? 1923 or 1924*]

CAF, fo. 18r, ink autograph.
This poem shows the lingering influence of Davies, for instance his 'April Charms'.

Envoi

From the red chimneys smoke climbs slow and straight
    Martins twitter below the eave
Dawn spreads across the hills, solemn and great
    You must rise now and take your leave.

Does your heart ache? But you must not mind it
    Does your love cry? You must not heed.
There is a far goal and you must find it
    Though the limbs tire and the soul plead

A thrush bursts into song; stars disappear;
    Black hills grow brown; there springs a breeze   10
That sets the windmill stirring; the ripe pear
    Drops with a thump from orchard trees

Turn once at the road top and wave your hand
Then go you steadfast down the track
Though wind is sweet with smell of the hill land
And the mill waves to you 'Come back!'

[*1923 or 1924*]

CAF, fo. 18v, ink autograph.
   Auden wrote three related poems: 'Envoi', 'Envoi No. 2', and 'Envoi' ('Take up your load and go, lad'); see note, p. 8.

Song

I have a little book
    With paper white and fine
And the people in it
    Are all great friends of mine

I have a well-worn coat
    Goes everywhere with me
It has all sorts of things
    That only I may see.

I have a memory
    Nobody knows but me   10
And when I think of it
    A face comes up to me.

[*1923 or 1924*]

CAF, fo. 19r, ink autograph.

Arthur's Quoit, Dyffryn

O Cold grey stones! What mighty warrior lies beneath thy shade?
What deeds of valour wrought his battle blade?
Was it that a people mourned his loss with bitter tears,
And was his legend told in after years

By bard and poet while an awed multitude sat round and listened
And the ancient minstrel's bright eye glistened?

There he lies! Let no unhallowed hand disturb his sleep.
He gazes out across the valley deep.
Oft-times I have seen him thus, sunk as if in thought profound
While round him the white moon doth silver all the ground.   10
A brazen helm he wears, and down his back there falls a yellow lock.
He sleeps, and hopes, and waits his Ragnarok.

[*1923 or 1924*]

CAF, fo. 21r, ink autograph. Variants: TITLE Arthur's Quoit, Dyffryn *this edn*] Arthur's
Quoit Dyffryn *CAF*.
   Arthur's Quoit (Ceotan Arthur) is a cromlech supposed to have been hurled down
by King Arthur from the top of Moelfre, near Dyffryn Ardudwy (also known as Dyffryn),
about five miles north of Barmouth, Gwynned, Wales. John Auden recalled a family holi-
day sometime between 1915 and 1918 that included a visit to Dyffryn (*Tribute*, 26). Rag-
narok (12) is the Götterdämmerung (twilight of the gods) in Scandinavian mythology.
   The opening line of this poem echoes 1.2 of Tennyson's 'Break, break, break': 'On
thy cold gray stones, O Sea!'

In the Nursery

Old Nurse sits mending by the fire
Her kind grey eyes are bright with happy light
Her busy fingers never seem to tire
While the cold wind is crooning in the night

She tells us tales of fairyland—
Princesses radiant and fair
Are rescued from the ogre's hand
By Princes tall with golden hair.

She leads us up the steeps of dream
Till in the fire we try to see   10
A thousand flashing eyes which seem
To beckon to us joyfully

Then round the room the shadows dark
Take one step nearer to our hearts
We can hear their listening footsteps—hark!
Outside the rain its whispering starts

And down the chimney sing the winds
Whistling a hundred plaintive airs
Till even we with our untutored minds
Feel strangely stirred by dead men's cares.   20

[*1923 or 1924*]

CAF, fo. 22v, ink autograph. Variants: 9. leads us up *this edn*] leads up *CAF.*

Christ in Hades

When Christ descended into Hell
    To fill a myriad ghosts with breath
    Living in the sunless courts of death
That they might know their God as well

He did not tell them how they might have lived their lives
    He did not call them Pharisees
    Or bid them pray upon their knees
Or tell them that it was wrong to have two wives

He told them that in beauty still dawned the day
    That silver in the night did shine the moon   10
    As flamed the glorious sun at noon
That hope still blossomed by the way.

Then all the ghosts rose up from off the ground
    Singing to feel such sweet remembered joys
    Till Hell reechoed with unwailèd noise
And all creation danced to hear the sound.

[*1923 or 1924*]

CAF, fo. 22r, ink autograph.
    For the legend of Christ descending into Hades to lead out the souls of the just, see the apocryphal Gospel of Nicodemus.

Sonnet I

There was desolate silence on the world
For who shall say how many million years
Only a roar where cold hill waters hurled
Themselves upon the jagged basalt spears
Grasses rustled; the little hills clapped hands;
Wind sang; and still no living voice was heard.
An age; then frogs croaked love in marshy lands;
An age; then came that miracle the bird.
And last came Man, who with wide marvelling eyes
Gazed at his mate, the flowers in the wood,   10
Beheld the Sun run splendid through the skies
Beheld and shouted for he found life good.
    God who had slumbered until now awoke
    The Word made flesh, the Spirit, moved and spoke.

[*1923 or 1924*]

CAF, fo. 24r, ink autograph.
   This poem does not appear to be the work of someone who has ceased to believe in God so much as of someone trying to fit together Christian beliefs with a modern, scientific view of creation and evolution. God's awakening *after* the evolution of man possibly reflects the promise of Hardy's epic *The Dynasts*, which suggested that the final outcome of the evolutionary process might be the coming to consciousness of the Immanent Will. See the final chorus of the 'Afterscene', which Auden quoted in his 1940 essay 'A Literary Transference'.

Sonnet II

It matters not that we shall cease to be
Our sons will tarry though our souls be gone
Our dreams shall be the common things they see
The deeds we dared not do, by them be done.
All things must change; and yet how little change
Appears; the blackbird in the apple tree
Sings the same song as lovely and as strange
As when Eve stood beneath gazing fearfully.
But these will go, and even that bright thing
Which we call life must flicker up and cease,   10

Leave but a night with blind stars wandering
Yet in that lonely darkness, some vast Peace
Some mighty Purpose, fashioned high by Pain
Some Mind eternal, this must still remain.

[*1923 or 1924*]

CAF, fo. 24v, ink autograph.

Auden's first line offers a rebuke to Keats's sonnet beginning 'When I have fears that I may cease to be', and the image of Eve underneath the apple tree listening to the blackbird (6–8) reworks Keats's image of Ruth amid the corn in 'Ode to a Nightingale' (65–67). Also, ll. 9–10 seem to echo the start of Shelley's sonnet beginning 'Lift not the painted veil which those who live / Call Life.'

Vision

The firelight gleams upon your hair,
    Leaping in shadows bright and broken:
I have been all my life asleep;
    It is but now that I have woken,
To gaze upon your brooding face
In its dark frame of wall and chair,
    In silent thought so sweet, so deep,
I cannot tell how long a space
    Has passed us by since you have spoken.

If ages, as I watch you, glide,   10
    Or if this dream's bright character
In one short breath is writ and scanned,
    Than all those ages lovelier,
I know not; yet I could, as now—
Eternally unsatisfied—
    Gaze on you sitting, chin on hand,
With dancing light on cheek and brow,
    And never wish to speak or stir.

[*1923 or 1924*]

CAF, fo. 34r, purple TS (carbon).

Stone Walls

Where do they travel to
Sleepily wending
Over the waste fells,
Silent, unending?

Do they seek the Wind
As he calls and calls,
To the end of things,
Those creeping walls?
So secret they are
No man can know   10
Through what strange kingdoms
They come and go.
So lonely, so old
Each stone appears,
As dead hands laid them
In dream-lost years.
What if I follow them,
Upward, afar?
What if I come to
Where burns no star,   20
Dark hidden places
Where memories are,
And cold dead faces
Despairs do mar?

[*1923 or 1924*]

CAF, fo. 35r, TS with ink autograph revisions.
    Like Auden's similar poem, 'The Lost Secret', this shows the influence of de la Mare, but now apparently overlaid with the diction of Hardy.

The Owl

An owl I hear
That hoots so shrill
Through the June air
From up the hill.

And somewhere there
As those wings pass,
Two bright eyes peer
Through dew-drenched grass.

In trembling fear
There waits a mouse;　　　　　　10
No hiding near,
And far his house.

No light lays bare
That hill of stone,
As he waits there
Forlorn, alone.

Till through a tear
In cloud-thick skies
Moon shows him clear
To watching eyes.　　　　　　20

No sound to hear
Save one small cry,
And whispers where
The night drifts by.

[*1923 or 1924*]

CAF, fo. 35r, TS.
　Possibly this poem was inspired by de la Mare's 'Evening', which appeared in his *Poems 1901 to 1918*.

Farglow

The room in the soft lamp glow
    Wears a peaceful look,
Though a storm shakes the window,
Where One, sunk deep in his chair,
    Over a book
    Bends eagerly.

And he scarcely seems to hear
    The wind and the rain;
Heeds not that midnight draws near,
Nor recks One standing out there,   10
    Who at his pane
    Stares yearningly.

March 1924

CI, TS, with ink autograph corrections and pencil autograph date 'March 1924'; D, blue
TS (carbon of CI), numbered '25' in [Davidson's] hand; CAN, 44, ink autograph.
    In a letter to Isherwood, Auden defended this poem: 'Re the list of 3rd rate, I dis-
agree only about "Farglow", "There is so much" and "Friendship," all of which I like!
Probably however you are quite right' (AL signed 'Dodo', possibly from Christ Church,
[early 1926]). Fisher noted the poem's Hardyesque character ('Auden's Juvenilia',
371). In a later poem, 'Helen', written in the style of Edward Thomas, Auden used the
name 'Far-glow' for a farm.

Inn Song

    Traveller, stay
    On your long way;
    Dusk falls on day,
    Dark grows the hour.
    Here is good ale
    That will not fail;
    Tell us your tale
    By the bright fire.

    Night will pass by,
    The stars will die,

Dawn winds will cry,
And you will go;
You will forget
By next sunset
The friends you met
A day ago.

Pleasures will pall,
Great love grow small,
Sad things befall
You had not guessed;   20
Yet, though you weep,
Though cares burn deep,
How great is sleep.
Traveller, rest.

March 1924

CI, TS, with pencil autograph date 'March 1924'; CAF, fo. 13v, ink autograph. Variants:
3. Dusk] Eve *CAF*. 21. weep] reap *CAF*. 22. Though cares burn deep] Tares, though
you weep *CAF*.

The Miner's Wife

She sat in her cool parlour
While the sun streamed through and through
The kettle sang on the hob
And a small fly buzzed and flew

There came a knock at the door.
And a young man white and pale
Stood at the threshold silent
Then quickly he told his tale.

'An accident at the mine
The pumping rod broke,' he said,   10
'Your husband, he was climbing,
And it caught him; he is dead'

She watched him down the garden
Then gently she latched the door
And hummed to herself a tune
As she bent to work once more.

[*1924*]

CAF, fo. 13r, ink autograph.
  Auden reused the theme of the miner killed by a fall at the mine in his 1926 poem
'Lead's the Best'.

In a Train

The carriages slow,
And a name I know
Is shouted outside,
As porters go
To and fro.

The farm on the hill
Gleams there whitely still,
And the splashing beck
Tumbles until
It turns the old mill.   10

Once my heart would race
As I neared this place,
And feverishly scanned
The platform space
For a well-known face.

Who'd have dared to say
There would come a day
When, passing this spot,
I should not stay,
But go on my way?   20

March 1924

CI, TS, with ink autograph corrections and pencil autograph date 'March 1924'; D, blue
TS (carbon), with ink and pencil corrections and numbered '26' in [Davidson's] hand.
CI and D are identical, including several typos.
  This poem is another from Auden's most Hardyesque phase.

Rookhope (Weardale, Summer 1922)

The men are dead that used to walk these dales;
The mines they worked in once are long forsaken;
We shall not hear their laughter or their tales
Now, as in bygone days, all these are taken.
Dead men, they say, sleep very soundly, nought
Remaineth as a mark to signify
The men they were, the things they did, nor aught
That this unheeding world may know them by.
Yet—I have stood by their deserted shafts
While the rain lashed my face and clutched my knees,   10
And seemed to hear therein their careless laughs,
To glimpse the spirit which engendered these;
     Feel in the might of that exulting wind
     The splendid generous Soul, the simple Mind.

April 1924

CI, TS with ink and pencil autograph revisions and pencil autograph date 'April 1924'.
Variants: 4. in bygone *this edn*] in the bygone *CI*; Auden added 'now' to the line in
pencil and probably meant to delete the extra syllable. The pencil revisions to this
poem may have been made as late as the mid-1930s, when he possibly added pencilled
dates to the early poems in the Isherwood collection (see Textual Note, p. lviii). These
affect l. 2, which, before the pencil revisions, read 'The mines they worked in are long
forsaken', and l. 4, which read 'As in the bygone days, all these are taken.'
   The village of Rookhope, in Durham, is in Auden's beloved Pennines lead-mining
district, not far from Alston and Allendale. He briefly gave the title 'Rookhope' to his
1927 poem beginning 'Who stands, the crux left of the watershed'; see also 'The Old
Lead-mine' and note.

The Cat

They drowned her kittens only yesterday;
Tom buried them behind the stable wall.
And now she wanders on from place to place
About the farmyard, seeking them and crying.
She does not understand, she only knows
Her breasts are full, and she must feed them now.

June 1924

CI, TS, with pencil autograph date 'June 1924'.

The theme for this poem may have been suggested to Auden by the first stanza of Edward Thomas's poem 'A Cat'.

By the Gasworks, Solihull

This spot is loved by all wild things since men
Left some old drain-pipes here; all the weeds then
Had their way with them, until cow parsley,
That the flies seem to love, stands five feet high
At least; nettle and dock grow up together,
And to the wren of all places, this is dear
To pour his joy into; he always sings
His loveliest among these broken things.

June 1924

CI, blue TS (carbon) with ink autograph title and pencil autograph date 'June 1924'.

Solihull is the village outside Birmingham (now a suburb) where Auden grew up. The poem is reminiscent of Edward Thomas's 'Tall Nettles', one of the poems Auden marked in his copy of Thomas's *Collected Poems*; see note to 'To E.T.'

The Robin

Yes, always now
He follows me
About the lawn,
From tree to tree.

For if I go
Raspberry picking
He'll perch among
The canes to sing.

And when I dig
He stands quite close,   10
And pecks for food
About my toes.

Often we talk
Whole hours away,
Though neither knows
What each would say.

God bless the bird!
What grace have I,
That he should love
My company?   20

If he but knew
What we men be,
He would not thus
Hop after me.

July 1924

CI, TS with pencil autograph date 'July 1924'; CAN, 42, ink autograph; CAF, fo. 28r, ink
autograph. Variants: 5. For] And *CAF.*
   The colloquial amiability of tone in this poem suggests the influence of Robert Frost.

Early Morning

Perched on a nettled stump he stands,
One yellow leg drawn up, and crows.
Farther and farther off from lands
Of waking dreams, the answer goes.

Sun flashes on the barn's red tiles;
A hen stirs on the turnip heap;
And far around for miles and miles
People turn over in their sleep.

July 1924

CI, TS with pencil autograph revisions and pencil autograph date 'July 1924'; D, blue
TS (carbon), with ink autograph revisions, numbered '11' in [Davidson's] hand; CAN,
fo. 43, ink autograph. Variants: 4. waking dreams] dream almost *CAN.* D appears to
be a carbon of CI, and both show the same autograph revision in l. 4, but CI is not
numbered.
   These quatrains may be loosely modelled on the ones in Thomas's 'Adlestrop'; see
his *Collected Poems* (London, 1920). Auden's image of the solitary rooster and the
spreading response to his crow perhaps recalls Thomas's final stanza:

And for that minute a blackbird sang
Close by, and round him, mistier,
Farther and farther, all the birds
Of Oxfordshire and Gloucestershire.

Auden included this poem in a list he sent to Isherwood, probably in early June 1927, of pieces written before July 1926 that he intended to preserve (ALS, from Christ Church, before 9 June 1927). In July 1926, he visited Isherwood at Freshwater Bay in the Isle of Wight, where they apparently looked at Auden's poems together in detail.

In the autumn of 1926, Auden wrote another poem called 'Early Morning'; it begins 'Earth rolls these houses out into the sun' and uses a similar image of a solitary bird perched on a tree.

The Walk

The storm had passed and now the sun
Set the black wintry hedge aflame
Save for my splashing footsteps, none
Broke the long silence there, none came.

A dogcart, yellow-wheeled and high
Came sudden round the hedge's fold
A farmer and his wife drove by,
They nodded to me; both were old.

They clattered past me; once or twice
A bird sang; it was still again   10
A secret peace, a Paradise
I could not enter filled the lane.

July 1924

CI, ink autograph with pencil autograph date 'July 1924'.
    Auden used the phrase 'they clatter past' (cp. l. 9) in his later poem 'Trippers'.

Elegy

Why was it that you gave us no warning,
But the night before, magic, and candle-flamed,
Talked, yea and laughed with us? We did not dream
How drenched with weeds the mere of hours might be
We sported so in, nor how swift the stream;

Little guessed that in the splendid morning
One we loved would lie as cold, as strangely still
As the black tarn deep-hollowed in the hill.
Death took you quickly, as though ashamed
To steal as fair a thing so wantonly.   10

Now, when after a June shower, grass smells sweet
And the drops flash slowly from bough to bough,
Or the river, peat-stained in its March spate
Sweeps down rapids foaming exultantly
Till rocks are covered that were bare of late,
Shall we turn from all these with weary feet?
Shall we sit no more flame-dyed by the fire,
But think as the whirring clock strikes each hour,
'These things, they meant more to us then than now,
For these were the things which he loved to see'?   20

Perhaps a little while? It may be so;
But Time, that drowsy-voiced waterfall,
Will wash the very hardest stone away;
Beauty will come into her own again,
And we, on some far bleak October day,
Will climb the hill as we did years ago
To watch them round the sheep in from the fell.
We shall see men as fine as you still dwell
Where wind and rain bring nobleness to all
This land of kings and simple-hearted men.   30

There is left little we may grasp to know
Where you have gone, what life before you was.
No more than of those winds that slashed the panes
Three weeks ago; they came over the land,
Leaping and sowing the glittering rains;
Now they have passed, and none know where they go.
We who are left behind, we only see
This English Spring is lovelier than we
Remembered it; only know a thing has
Touched us we are too small to understand.   40

September 1924

CI, TS with ink autograph revisions and pencil autograph date 'Sept 1924'; CAN, 38–41, ink autograph; D, TS. Variants: 2. magic, and candle-flamed] radiant candle-flamed *CAN*; magic, candle-flamed D. 6. Little] And little *D*. 16. all these] these now *CAN*. 17. flame-dyed] flame-eyed *D*. 23. stone] grief *D*. 30. This] A *CAN*. 36. where] whence *CAN*. An additional final stanza is cancelled in CI, but allowed to stand in both CAN and D. In CI it reads:

> And we, do we indeed go when we die
> Into a night past love or fear or pity?
> We cannot answer, yet at times there gleams
> A light about us, a sign, a token.
> We are no puling children then; it seems
> That all this patient earth, this wandering sky
> Are but mere swaddling clothes; we are stars set
> In the Eternal and the Infinite;
> We are strong citizens of no mean city.
> Out of the silence a trumpet has spoken.

In l. 3 of this stanza, D has 'sigh' for 'sign'. Its penultimate line loosely quotes Paul of Tarsus, Acts 21.39.

The last seven lines of stanza 4 are a slightly revised version of Auden's earlier poem 'March Winds'.

The Old Colliery

The iron wheel hangs
Above the shaft
Rusty and broken
Where once men laughed.

The boards over the shaft
Are gnawed and rotten
The engine lies
Dismantled forgotten.

Nought night or day
But the wind's noise   10
No cry is heard
Of human voice

But close beside
Stunted, forlorn
And scarcely green
There grows a thorn

Where often now
A thrush will lurk
Whose singing blesses
Man's handiwork.   20

September 1924

CI, ink autograph with pencil autograph date 'September 1924'; CAN, 45–46, ink auto-
graph; D, blue TS (carbon) with ink corrections and numbered '3' in [Davidson's]
hand. Variants: 3. Rusty] Rusted *CAN*, *D*. 9. night or day] night and day *CAN*; day or
night *D*. 10. But] Save *CAN*, *D*.

  Fisher included this among Auden's poems written in the style of Hardy ('Auden's
Juvenilia', 371). The penultimate stanza, with its rhyme of 'thorn' and 'forlorn', recalls
the opening of Wordsworth's 'The Thorn':

It stands erect, this aged Thorn;
No leaves it has, no prickly points;
It is a mass of knotted joints,
A wretched thing forlorn. (6–10)

Auden's phrase 'close beside', in the same stanza, appears several times in Words-
worth's poem, in stanzas 4 and 5.

The Rookery

When we were half asleep we thought it seemed
Stiller than usual; but no one dreamed
That aught was wrong until we came downstairs,
And looked, as we had done these many years,
At the huge wall of elms that flanked the lawn
And shouted every time a wind was born.
Someone cried, 'Look': we crowded to the pane:
Their tops still glittering from last night's rain,
They swayed a little, and upon their boughs
Swung to and fro each black untidy house   10
The rooks had made in some past century,
And mended every Springtime. But no rook
Showed dark against the early sky, or shook
Down twigs, or cawed; a hungry fledgeling's cry,
Waiting a breakfast that would never come,
Was all there was; the world seemed stricken dumb.
'The rooks have gone, have gone . . .' We said no word;
But in the silence each one's thought was heard.

September 1924

CI, blue TS (carbon), with ink autograph and pencil autograph revisions and pencil autograph date 'Sept. 1924'; D, blue TS (carbon), with ink revisions and numbered '9' in [Davidson's] hand. The CI and D carbons are identical except where altered by hand. Variants: 12. Springtime] Autumn *D*. Printed in *Lions and Shadows*, 188–89.

In l. 16, CI and D show as cancelled the better reading 'was all we heard'. On D, the change is made in [Davidson's] hand, suggesting that it was his, and not Auden's, revision. Apparently, Auden accepted it at the time and made the change on Isherwood's copy as well, although he later reverted to the version he had first written. 'Was all we heard' was the version used when 'The Rookery' was printed in *Lions and Shadows*, but presumably Auden cancelled it because it seemed too similar to the final line of the poem.

In Fisher's view this poem clearly shows the influence of Edward Thomas, and he suggests that it describes the 'rooks' sudden desertion of their rookery in the great wall of elms in the school grounds at Holt' ('Auden's Juvenilia', 372).

After the Storm

It was a lovely day
　　　　When the storm passed,
And I left the ruined
　　　　Sheepfold at last.

Far away on the hill
　　　　I caught the roar
And flash of waterfalls
　　　　Unknown before.

All things sang in the sun;
　　　　Telegraph wires   10
Even, and the birds'
　　　　Ecstatic choirs.

And a strange singing rose
　　　　In my breast too;
Glad, yet half-regretful,
　　　　It grew and grew;

Sad for I knew not what,
　　　　A strange desire
For things not understood,
　　　　It mounted higher.   20

Vainly it sought to grasp
　　　　This thing; the tide

Ceased; then into silence
Flowed back and died.

I have sung many songs
Of life and earth,
But none so sweet as that
Which had no birth.

September 1924

CI, blue TS (carbon) with ink autograph and pencil autograph revisions and pencil autograph date 'Sept. 1924'.

Stanza 2 was revised several times, the last time in pencil, possibly though not certainly some years later (see Textual Note, p. lxix). The earlier revision of l. 7 reads 'Of hidden waterfalls'.

The Tarn

Some say the tarn is bottomless.
Dark rocks run sheerly downward on three sides
Into darker waters; little grows there
Except the lichens old ere man was born.
Often and often I sat beside it,
Noticing how the reeds grew where the stream
Ran out, for it was shallow there and strewn
With boulders; hearing the stonechat's twitter,
A ghost asking to be let out of Heaven.
Always it seemed a lonely silent place,   10
Until I climbed the rocky slopes behind
One July day. It looked so blue below,
As if a thousand April skies were caught
And lay imprisoned, yet were glad of it.
Two boys were bathing there, splendid of limb,
Ruddy and beautiful; while the sun seemed
As if it glowed within them. Always now
The place seems haunted by their laughing voices.
Glory is there I had not seen before,
Which shall not be revealed a second time.   20

September 1924

CI, blue TS (carbon), with ink autograph and pencil autograph revisions and pencil autograph date 'September 1924'.

L. 9 is cancelled and revised in pencil, possibly a change made much later (see Textual Note, p. lxix). The previous reading was 'Like a pale ghost lost in Eternity.'

Before

I mark not without
That the darkness there
Will swiftly be here
When the flame dies out

The damp logs that sing
And the clock's grave whir
Make but little stir
In my visioning

As the days to be
Appear to my sight   10
And love and delight
Come singing to me

Yet thus I shall sit
I know just the same
My hands to the flame
But weary of it

With many a dream
Memory-nourished
Of Her I had kissed
Of faces that stream   20

On driven like leaves
Glad, noble and kind
Past doors of a mind
That vacantly grieves

While formless without
The night awaits there
Its mastery here
As the flame dies out

September 1924

CAN, 52–54, ink autograph; CI, ink autograph with pencil autograph date 'Sept 1924'. Variants: TITLE Before] Visions *CI*. CI offers an alternative stanza 3:

> Of the days to come
> When this life shall rise
> To my full surmise
> Nor will love be dumb

26. night awaits there] darkness waiteth *CI*. 27. Its mastery here] All it covereth *CI*. 28. As] When *CI*. Following stanza 1, both versions have an additional stanza, which is cancelled in the notebook version. The cancelled stanza reads:

> As I sit alone
> By the glowing grate
> And envisage Fate
> In my years unknown.

In the CI version, not cancelled, the last three lines of this stanza read differently:

> By the dying fire
> With each present hour
> Throbbing by unknown

The history of this Hardyesque poem is not entirely clear. With most of Auden's early poems, the Isherwood versions apparently post-date the Constance Auden versions, but this is the next to last poem in the notebook and could have been added at almost any time (see also 'Stone Walls', beginning 'One almost takes a hedge for granted'). It appears that Auden tried to revise the second stanza when he wrote it out in the notebook, and then decided to cancel it altogether. However, it is also possible that the Isherwood version is actually the later draft, and that he wrote an entirely new version of the second stanza when he sent the poem to Isherwood.

Buzzards

> Quite suddenly they flew
> Across the mountain dale,
> Far up, cleaving the blue
> With wings of steel.
>
> 'Buzzards.' I heard you cry,
> And both of us stood still
> Till they swept down the sky,
> Behind the hill.
>
> I, though a watcher too,
> Marked little how they sped: 10

Who could have dreamed that you
Would turn your head?

October 1924

U, TS on 'British Bond'; CI, TS with ink autograph title and pencil autograph date
'October 1924'; D, purple TS (carbon of CI), with ink autograph title and numbered
'30' in [Davidson's] hand. CI and D are identical, but the punctuation in D has been
altered so carefully by hand that it appears to be differently typed. Printed in the two-
stanza *P(28)* version in 'Auden's Juvenilia', 373; see below.

Auden included this poem in the list he sent to Isherwood in about June 1927 of
pieces written before July 1926 that he intended to preserve (see note to 'Early Morn-
ing', beginning 'Perched on a nettled stump he stands'). Eventually he incorporated a
two-stanza version into his 1927 poem 'The Megalopsych', which, untitled and much
revised, later became the first poem sequence in *P(28)*.

The theme of the poem may have been suggested to Auden by Martin Armstrong's
'The Buzzards', published in *Georgian Poetry 1920–1922*. Richard Ellmann pointed out
that the final couplet echoes Yeats's 'O heart! O heart! if she'd but turn her head' (14)
from 'The Folly of Being Comforted'; *Eminent Domain* (New York, 1967), 102.

□   □   □

There is so much that I can share with you
Which once was only dear to me alone:
The new day's lambent secrecy,—the yew
Casting her shadow on the greening stone,
The solemness of pines, the finch's voice
Like a creaking gate; now no swift that sings
On wires after rain, nor sawmill's noise,
But speaks to both of breathless starry things.

October 1924

CI, TS, with pencil autograph revisions and date 'Oct. 1924'.

This is one of the poems that Auden defended in a letter to Isherwood after Isher-
wood had apparently included it in a list of the third-rate (see note to 'Farglow'). The
'sawmill's noise' (7) figures centrally in Auden's later full-length poem entitled 'The
Sawmill'.

On the same folio are the following TS lines cancelled in pencil:

We who were small have found so great a thing:
Mightier than deep waters, more fearful than
Darkness, swifter than flame; lo, a strange thing
And beautiful now is come upon us,
And for the sign we bear the very stars
Must worship. Let us be humble then.

After the Burial

Words have been said, well polished by use,
                    Your name befriending;
A sense of impotence made me muse,
                    As we laid the earth,
                    On the ultimate worth
Of all those things that men fear to lose
                    Here, at an ending.

What are we men but puling and small,
                    Fit for derision:
When things seem fair we see good in all,   10
                    But utter a cry
                    When we have to die,
Or griefs that will soon be forgotten fall
                    Past our prevision.

What are we men, whose mind to life brings
                    Unpatterned gauges,
Whom suns may stir to imaginings,
                    Who hold a mere chance
                    Of significance,
And call the scratch on the surface of things   20
                    Wisdom of ages?

What are we men who find in a face
                    A secret glamour,
Who see in friendship some unknown grace,
                    But a millpond wave,
                    Or a stream in a cave
That falls through the dark of a silent place,
                    In self-made clamour.

November 1924

CI(1), TS with pencil autograph date 'November 1924'; CI(2), ink autograph; CAN, 47–48, ink autograph; D, blue TS (carbon), with ink revisions in [?Auden's] hand and numbered '33' in [Davidson's] hand. Variants: TITLE After the Burial] At the Burial *CAN*. 6. that] which *CAN*. 13. that] which *CI(2), CAN*.

As Fisher observed, this poem reflects the strong influence of Hardy ('Auden's Juvenilia', 371). Auden again uses the image of men as 'puling children', which he tried out and abandoned in his earlier 'Elegy'; see the cancelled stanza in the note to 'Elegy', p. 59.

The Traction-engine

Its days are over now; no farmyard airs
Will quiver hot above its chimney-stack; the fairs
It dragged from green to green are not what they have been
　　　In previous years.

Here now it lies, unsheltered, undesired,
Its engine rusted fast, its boiler mossed, unfired,
Companioned by a boot heel, and an old cart-wheel,
　　　In thistles attired,

Unfeeling, uncaring; imaginings
Mar not the future; no past sick memory clings,　　　10
Yet seems it well to deserve the love we reserve
　　　For animate things.

November 1924

U, TS on 'British Bond'; CI, TS with pencil autograph date 'November 1924'; D, blue TS (carbon), with ink revisions and numbered '21' in [Davidson's] hand; CAN, 51, ink autograph; CAF, fo. 33r, ink autograph. Variants: 8. In] With *D*. 10. the] its *CAF*. As with many of Auden's earliest poems, the punctuation varies widely among these copies. U is the cleanest and latest fair copy, but (characteristically for Auden) it uses a colon where a semicolon might normally be preferred, in ll. 1, 2, 9, and 10; however, it appears that the typewriter may have been worn in such a way as to make the semicolon look like a colon. CI and CAF both use semicolons in place of all four of these colons, CAN uses the semicolon in place of three of them, and D uses it in two, so I have made the substitution throughout. Printed in *Lions and Shadows*, 186; reprinted in *Seeds in the Wind: Juvenilia from W. B. Yeats to Ted Hughes*, ed. Neville Braybrooke (London, 1989), 141.

　　Fisher suggested that the style of the poem is borrowed from Hardy ('Auden's Juvenilia', 371); it may be at least as indebted to Edward Thomas.

J. S. Bach

No pine so firmly set, no lofty towers
But in the end, will to the dust be hurled;
Your voice will hush, Sebastian as ours
Before the silence of a dying world.
Yet live on now; mights fall and cease to be
Man goes and man succeeds but you still stand
A beacon fire to lost humanity
A great rock shadowing a weary land.

You tell of infants smiling in their sleep,
Of what the singing mountain shepherd saith;   10
A noble spirit toiling in a deep
Of pain, the thunder of a nation's faith,
A voice in Ramah weeping, and that cry
Of desolation wrung on Calvary.

[*Autumn? 1924*]

CAF, fo. 33r, ink autograph. Variants: 2. dust be *this edn*] dust to be *CAF*.
    Ramah (13) refers to the prophecy of Jeremiah 31.15, which is fulfilled in Matthew
2.18. Jesus's cry of desolation on the cross is given in Matthew 27.46 and Mark 15.34
(although in the King James version both these gospels refer to the place of crucifixion
by its Greek and Hebrew name, Golgotha, and only Luke 23.33 uses the Latin, Calvary).

The Candles Gutter Low

Candles now gutter low; there is no priest to bless,
But we do not need his prayers; the night is kind,
And will cover up our shame when we look to find
We that were great gave up ourselves to littleness.

We have vowed vows, we have not kept them; dreamed our dreams,
Noble, beautiful, but have not made them living;
We bought and sold, but we never thought of giving;
Now we must go where no gift matters much it seems

We have done little worth the doing, none will mind us
When we turn from all the moils of gain and getting;   10
Our time is ended; the dying sun is setting;
Up; we will journey on now; fear not; none will find us.

[*1923 or 1924*]

CAF, fo. 33v, purple TS (carbon) with ink autograph corrections.

□ □ □

Though thy rafters are grown rotten
Though the foaming torrents sweep
Thee down unloved, forgotten,
Though fear claw thee deep,
Though waves beat to thy knees,
Yet thou art not broken, rise
All the fires within thy eyes,
Thou art grander than all these.

Though ravens flap above thee,
Though the thunder showers sting   10
And scatter all that love thee,
Thou art still thy king;
Though cold pierce thee to the bone,
Clench thyself, lift up thy head,
Till the storm pass and naked
Leave thee weary and alone.

Thy mighty bulwarks shattered,
Thy leaves all fallen and dead,
Thy cloak all shreft and tattered,
Thy singing birds fled;   20
Thy great winds silent and dumb,
Mute and lonely thou must stand,
A stark figure in the land
Till thy charnel-house be come.

[*1923 or 1924*]

CAF, fo. 33v, purple TS (carbon).
   Auden's use of 'shreft' is anomolous. *The Oxford English Dictionary* (2nd edn) cites it
as an archaic form of 'shrift', but here it seems to have the sense 'shredded' or 'worn'.
This poem may show the influence of Swinburne; compare 'The Garden of Proserpina',
which Auden included in his 1950 *Poets of the English Language.*

Allendale

The smelting-mill stack is crumbling, no smoke is alive there,
Down in the valley the furnace no lead ore of worth burns;
Now tombs of decaying industries, not to survive here
        Many more earth-turns.

The chimney still stands on top of the hill like a finger
Skywardly pointing as it were asking 'What lies there?'
And thither we stray to dream of those things as we linger,
        Nature denies here.

Dark looming around the fell-folds stretch desolate, crag-scarred,
Seeming to murmur 'Why beat you the bars of your prison?'   10
What matter? To us the world-face is glowing and flag-starred,
        Lit by a vision.

So under it stand we, all swept by the rain and the wind there,
Muttering 'What look you for, creatures that die in a season?'
We care not, but turn to our dreams and the comfort we find there,
        Asking no reason.

December 1924

CI(1), TS, with pencil autograph date 'December 1924'; CAN, 49–50, ink autograph;
CI(2), TS, probably typed by Isherwood. Variants: 3. here] there *CI(2)*. 7. And . . . stray]
But . . . turn *CAN*. 9. fell-folds] fell fold *CAN*. 13. rain . . . wind] wind . . . rain *CAN*.
CI(2) was possibly prepared for publication in 'Some Notes on Auden's Early Poetry',
5. As this appeared more than ten years after the poem was written, I have preferred
what appears to be the contemporary typescript.

   Allendale is in the Pennines lead-mining district, north-east of Alston Moor. The
chimney described in stanza 2 is evidently the one that once rose from Bolt's Law, above
Rookhope, to the east of Allenheads. Auden described the terrain again in 'New Year
Letter':

            The derelict lead-smelting mill,
            Flued to its chimney up the hill,
            That smokes no answer any more
            But points, a landmark on BOLT'S LAW,
            The finger of all questions. (*CP*, 228)

At Parting

Under the lamp's exhausted glare
    We stand two souls
Oblivious of the passer's stare
    While life unrolls
Its tangled skeins bewildered down the thoroughfare.

But a few moments now remain
    Before a day
We do not often dream to gain
    Will pass away
And, having been, no rack be left to mark its train   10

Long weeks it as a light was seen
    We travelled to
Fearing a chasm would intervene
    Ere I and you
Could make it, but it came, and even now has been.

Imminent things wag not their tongue
    But joy was not
The friend of any man for long
    Or any spot
And barriers build in a night and they are strong.   20

Well, though the future pave us knives
    To walk upon;
Though of our passion nought survives
    This day now gone
Will loom a pinnacle of grandeur in two lives.

December 1924

CI, ink autograph with pencil autograph date 'December 1924'; on the same folio with 'Before' (beginning 'I mark not without' and entitled 'Visions' on CI copy).

   'No rack be left to mark its train' (10) perhaps alludes to Prospero's speech after the masque in *The Tempest*: 'And, like this insubstantial pageant faded, / Leave not a rack behind' (4.1). (At Gresham's Auden played Caliban in the *The Tempest*, but not until the summer term of 1925.) Hardy's influence is also notable in this poem.

The Engine House

It was quiet in there after the crushing
Mill; the only sounds were the clacking belt,
And the steady throb of waters rushing
That told of the wild joy those waters felt
In falling. The quiet gave us room to talk:
'How many horsepower is the large turbine?'
'Seventy. The beck is dammed at Greenearth Fork—
Three hundred feet of head. The new pipe line
Will give another hundred though, at least;
The mill wants power badly.' He turned a wheel;   10
The flapping of the driving belt increased,
And the hum grew shriller. He wiped a steel
Rail with a lump of waste. 'And now,' he said,
'I'll show you the slimes-house and the vanning shed—
This way.' He opened a small wooden door,
And the machinery leaped into a roar.

December 1924

CI, TS with ink autograph revision and pencil autograph date 'December 1924'; CAF, fo. 31r, ink autograph. Variants: TITLE The Engine House] The Turbine-house *CAF*. Printed in *Lions and Shadows*, 186; reprinted in *Seeds in the Wind: Juvenilia from W. B. Yeats to Ted Hughes*, ed. Neville Braybrooke (London, 1989), 142.

Fisher recalled that at Christmas 1925 Isherwood singled out this poem 'for special praise' ('Auden's Juvenilia', 371). It is full of mining terminology, mostly to do with the processing of ore. The crushing mill (1–2) is for breaking up quartz. 'Head' (8) is the measurement of pressure created by the dam. 'Slimes' (14) are finely crushed or powdered metallic ores in the form of mud; these are sometimes separated on vanning tables. 'Vanning' (14) is washing or separating ore on a shovel or pail. 'Greenearth Fork' (7) probably refers to part of the Greenhurth lead-mine in Teesdale, north-west of Middleton and not far from Alston. This mine is among those described in Forster's *A Treatise on a Section of the Strata from Newcastle-upon-Tyne to Crossfell* (see note to 'Appletreewick'). Auden was to use a similar name in 'Lead's the Best' (Greenearth Side) and in 'Control of the Passes was, he saw, the key' (Greenhearth). The variation in 'Lead's the Best' suggests he could have been thinking of another mine, Greenside, a rich lead-silver mine in the north of England, not far from Keswick where his family had a holiday cottage, but the spelling in 'Control of the Passes' suggests he may—characteristically—simply have misremembered the name, or mistakenly combined the two names.

The poem's matter-of-fact, almost flat dialogue is reminiscent of Frost. Auden used parts of the scene again in ll. 330–54 of his unfinished epic 'In the year of my youth when yoyos came in' which he worked on in 1931 and 1932. In particular, l. 353 in the epic, 'A man with a rag was rubbing a rail,' recalls ll. 12–13 of 'The Engine House'. For the epic, see Lucy S. McDiarmid, 'W. H. Auden's "In the Year of My Youth . . ."', *The Review of English Studies*, n.s. 29, no. 115 (August 1978): 267–312.

□ □ □

Since the Autumn day
When she went away
There is little change
Still friends are here
As kind, as fair;
Why seems the old strange,
And bright things grey?

What do I lack
That I wish her back?
Why do I hear   10
In the twitching flame
Her whispered name,
Dream of her everywhere
Fair days or black?

Why ache I to greet
In room or in street
Her face once more,
Or in lamplit rain
Glimpse her form again,
Feel once as heretofore   20
Her bosom beat?

Unreasoning say you,
But this I do
And question not;
For what heart's-ease brings
Much thinking on things;
Such was man's lot
Old times or new.

Reason or no
These things are so;   30
And I visit the place
Where we used to meet,
When we found life sweet,

Thereupon to trace
My vision show.

Years must I spend
Ere this matter mend;
Till I lie underground
In my little room
Of rook-haunted gloom   40
No change will be found
Or feeling end.

Then I shall not care
That she lie so near
No more to be leaving;
The vision that stayed with me,
Then it shall fade with me,
And pondering, grieving
Shall vanish there.

[*1924*]

CAF, 31v, purple TS (carbon) with ink autograph revisions; CI, ink autograph, entirely cancelled in pencil with a single large X, on the same folio with 'The Hidden Lane (Near Selbrigg, March 1925)'. Variants: 8. do] is it *CI*. 13. Dream of her] Dream her *CI*. 14. or] and *CI*. 29–35. Reason . . . show] not in *CI*. 36. Years] Long years *CI*. 38. lie underground] kiss the ground *CI*. 47. Then] Then, then *CI*.

Possibly Auden discarded this poem because it was too much like Hardy, especially Hardy's 'Poems of 1912–1913'.

The Pumping Engine, Cashwell

It is fifty years now
Since the old days when
It first pumped water here;
Steam drove it then.

Till the workings were stopped,
For the vein pinched out;
When it lay underground
Twelve years about.

Then they raised it again,
Had it cleaned a bit,   10
So it pumps still, though now
The beck drives it.

As it groans at each stroke
Like a heart in trouble,
It seems to me something
In toil most noble.

[*1924*]

D, TS.

Fisher included this in his list of poems Auden had written in the style of Hardy ('Auden's Juvenilia', 371). The 'vein' (6) is a lode of ore, and 'pinched out' means that it narrowed down to nothing. Auden again described the restored pumping engine at Cashwell in his 1927 poem beginning 'Who stands, the crux left of the watershed.' Cashwell mine is just below Crossfell in the mining district of Alston Moor. Auden still possessed as part of his library when he died his copy of E. H. Davies, *Machinery for Metalliferous Mines* (London, 1902); it is inscribed 'Christmas 1918' with his name in his mother's hand (now at HRHRC).

□   □   □

Whenever I see for the first time
    From road or train,
No hedges along the field, but grey
    Stone walls again,

That summer flies back to me at once—
    A week of it
At least, we two spent up on the moors,
    Happiness-lit.

If rain fell at all I cannot tell;
    I only find   10
In memory visions of white clouds
    That raced the wind.

And over all lingers with me now
    The laughing sound

Of waters that flashed sun-kissed, or sang
    Deep underground.

Who deafened our ears during those days,
    Who dulled our eyes,
That life's great doxology we failed
    To recognize?   20

No whisper fell when we watched the wheel
    Toss at the mill:
'You never knew days richer than these,
    Nor ever will.'

Then standing at sundown on the cliff,
    It fired your hair;
No voice said to me: 'You will not find
    Two souls as rare.'

For little we sensed of the delight
    Hid in our laughter;   30
Yes, little we recked of things that we
    Would prize hereafter.

                                     [*1924*]

D, TS.
   This poem may refer to the week Auden spent with Medley and his family in August
1923 in Appletreewick in the Yorkshire dales. Fisher notes in it the persistent influence
of Hardy ('Auden's Juvenilia', 371).

The Mail-train, Crewe

Under the hundred lamps whose flare
    Turns night to day,
I stand to watch the huge train there
    Move slowly away,
And reck not of the load it has to bear;

Knows not if sinister or kind,
    But swiftly rolls
Southward; the silence calls to mind
    How many souls
That watch the morning dapple on the blind,   10

Who at the postman's slow advance
    Trill like a bird,
Will stand and throw a frightened glance
    At each clear word,
Uncomprehending its significance

Postmen perform without a thought
    Their daily task,
But some there be whom life has brought
    To turn and ask
Wherefore the world is ordered in this sort.   20

Crying small comfort ever brings;
    Of little worth
Are wild and sullen questionings;
    No man on earth
Can cast a spoke into the wheel of things.

And if the waters grow not less
    Nor ever will,
Of human sorrow, nobleness
    Is with us still,
And here and there a sail of tenderness.   30

[1924]

D, TS.

   Crewe is in Cheshire, in the Midlands, about twelve miles north-west of Stoke-on-Trent, and has an important railway station, junction, and works. Through the Hardy-esque clumsiness of this carefully rhymed poem, the themes of train travel and communication by post look forward to Auden's preoccupations of the 1930s, and the lines 'Who at the postman's slow advance / Trill like a bird' (11–12) could have been written a decade after they were.

□ □ □

So I must go my way:
I am not first nor last
Of those who, as they passed,
Have found in you a stay.
Others have known and heard
The tender helping word.

For what are you? A spring
Unto a thirsty child;
A dark lair to some wild
And desperate hunted thing;   10
A fire where lonely men
May warm their hearts again.

[*1924*]

D, TS.

He Revisits the Spot

Yes, this is the place,
There are many such
To be found elsewhere
Quite as silent, fair.
Here's nought to let
The mind linger on—yet
To some it meant much.

Few people will guess,
If they chance to fare
To this lonely place,   10
That a woman's face
Was scored with grief,
And a man's whole belief
Was shattered here.

[*1924*]

[D], TS, transcribed by B. C. Bloomfield in the early 1960s, now lost. Printed in
'Auden's Juvenilia', 371.

Fisher calls this 'too good an imitation to be true' of Hardy ('Auden's Juvenilia', 371).
It bears comparison with Hardy's 'A Spot'.

□   □   □

The dew steams off the thatches
The drops fall from the bough
And brightly flash the bridles
As teams go out to plough.

On hot and crumpled pillows
The eager sunbeam burns
The dreaming lover wakens
And yesterday returns.

[*Late 1924*]

F, ink autograph, with Fisher's pencil autograph corrections. In l. 1 Auden wrote 'of' for
'off' and Fisher corrected it. The verso shows a very rough draft, fully cancelled, of the
poem beginning 'Like other men, when I go past'.
    For these quatrains Auden again took Housman as his example, though ll. 3–4 per-
haps borrow their imagery from the opening line, 'As the team's head-brass flashed out
on the turn', of Thomas's poem.

□   □   □

Now from far eastern wolds, the bay
    Of the hounds of morning peals;
Night lifts her head and springs away
    With the whole pack on her heels.

Wake! and be merry, you are strong;
    You may have it as you please
A little while, though God ere long
    Break your back across his knees.

[*Late? 1924*]

D, blue TS (carbon), numbered '39' in [Davidson's] hand. Printed in 'Auden's Ju-
venilia', 372.
    Fisher suggests that these verses are written in the style of Housman ('Auden's Ju-
venilia,' 372).

Nightfall

As ghosts peer over a bedroom curtain
The moon looks over the tree-topped hill
    A star burns cold, uncertain.
        The birds are still.

No mouse rustles in the lane's dark hedges
The last weary traveller is home
    A sigh breathes through the sedges
        And night has come.

For children sweet dreams until to-morrow
For lovers the shadow of the thorn   10
    And for the sons of sorrow
        A day well-born.

                     [1924 or 1925]

CI, ink autograph with pencil autograph revisions.
   An echo of Housman is audible in this poem, particularly its last stanza.

Skyreholme Mill

The mill-wheel never seems to tire,
But tries his hardest to leap higher;
The shouting stream is young enough,
And has not yet become too proud
To run a race with every cloud;
The millstones drone their patter off
            Like a school child

This tossing water-wheel will soon
Lift rigid arms towards the moon;
This stream that flashes in the light   10
Will in a tunnel underground
Fret sullenly in darkness bound;
These stones will lie as still to-night
            As a dead world.

                    February 1925

CI, ink autograph with pencil autograph date 'February 1925'; CAN, 30, ink autograph. Variants: 2. his] its *CAN*. 5. cloud] child *CAN*. 9. towards] toward *CAN*. 10. that] which *CAN*. CAN may, in fact, be a later fair copy, and, as with many of the poems in the Isherwood collection, the CI copy may have been typed by Isherwood, and possibly the punctuation, was supplied by him. Still, I have preferred CI because some of the variants in CAN appear to have been created in hasty transcription: there is hardly any punctuation, and in l. 5 Auden wrote 'child' where he almost certainly meant 'cloud,' as in CI.

Skyreholme is in North Yorkshire, near Appletreewick. Auden had previously written another poem entitled 'Skyreholme Mill'; see p. 33 and note.

Stone Walls

One almost takes a hedge for granted
And finds in it small interest
For when one's seen the nettles planted
Why, nature has to do the rest

But with a wall it's otherwise
Seeing that every single stone
Is hunted for with human eyes
And set in place by hands alone.

They've no bud-bursting feats in Spring
To stir up vain hopes in one's head   10
In Autumn no unblossoming
To remind one of the dead.

February 1925

CAN, 54–55, ink autograph; CI, purple TS (carbon) with ink and pencil autograph revisions and pencil autograph date 'February 1925'; CAF, fo. 32r, ink autograph; D, purple TS (carbon) with ink revisions and numbered '8' in [Davidson's] hand. Variants: Title Stone Walls] Walls *CI, CAF*. 3. nettles] bushes *CI, CAF, D*. 10. up vain hopes] vain hopes up *CAF*; up false hopes *D*. CAN shows a cancelled penultimate stanza:

> The hills are used to walls about them
> If looks have anything to tell
> And could one think of hills without them
> One would not love hills half so well

In all three other versions, this stanza is not cancelled; in CI it is typed as the first stanza but with a pencilled arrow indicating that it is to be moved into the penultimate position; in CAF it appears as the first stanza; and in D it is typed in the penultimate position, but with an arrow and the number '1' indicating that it should be moved to the opening position (all the stanzas in D are numbered in [Davidson's] hand to show their resulting new positions). Also, in all three of these other versions, there is a further stanza in the penultimate position, for a total of five draft stanzas:

> A hedge is easier to keep
> Perhaps, but then it's never warm;
> If you want proof, just ask a sheep
> Which he would rather have in storm. *(CI)*

However, in CI, this penultimate stanza is cancelled with a large purple X (probably made on the original TS and showing through in purple on the carbon). In D this stanza shows minor variants and several revisions, and the changes made to CI and to D suggest that Davidson rearranged the original five-stanza poem, that Auden accepted his rearrangement along with a few changes to individual words, and that the poem was retyped and also written out by hand accordingly. Then Auden changed his mind about the order of the stanzas, and, on CI, made alterations by hand indicating a return to the order in which he had originally written them. CI thus follows CAN as it stood, in four stanzas, before Auden made further revisions, cancelling the newly replaced penultimate stanza and reducing the poem to just three stanzas. This tends to confirm that CAN is the final fair copy, and so does the poem's position as the last one in the notebook. As with the preceding poem in the notebook, 'Before', the sloppy writing and haphazard punctuation probably result from hasty copying. Printed in 'Auden's Juvenilia', 373.

Auden's understated, colloquial tone in this poem was probably influenced by Robert Frost, and the subject may have been suggested to him by Frost's 1914 poem 'Mending Wall'.

□   □   □

> Like other men, when I go past
>   A mine shaft or a well,
> I always have to stop and cast
>   A stone to break the spell
>
> Of wondering how deep they go;
>   And if the clatter end
> Too soon, turn grieved away as though
>   Mistaken in a friend.

February 1925

U, TS on 'British Bond'; CI, TS with pencil autograph date 'February 1925'; D, purple TS (carbon of CI), numbered '13' in [Davidson's] hand; CAF, fo. 32v, purple TS (carbon). Only CI and D, not U or CAF, appear to be identical. A cancelled rough draft for this poem is among the Fisher manuscripts, on the verso of 'The dew steams off the thatches'. Printed in 'Auden's Juvenilia', 373, and Mackinnon, 55.

□ □ □

The crocus stars the border
In silver struts the dawn
The rooks put nests in order
And helpless things are born.

They sing, preen fur or feather
And soon return to dust.
So we two step together
And part because we must.

[*1925*]

CAF, fo. 32v, ink autograph.
   See 'Song' ('The crocus stars the border') for another, probably later, version of this poem. Auden revised the first stanza yet again for 'Chloe to Daphnis in Hyde Park'. The quatrains are modelled on Housman, for instance, poem 21 in *Last Poems* (1922), also a pair of quatrains, of which the first reads:

> The fairies break their dances
>   And leave the printed lawn,
> And up from India glances
>   The silver sail of dawn.

Damming Stream

It's time we went out to finish the dam,
For there are still several stones to fix,
And clods of turf to find to stop the leak;
The water ought to have covered the sticks

We placed before tea to measure its level,
Which means we'll have the flood-channel to do.
So we'd better start now—you'll catch us up;
Remember to shut the gates after you.

February 1925

CI, purple TS (carbon) with ink autograph revisions and pencil autograph date 'February 1925'.
   This poem is closely modelled on 'The Pasture' by Robert Frost, which is the prefatory

poem to his first volume of verse, *A Boy's Will* (London, 1913); William Heinemann Ltd. published Frost's *Selected Poems* in 1923, and 'The Pasture' appeared as the first poem in this volume as well:

I'm going out to clean the pasture spring;
I'll only stop to rake the leaves away
(And wait to watch the water clear, I may):
I shan't be gone long.—You come too.

I'm going out to fetch the little calf
That's standing by the mother. It's so young,
It totters when she licks it with her tongue.
I shan't be gone long.—You come too.

Sunday Morning

Across my dreams the bell
Clangs sullenly; I turn
And listen; twice it fell—
Then silence; so I learn.

The wind has changed to-night,
For now it blows this way.
There are two hours till light,
And two since yesterday.

How easy it would be
To move those hands, and say   10
To men to-morrow 'See,
It still is Saturday!'

One could so soon deceive
Them with its altered boom.
Perhaps some pain would leave
A heart, some soul a tomb.

[*March 1925*]

CI, TS with ink autograph revision and pencil autograph date 'March 192[5]'.

A Visit

The hedge has torn some blossom from the cart of May
    Two seagulls play
About the church's lantern tower; below salt-marshes stretch away
To where against the pebble beach the long sea flings its line of spray
    And you have come to me and come to stay

The grey church quivers drowsily, shut in its hollow;
    The marshes borrow
The burning heaven blue and turn it cool; the eye can scarcely follow
The glint of sails out through the haze; I walk alone but have no
                      sorrow
    Though you are gone for you return to-morrow.   10

I squelch through clay past sodden ricks; the hedge is raw
    The marsh we saw
Is now a desolate mudflat; as through a rotting factory floor
The sun strikes through the cloud in shafts; I walk the lane I walked
                    before
    But you are gone and will return no more.

March 1925

CI, ink autograph with pencil autograph date 'March 1925'. The manuscript shows a
cancelled title, 'No More'.
    Auden reused the first half of l. 11, slightly altered, in part 3 of 'Lover's Lane', written
probably in the summer of 1926. The image of the sun shining in shafts through a
rotten factory floor (ll. 13–14) he repeated in the opening lines of 'Thomas Epilogizes',
written in the spring of 1926, and again as ll. 9–10 of the 1929 poem beginning 'Which
of you waking early and watching daybreak' (*EA*, 41–42).

The Hidden Lane
(Near Selbrigg, March 1925)

I'd gone for walks upon that land
Ploughland and grass, ten times or more,
Even the fields adjoining it
But never seen the lane before

So like a hedge it looked outside
But even so I might have guessed
From the long line of stunted oaks
Where missel-thrushes had a nest

Not that it seemed much of a find
Choked as it was with blackberry—long   10
It must have been since anyone
Interrupted the robin's song

I walked a little way until
I found a gate to lean upon
Though thistles rose above my knees
And half its bottom bars were gone

Huge clouds lay quietly on the sky
The road ran on till lost to view
Behind a shoulder of the hill
To Paradise for all I knew   20

I broke the tallest thistle's back
Smiling to see its head hang yet
By one small strip, then turned to go
But half aware I may regret

That never shall I know what lies
Beyond the hill where that lane goes
Perhaps a lover like myself
Who tries to look this way, who knows?

[*March? 1925*]

CI, ink autograph, on the same folio with 'Since the Autumn day'. Variants: TITLE
Selbrigg, March *this edn*] Selbrigg March *CI*. 23. one *this edn*] once *CI*.
    Auden wrote 'Holt' in front of the words 'near Selbrigg' in the poem's title, then
cancelled it. Selbrigg Pond and Selbrigg Woods are both mentioned in *The Annual
Report of the Gresham's School Natural History Society* for 1925. Like many of the place
names mentioned in Auden's school poems, they were favourite spots for bird-watchers.
    This poem may be compared to Frost's 'The Road Not Taken' and Thomas's 'Over
the Hills' and 'Roads'.

April in a Town

Outside the factory window April came
    At last; a square of tender blue
Cut by the orange chimney like a flame
    Slimmer than cypress, grave as yew

Down in the street below was quiet as yet,
    From the canal nearby one cried,
A child perhaps? At dawn you soon forget
    One beauty for the next beside

No race of mating hares in March can please,
    No primrose by the brook that brings   10
A dream of April wonder deep, as these,
    The symbols of more noble things

Of seeds, man-sown, that leap beneath the soil
    Of damp earth cleft by chiming ploughs
A world made beautiful again by toil
    And scarred hands lovelier than the rose.

April 1925

CI, ink autograph with pencil autograph date 'April 1st 1925'.

The Mill (Hempstead)

All features of the wood are known to me
For I have latched the gate which borders it
And scrambled through its fences many times.
The long straight avenue of sombre larches
The lofty spruce where sparrowhawks once nested,
The ruined cottage in the open clearing
With its old well all filled with heartstongue fern
And noonday stars; all these are dear to me
But most I love the mill-pond and the mill
Which shall not be forgotten in my time.   10
The pond was large till reeds invaded it
And with them coots, dabchicks, and all those things

That hide or nest in reeds; but still the pond
Is stocked with fishes; sharp-finned tench, great pike,
And eels which share with rats the mill-race darkness.
Some too, have seen an otter in the pond
Wrinkling the taut-stretched surface with his snout.
The mill is not so ancient, yet it seems
As old as Britain, not to be destroyed
While men reap harvest, and while starlings build   20
Their villages beneath old hanging eaves.
I have but seen the miller now and then
But heard him singing often; such a one
As He who cared for nobody, or He
The lusty hairy-nosed whom Chaucer spoke of
Whose wife was gent and small as any weasel
And sang sweeter than swallow on a barn.
Often and often I have walked down there
To stroke his pair of dogs or hunt for nests,
A dozen? ten? I cannot count the times   30
But of them all, today there stands up one
Like one tall fir amid a hazel copse,
Seen over all, though all are beautiful,
A glowing evening early on in spring.
Ten minutes' rain had hushed the birds and left
A lambent smile upon the wet fresh earth,
The pool was half a mirror and the rest
Lay in the deepening shadow of the mill
Which pushed its bulk up at the evening sky
Clear-cut, dark, and rigid. The miller came   40
Outside to screw his sluices down; the sound
Of grinding which was heard all day was stilled.
All was silence save for one robin's song
Cold and remote as some far waterfall
Washing the basalt crags which edge the world
Flushed by a dying sun, and over all
The weir's music, more ancient than the bird,
Which hushes not for rain or wintry days,
Sung since Man built on earth, and not to cease
Till darkness shroud a ruined world's decay.   50

April 1925

CI, ink autograph with pencil autograph date 'April 1925'. Variants: 18. seems *this edn*] seems. *CI.* Auden submitted this poem to *The Gresham* during the summer term of 1925, but it was never printed. In a letter to the editor, John Saltmarsh, he responded to some criticisms of the piece and agreed to make two revisions of which I have incorporated one: in l. 1 he altered 'Each feature' to 'All features', and I have emended the verb accordingly. The second alteration cannot be fully established from the text of the letter, but presumably describes changes suggested for lines 4–6: 'As to feminine ending; I must confess to a liking, perverse doubtless, for what is after all a perfectly legitimate prosodical variation in the heroic line. Also I wanted to perceive a connection between the three things mentioned. However I will alter it as you suggest if you like.' Auden refused to alter the end of the poem, saying, 'The fault is partly mine as I omitted punctuation marks in your copy I fancy. If you dislike the simile about the Robin, I shall retort "Go and be damned". To say the robin's song is not cold is not legi[ti]mate criticism. I think it is, and you think it isn't. Well what about it?' He offered a scheme of punctuation (exactly matching that in Isherwood's copy) to clarify the lines, and explained 'You will see that the music is the weir's and not the bird's as your criticism seems to imply. A bird does stop singing for rain and a weir doesn't.' According to a note Saltmarsh left with the letter, the criticisms were made by a master, the Reverend F. G. E. Field, who advised the editor of *The Gresham* on verse (ALS, from Farfield, Holt, now in King's College Library, Cambridge, Coll. 34/20).

Hempstead Pond, sometimes called Hempstead Mill Pond, is about a mile south-east of Holt, but was apparently forbidden to the boys. In his essay 'Honour', Auden recalled the pleasures of solitary walks at Gresham's where almost no bound was set on his wanderings: 'Watching a snowstorm come up from the sea over the marshes at Salthouse, and walking in a June dawn (not so legally) by Hempstead Mill are only the two most vivid of a hundred such experiences'; *The Old School,* ed. Graham Greene (London, 1934), 10. See also Auden's poem 'November at Weybourne'.

L. 24 refers to the song 'There was a jolly miller once', still well known as a nursery rhyme but originally contained in the comic opera *Love in a Village* (1762) by Isaac Bickerstaffe with music by Thomas Arne. Ll. 24–27 borrow from Chaucer's *The Canterbury Tales* (the 'Prologue' and, in particular, 'The Miller's Tale', 3234–35 and 3258). The borrowing from Chaucer is near quotation and brings with it the Middle English 'gent', in the sense of graceful or slender. Otherwise the poem is written in the style of Edward Thomas, and bears close comparison with 'Haymaking', one of the poems Auden marked in his copy of Thomas's *Collected Poems* (see note to 'To E.T.'). The turn of phrase in l. 9 is probably remembered from Thomas's 'Birds' Nests'—'And most I like the winter nests deep-hid'—another poem Auden marked in his copy of Thomas. Also, 'The Mill (Hempstead)' perhaps alludes in some of the features of its setting to Wordsworth's 'The Ruined Cottage'. Later Auden quarried 'The Mill (Hempstead)' for his 1927 poem 'Narcissus'.

Elegy

A wagtail splutters in the stream,
Two sparrows quarrel at the door
And make the kindling season seem
A lovely motion as before;
But bird's wild music cannot bring
The dead unto a latter Spring.

He found the earliest thrush's nest
Before us all, his was a grace
Like poplars with their leaves at rest,
Or pony in the wind; his face   10
Was keen with solitude, his ears
Scarce tuned to grief in sixteen years.

That Spring came early, and the time
Was swift with us from day to day
Far into April, till his climb
To look into a squirrel's drey;
The rotten branches bore him well,
For he had reached it when he fell.

Three weeks he lay and watched a rook
Or lilac hanging in the rain;   20
A pair of wrynecks came and took
The nesting-box outside the pane
And hatched their brood. The first one cried
Upon the morning that he died.

No dog barked in the street below
The churchyard where they dug his grave;
The day wore nothing strange to show
That earth took back the dust she gave;
And cuckoos, they were calling still,
When we had left him in the hill.   30

                                    May 1925

U, TS on 'British Bond'; CI, TS with pencil autograph date 'May 1925'; D, ink auto-
graph, with first stanza revised on an ink AP postmarked '13 May 1925' (I have not

recorded the earlier variants). D has an ALS on it; see note to 'Richard Jefferies'. Variants: 11–12. his ears / Scarce tuned to grief] to fears / And griefs unknown *D*. Printed in Carpenter, 39–40.

Fisher detects Hardy's influence in this poem ('Auden's Juvenilia', 371–72), though it also recalls the Wordsworth of 'The Danish Boy' or the boy of Winander passage in *The Prelude*, book 5. The lingering death after a fall while climbing to a nest combines the circumstances of two boyhood deaths that occur in one of Auden's favourite nursery books, *Eric, or Little by Little* by F. W. Farrar (Edinburgh, 1858).

Job

The tempest plucks the wood at last; on high
Scud fleeting glimpses of a shrunk moon bowed
Upon herself and storm-tossed; far and nigh
The crash of branch on branch, wind's anguished cry
And hissing of the rain as huge and proud
The thunderstorm sweeps grandly up the sky
Peals for an instant shatteringly loud
Then rolls away; the rain is held; a cloud
Mutters afar; slowly each corner fills
With heavy silence, motionless and deep   10
Until dawn's finger touches it to words;
Drops plashing to the ground; the song of birds
On fallen tree trunks; tired eyes asleep
At last while morning glitters on the hills.

May 1925

CI, ink autograph with pencil autograph date 'May 1925'.
    See Job 38; Auden referred again to this part of Job in 'Thomas Prologizes'.

Richard Jefferies

What of this Man? No striding Amos sent
Down from his native crags to thunder war,
No Shelley to light up the firmament
And plunge to darkness like a shattered star;
Rather winds found a pipe and blew thereon,
Sometimes with bubbling joy, now wild with griefs
But fresh as elder scent; his voice cries on
Among his Wiltshire downs; in strange beliefs
And rough slow-moving speech of village folk:
What more? When dying he could praise the light   10
And watch larks trembling over fields of corn
Until the whole sky sang, with eyes as bright
As kestrel perched upon the splintered oak,
A sentinel, dark, motionless, at dawn.

May 1925

CI, ink autograph with pencil autograph date 'May 1925'; F, Fisher's ink autograph transcription with pencil date '1925'. Variants: 5. winds] wind *F*.

The writer and naturalist Richard Jefferies (1848–87) was greatly admired by both Hardy and Thomas. Thomas wrote a biography of him published in 1909, and Davidson apparently gave the book to Auden in about May 1925, for Auden wrote to him: 'I had no copy of *Richard Jefferies* and have long wanted one' (ALS, probably from Gresham's, Holt; written across the bottom of the 'Elegy' beginning 'A wagtail splutters in the stream'; Christ Church Library). Fisher recalled that Auden thought Jefferies' *Bevis, the Story of a Boy*, 'the only tolerable book about a boy; all the others were shameful wallowings in sentimentality'. He also noted that 'Richard Jefferies' and 'To E.T.' are the first examples of the 'personal tribute' which Auden later wrote for Housman, Lear, Rimbaud, and many others ('Auden's Juvenilia', 372).

Amos is the herdsman and minor prophet of the thirtieth book of the Old Testament. The comparison with Shelley recalls several passages from his work, for instance, his 'Lines: "When the lamp is shattered"'; his statement in 'A Defence of Poetry' that the 'mind in creation is as a fading coal'; or the last lines of Urania in 'Adonais':

> A godlike mind soars forth, in its delight
> Making earth bare and veiling heaven, and when
> It sinks, the swarms that dimmed or shared its light
> Leave to its kindred lamps the spirit's awful night. (258–61)

The last two lines of 'Richard Jefferies' later reappeared as part of the conclusion to the 1926 poem 'Early Morning' ('Earth rolls these houses out into the sun').

The Sawmill

That's the sawmill—everyone can hear it
Day in, day out, the loud harsh, grating cry
Louder and harsher than the jay's voice even,
But still no less a voice among the trees
And clear enough to sweeten memory with;
Then the brief panting pause to wait for breath
Before the next deep plunge, or ask for time
To sniff the fresh-cut pine log's oozing gum.
So it toils on under the beech's shadow
Till Sunday comes; the woodman looks upon   10
The pile of logs which he has made to find
It good perhaps, and leaves the mill, alone,
With no voice left to answer all the birds
Which mock or stare at it. To enter then
And ask for shade as I did seemed profane;
The cuckoo trying for the hundredth time
To catch the tune which he has quite forgotten,
The sudden wild shout of the woodpecker,
Laughing at some old joke now seen at last,
These and the silence told me where men stole   20
The legend of the Sleeping Beauty from;
I could not end the cuckoo's song for him,
Nor understand the other's mirth, the day
Had slipped into this June from some past age,
An alien swallow from a ghostly flock
Which helped to make a summer years ago
Days which no child had smiled on in the making,
No fairer than our own but different
Nor, like love and sorrow, to be again.

May 1925

CI, ink autograph with pencil autograph date 'May 1925'; CAF, 16r–v, ink autograph.
Variants: 11. pile of logs] piles of planks *CAF*. 19. joke] jest *CAF*. 22. end the cuckoo's
song for him] finish the song for the one *CAF*. 24. age, *this edn*] age. *CI*. Printed in
Mackinnon, 52–53.

The influence of Thomas persists in 'The Sawmill' and with it perhaps the influence
of Frost; see for instance Frost's 'The Wood-Pile'.

□   □   □

Below me Ticknall lay but in the light
Which yet remained the roofs looked strange and blurred
My footsteps rang aloud but nothing stirred
Until a fern owl from the copse upon the knoll
Uttered his easeful note of victory
That immemorial cry so stern, and proud,
Seemed an old man calling at the edge of night
Above dark valleys, making a stone roll
Scattering down the slope and hearts be glad
Stung by the music and the wounded cloud   10
And horse and horseman huge against the sky
But then some change of mood as home I came
Made me remember shagged men, who had
An older name for home than Derbyshire
Or Britain, who on Autumn nights like these
Hearing that cry, woke sleeping logs to flame
Shivered and huddled closer to the fire
Feeling the dead peer downward through the trees.

May 1925

CI, ink autograph with pencil autograph revisions and pencil autograph date 'May 1925', on the same folio as 'Landscape' and 'The Road's Your Place'. The alterations to this poem make it difficult to decipher; the opening line originally read 'Below me was the village in the light'. Auden revised this in pencil, possibly some years later (see Textual Note, p. lxix).

   Ticknall, which Auden spelled 'Ticknal', is probably the village near Derby and near Repton. Auden might have visited there for several reasons. His father was educated at Repton, and the Saxon crypt in the parish church there had attracted Dr Auden's attention in his youth; the church is dedicated to St Wystan, the ninth-century Mercian prince after whom Auden was named (Carpenter, 4). Auden's brother John recalled that in childhood they occasionally visited their father's mother at the nearby village of Horninglow (*Tribute*, 26), about eight miles from Ticknall; their grandfather, another John Auden, had been vicar of St John's Church at Horninglow until his death in 1876. Auden's grandmother, Sarah Elizabeth Hogkins Auden, lived on in Horninglow until her death in December 1925. St John's has a window in her memory.

'The Road's Your Place'

The stream I think persuaded me at first
A tarn lay somewhere at the end of it
I felt quite positive; perhaps it was
The crunch of stones I tired of, anyhow
I left the road and struck up by the burn
Along a track which heaved and plunged and leapt
From side to side to gratify the whim
Of some once famous leader of the sheep
To-day scarcely a name to mountain-lambs.
In front the burn turned quickly to the left   10
I hurried on, eager and out of breath
And soon had turned the corner, all at once
Three crags rose up and overshadowed me
'What are you doing here, the road's your place'
—Between their bodies I could see my tarn—
What could I do but shift my feet awhile
Mutter and turn back to the road again
Watched out of sight by three tall angry hills.

May 1925

CI, ink autograph with pencil autograph date 'May 1925'; F(1), fragment, ink autograph of first seven lines; F(2), Fisher's ink autograph transcription with note 'Recited to me in Meadow Buildings, 1925'. Variants: 5. burn] beck *F(2)*. 6. Along a track which heaved and plunged and leapt] Which plunged and heaved and leapt from side to side *F(1)*; Along a track which plunged and heaved and leapt *F(2)*. 7. From side to side to gratify the whim] To gratify the whim of some once famous leader of the sheep *F(1)*; From side to side to satisfy *F(2)*. 9. To-day scarcely ... mountain-lambs] Scarcely ... mountain-lambs today *F(2)*. 10. burn] beck *F(2)*. 11. hurried] scrambled *F.* 13–14. me / 'What] me— / Stood there and stared down at me threateningly; / 'What *F(2)*.

Fisher noted that the three crags recall Wordsworth's description of the cliff which seemed to stride after him as he rowed his stolen boat across Lake Windermere in the first book of *The Prelude* ('Auden's Juvenilia', 371); see *The Prelude* (1850), 1.377–85. This passage seems to have haunted Auden's imagination for some years; it is the only excerpt from *The Prelude* that he included in his 1935 anthology *The Poet's Tongue*. Fisher also pointed out that 'The Road's Your Place' owes a great deal to the style of Edward Thomas ('Auden's Juvenilia', 372).

Landscape

The horse could scarcely pluck its stumbling heel
Out of the mire which floored the dreary way
Sunk in his thoughts the rider could not feel
　　　　　The sunken day.

No rock, nor twisted thorn was there to fill
The uneasy silence of those wasted lands
Mile after mile, save once a ruined mill
　　　　　Raised heavy hands.

June 1925

CI, ink autograph with pencil autograph revisions and pencil autograph date 'June 1925', on the same folio as 'Below me Ticknall lay but in the light' and 'The Road's Your Place'; CAN, 50, ink autograph. Variants: 6. The uneasy] Th'uneasy *CAN*.

Auden reused the imagery in the second stanza of 'Landscape' in his 1926 poem 'Thomas Epilogizes'. The mire and the 'sunken day' of the first stanza reappeared in 'Lovers' Lane', also written in 1926. The bleak atmosphere of 'Landscape' may derive from Hardy's influence; Auden's 'stumbling' horse recalls in particular the 'old horse that stumbles and nods' in the first stanza of Hardy's 'In Time of "The Breaking of Nations"', one of the many poems Auden marked in his 1925 edition of Hardy's poems. (By the end of his life, Auden owned three copies of Hardy's poetry, all heavily marked and one with many pages removed. They are now in HRHRC.) Yet the metre, mood, and diction of 'Landscape' also recall Edmund Blunden's 'The Waggoner' (1919), on a similar theme.

The Dying House

The house was dying when I saw it; gaunt
And hollow its eyes looked, which once had shone
So bravely from the wood on winter mornings
Across the fields; now even moss and leaves
Were getting ready for the burial

I knew but little of the house save what
They told me at the inn; a woman lived
There last who bore a boy and dropped him
Three days later—The stair was always dark—
She would not live in houses after that.　　　　10

The house still seemed an old and kindly one
Which shut no door on martin or on ghost

I only stopped to watch a silver squirrel
Chasing a red across the broken tiles
My odds were on the English one, I lost

Nought could be done to help it so I left
Like Hagar wishing not to see the end
There are worse ways of death than this to choose from
Beneath the sky and rain, alone, with birds
And no grief but a stranger's casual tears.   20

June 1925

CI, ink autograph with pencil autograph date 'June 1925', on the same folio with 'The Sawmill'.

Red squirrels are native to England, silver (or grey) squirrels are not, although they are now by far the most common type; the poet bets on the dying English breed. His emblematic nostalgia for a former England, and the style of the poem generally, are borrowed from Edward Thomas. For the reference to Hagar after she is expelled by Abraham with their son, see Genesis 21.16, 'Let me not see the death of the child.'

Friendship

The earth was grateful for a day of rain
Not I, silent and weary with the thought
Of Friendship which I fancied lost again
And happiness long looked for brought to nought.

It meant no more to me than tree or stone
Until a hedge fell, showing as I passed
An old man picking flints, wet and alone,
Who gave a meaning to the rain at last

The rain spoke to me then but not for long
Telling of things between me and my friend   10
Heard and forgotten like a thrush's song
Made in an hour yet not perhaps to end.

July 1925

CI, ink autograph with pencil autograph date 'July 1925'.

This is one of the poems Auden defended against Isherwood's criticism that it was third-rate (see note to 'Farglow'). The 'old man picking flints' (7) is modelled on the leech-gatherer in Wordsworth's 'Resolution and Independence'.

The Sunken Lane

Fine evenings always bring their thoughts of her,
But beech woods chiefly—their silence astir
So like her movements. Here I have them both.
Like small birds rustling in the bramble-growth,
Questing among the rotting leaves unseen,
I ransack memory for what has been
And is not, finding here perhaps a look,
There a shadow of the sun-browned neck which took
My wonder and my lips; then blankness; yet
One little thing I never can forget: 10
Nothing of hers but the one treasured thing,
Except for love, of all that fairy Spring:
I think of her and straightway wild and clear,
As a stream bubbling in a wood I hear,
Just as I heard it then and since, a voice
Singing of beauty far beyond my choice
Or hers, and sweet as Marvell or the rain,
A linnet piping in a sunken lane.

July 1925

The Oxford Magazine, Commemoration Number (19 June 1926): 8, with Auden's name
misprinted as 'W. A. Auden'; CI, TS with pencil autograph date 'July 1925'. Variants: CI
has no title. 5. rotting] rotten *CI*. 16. Singing] Telling *CI*. 17. Marvell] Chaucer *CI*.
    This poem intertwines the themes of Thomas's 'Celandine', 'The Unknown Bird',
and 'The Word', three poems Auden marked in his edition of Thomas's *Collected Poems*
(see note to 'To E.T.'). He included the last line of 'The Sunken Lane' in 'Narcissus',
written in the spring of 1927.

Punchard

This is the place for you if you love quiet
Hills to keep the wind off but never sun
No sudden voices but the chickens' riot
At breakfast, the colley rattling his chain
At night sometimes, and now and then a gun
Tells that some jay will suck no eggs again

In pheasant woods across the valley; hot
It is out upon the fell here but not
Within the farm, where old Joe Punchard lies
On the cool kitchen flags until to-morrow.   10
Toil he knew, and love, but mostly toil—wise
And kind he's done with all of these and gone
No more to come again than to-day's dawn.
His son has not an hour for sorrow
The farm is his now, he must reap the corn
Bring out the sheep to pasture, eat and rest
Himself with sleep not tears. As for the barn
How should it know? Hay and a starling's nest
Perhaps are all a barn asks for. And none
Will drag the hidden barrow out into the sun   20
Or mend the handle of the broken rake
—The cock must crow though one will not awake.
A few years more myself? Who knows? I pass
Shading my eyes with one rose-glowing hand
And muttering 'All flesh is as the grass
To seek this solitude to find the word
Fit to speak of beauty and the dead and
Cannot being no child now nor a bird.'

July 1925

CI, ink autograph with ink and pencil autograph revisions and pencil autograph date 'July 1925', on the same folio as 'To Edward Thomas' (printed as 'To E.T.' in this edition). Most of the revisions to the manuscript were made in ink, but l. 21 was altered in pencil, possibly much later (see Textual Note, p. lxix). Before the pencil alterations, l. 21 was two lines reading 'Or pluck the stonecrop from the wall, or break / His grinding stone behind the cattle shed.'

This poem, reflecting Auden's passion for Thomas, was included in the list sent to Isherwood in about June 1927 of pieces written before July 1926 that Auden intended to preserve (see note to 'Early Morning' beginning 'Perched on a nettled stump he stands'). For l. 25, see Isaiah 40.6 and 1 Peter 1.24.

Auden was to draw heavily on 'Punchard' for the epithalamium he wrote for Cecil Day-Lewis's wedding at Christmas 1928. The remote cottage, the riot of poultry, and the rattling chain of the farmer's watchdog all reappeared in the wedding poem beginning 'This morning any touch is possible', printed in Sean Day-Lewis's biography of his father, *C. Day-Lewis: An English Literary Life* (London, 1980). Later, Auden reused the last line of 'Punchard' as the conclusion to the second part of his 1929 poem beginning 'It was Easter as I walked in the public garden' (later titled '1929').

To E.T.

Those thick walls never shake beneath the rumbling wheel
No scratch of mole nor lisping worm you feel
So surely do those windows seal.

But here and there your music and your words are read
And someone learns what elm and badger said
To you who loved them and are dead

So when the blackbird tries his cadences anew
There kindles still in eyes you never knew
The light that would have shone in you.

[*Summer 1925*]

Ink autograph signed 'W.H.A.', on the blank leaf facing the last poem in Auden's copy of Edward Thomas's *Collected Poems* (London, 1920), now at HRHRC; CI, ink autograph; F, Fisher's ink autograph transcription with his pencil autograph date '1925?'. Variants: TITLE To E.T.] To Edward Thomas *CI, F*. 5. elm . . . badger] elms . . . badgers *F*.

Fisher recalled this poem as having been written with 'Richard Jefferies' and 'The Road's Your Place' during Auden's school-days ('Auden's Juvenilia', 371). Probably it was written in the summer of 1925, between May and July. The idea for the poem may have been suggested to Auden by Frost's poem of the same title printed in *New Hampshire* (published in London in 1924). De la Mare wrote a similar poem, 'To E.T.: 1917', included in his collected *Poems 1901 to 1918*. The tangible weight and closeness of the grave, along with the rhyme feel/seal in stanza 1, recall Wordsworth's quatrains beginning 'A slumber did my spirit seal'.

HRHRC holds two copies once belonging to Auden of the 1920 edition of Edward Thomas's poems. While the copy with the poem inscribed in it appears otherwise unused, with many uncut pages, the second copy is battered and well-annotated in Auden's hand. On the front paste-down endpaper of the second copy is a Gresham's School prize bookplate with the following details completed in Auden's hand: 'W. H. Auden / Eccles Science Prize (Chemistry) / June 1924'. Some of the annotations in the second copy appear to be in Auden's late handwriting; others are perhaps much earlier.

The Canal, Froghall

There runs no road except the towpath through the valley
And oaks hang over it to make a dark green alley
Quite covering the weedy sunk canal it follows
Winding in and out among the hill-ribs and hollows.

Beneath the water trees hang downward in their stations
Glassed in a calm which might have been for generations,
And save for some few sleepy birds no note is spoken
The silence and the watercalm are both unbroken.
Until a barge with coal and iron ore laden passes
The swaying towrope swishing gently through the grasses.   10
At once tree images jostle and soon have vanished
The silences and solitudes are quickly banished
Because of one tired horse with jingling harness stalking
Slow, patient forward, one old man beside it walking,
And puffing at a blackened clay, or sometimes humming
All unaware of what is scattered by their coming.
They go their way and ripples are the only traces
Until the calm returns which everything effaces
And images of trees resume their standing places.

[*Summer 1925*]

F, ink autograph, on the same folio with 'The Carter's Funeral' and 'Christmas Eve'.
    Froghall, a hamlet in Staffordshire in the Midlands three miles north of Cheadle, is
the terminus of the Caldon Canal.

Song

The merriest cuckoo
Which haunted us in May
Is silent now, and you
Will go but not to-day

One moment sing with laughter
While heart and eye are young
That we may treasure after
The music which we rung.

One moment say and do
The things which cannot end   10
While memories renew
The dead tones of a friend,

As some old country wine
To winter nights can bring
The cowslips, which made fine
A far-off perished spring.

For this is surely known
To each man come the years
When he must sit alone
And eat his bread with tears.   20

[*August 1925*]

CI, ink autograph with pencil autograph date 'August 192[5]', on the same folio with
'Sonnet' ('April is here but when will Easter come?') and 'Memento Creatoris Tui'.

Sonnet

April is here but when will Easter come?
Men's bones are scattered in a gloomy pass
They lie with arched ribs crumbling in the grass
Each sunset adds its quota to the sum
Of bitterness, and prophecy is dumb.
Our end no nearer than it ever was
We wander like the phantoms in a glass
Pale, naked, nameless, and without a home.

Not once nor twice have those appeared who caught
The cry of anguish from this stricken world   10
Who knelt to wash the feet of slaves, who sought
With tears to lift the crowns of thorn which stab us
Day and night; ever in their teeth is hurled
The frenzied shout 'Not this man but Barabbas'.

[*August 1925*]

CI, ink autograph with pencil autograph date 'August 192[5]', on the same folio with
'Song' ('The merriest cuckoo') and 'Memento Creatoris Tui'.
   L. 2 perhaps alludes to the opening of Milton's sonnet 18, 'On the Late Massacre in
Piemont': 'Avenge, O Lord, thy slaughter'd Saints, whose bones / Lie scatter'd on the
Alpine mountains cold,' (1–2); the image of scattered bones also occurs in the Bible,
for instance Ezekiel 6.5 and Psalms 53.5 and 141.7. The poem's final line is quoted from
John 18.40. For Jesus washing the feet of his disciples, see John 13.5–12. Auden later
incorporated l. 3 into his 1926 poem 'Lead's the Best'.

Memento Creatoris Tui

I climbed a dazzling cliff which overhung the sea
While the south-west shepherded cloud flocks over me
And round I heard the young grass growing silently
But the voice of the surges beneath called strangely my dreaming
through
'The strong men shall bow themselves; the grinders cease because
they are few'

I walked through crags which frowned upon a pass
While the wind-gust froze and the hail-storm cut like glass
And I laughed and sang as I strode for glad I was
But the wind and the rain howled out what I would not hear—
'Soon they
Shall be afraid of that which is high, and fears shall be in the way.'   10

Joy came to me with the first blackbird's carolling
And the time I heard a passing peasant-girl sing
Is a day I shall remember with thanksgiving
But a sweet note tolls as clear as a bell—'He shall rise up and go
At the voice of the bird and the daughters of music be brought low.'

For miles across the fells lay the golden Autumn weather
When she of the dark-hair and I sat down together
And all the world was shrunk into a patch of heather
But the lovely tones of her voice told me love is of no avail
For soon 'The grasshopper shall be a burden, and desire shall fail.'   20

I wander through the earth and rejoice in it all
For the march of Spring, and the sunlit waterfall
And friends' faces grow day by day more beautiful
But ever my pulse has a word to whisper to me as it beats
'Man goeth to his long home and the mourners go about the streets.'

[*August 1925*]

CI, ink autograph with pencil autograph date 'August 192[5]', on the same folio with
'Song' ('The merriest cuckoo') and 'Sonnet' ('April is here but when will Easter
come?'). Variants: 14. shall *this edn*] has *CI.*
   The title 'Memento Creatoris Tui' is from Ecclesiastes 12.1: 'Remember now thy
creator in the days of thy youth.' The final lines of each stanza are also near quotations

from Ecclesiastes; see 12.3–6. Auden has introduced some important changes to this forbidding text, whose perhaps most famous admonition is in 12.8, 'Vanity of vanities saith the preacher; all is vanity.' See also verses 12 and 13, which are relevant to Auden's loss of faith and his choice of vocation.

The peasant girl in stanza 3 recalls Wordsworth's 'Highland lass' in 'The Solitary Reaper', a poem Auden echoed in 'California' (see note to 'California').

Earth's Praises

I will be silent, Mother earth
Will teach my love her beauty's worth

Two young larks kiss the sky above
Can I teach them new songs of love?

For metaphors of love why search
Her image? Look, this silver birch

So frail, so delicate, so tall,
A dream of the white waterfall!

[*September 1925*]

CI, ink autograph with pencil autograph date 'September 192[5]'. Variants: 5. search *this edn*] search, *CI*. Auden reused ll. 6 and 8 in his 1926 poem 'Lead's the Best' (ll. 25–26).

Daily Bread

The rolling mill
Though day is dead
Is burning still
A sunset red

A furnace door
Gleams orange bright
And seems to gnaw
The heart of night

And now and then
Within the glow   10
Half-naked men
Move to and fro

Steel clangs on steel
Shades flicker past
A window, cast
By some huge wheel.

Here, once the same,
Just such a mill
As good to fill
The night with flame   20

Look at it now
A rusted shard
A useless plough
In time's farmyard.

Its chimney stacks
Twisted awry
Its windows cracks
Its mill race dry.

Lovers must pray
Though love be dead   30
'Give us this day
Our daily bread.'

[*1925*]

CI, ink autograph, on the same folio with 'The Dark Fiddler' and 'Maria hat geholfen'.
Variants: 15. window, cast *this edn*] window cast *CI*.
  The final stanza of this poem suggestively foreshadows the conclusion to Auden's
?1957 poem 'First Things First': 'Thousands have lived without love, not one without
water' (*CP*, 584).

The Dark Fiddler

The ash tree hides her face
    Away and grieves
Her children scattered under
    Dying leaves

All Autumn the Dark Fiddler
    Has often sung
The poor and old can hear him
    Not the young

Far off the music wanders
    By forest meres   10
Dark valleys, lonely mountains
    Ruined weirs

Autumn passes but Winter
    Still hears the sound
Level the snow plain stretches
    Miles around.

Music struggling with sorrow
    A single cry
Pierces the night and passes
    Drifting by.   20

Silence at last, the stars
    Burn bright and glad
Only a moon climbs slowly,
    Frailly sad.

[*1925*]

CI, ink autograph, on the same folio with 'Daily Bread' and 'Maria hat geholfen'.
    The final line of this poem first appeared in 'A Moment', published in *The Gresham* in April 1922, and it reappeared in 'Humpty Dumpty' with a landscape similar to the one described here in stanza 3.

Maria hat geholfen

Old dead builder, how wise you were,
To build your church on mountains here
What better way to conquer ills
And grief is there than climbing hills?

How many pilgrims stoop to pull
Flowers from this pathway beautiful,
How many seasons' weary eyes
Have gladdened at these butterflies?

And here perhaps where tapers shine
Some early god had once his shrine   10
Some savage woman kissed the earth
Because her son was brought to birth

Wild presences who came before
Christ Jesus, Jupiter, and Thor:
Earth Mother—Mary—, what's the name?
The thankful heart is just the same.

'Mary has helped them'—me—a friend
Why, every sorrow has an end
Like any other earthly thing
But love, no more than Death, dies with the Spring   20

[*1925*]

CI, ink autograph, on the same folio with 'Daily Bread' and 'The Dark Fiddler'. Variants: TITLE Maria hat geholfen *this edn*] Maria hab geholfen *CI*.   17. them'—me *this edn*] them' me *CI*.

In l. 17 the poem offers a translation of its title. Auden went to Salzburg for the music festival and to Kitzbühel in the summer of 1925.

Sunshine

There's nothing like the sun, not even rain or children; see the grass
And flowers can tell from shadows now that overhead the rook
                                                        flocks pass.

The scythe blade in the field becomes a living thing of light, a song,
                                                        a gleam
As if the eye picked out at last the flash of a long hidden stream.

The factory chimneys cluster in the morning like so many trees
No forest is more silent and more beautiful to-day than these.

To each man's heart the sun speaks as to chimney, scythe, and
                                                        meadowland
'I see it all, the foolish and the great; I love, I understand.'

                                                [September 1925]

CI, ink autograph with pencil autograph date 'Sept 192[5]'.
    Auden borrows this theme from Thomas's poem 'There's Nothing Like the Sun'.

Autumn Evening

Hills and a cloud have hid away the sun,
The cottage lamps are lighted one by one.

Two lovers steal forth from the village street
Like two shadows from world and world they meet

And make one gloom, heart pressed to beating heart,
Then into the old night they fall apart.

A distant curfew bell merrily saith
'Night and morning, work and sleeping, life and Death.'

The ringer dies unknown; his ashes give
The corn whereby both larks and poets live.   10

                                                [October 1925]

CI, ink autograph with pencil autograph date 'Oct 192[5]'. The manuscript shows three cancelled stanzas. Two follow stanza 1:

> Silence holds up the pinewood like a wall,
> The birds roost in the boughs and cease to call
>
> The sheep have all been driven off the moor
> Lest snow should come and bleat amid their straw

The third follows stanza 4:

> Sing O my soul in this dark wilderness
> Some lonely traveller through the night to bless

L. 7 perhaps alludes, in a perverse manner, to the opening line of Thomas Gray's 'Elegy Written in a Country Church-Yard': 'The curfew tolls the knell of parting day'. And Auden's poem perhaps also borrows from Gray's the themes of evening and of the bell-ringer who dies unknown. The furtive lovers, on the other hand, are borrowed from Edward Thomas's 'Lovers': 'The two men in the road were taken aback. / The lovers came out shading their eyes from the sun'. (In 'As the Team's Head-Brass', a similar pair of lovers disappears into the woods.)

The Carter's Funeral

Sixty odd years of poaching and drink
And rain-sodden waggons with scarcely a friend;
Chained to this life—Rust fractures a link,
      So—the end

Sexton at last has stamped down the loam
He blows on his fingers and prays for the sun;
Parson unvests, and turns to his home,
      Duty done.

Little enough stays musing upon
The passing of One of the Masters of things;   10
Only a bird looks peak-faced thereon
      Looks and sings.

[October or November 1925]

F, ink autograph, on the same folio with 'Christmas Eve' and 'The Canal, Froghall'; CI, ink autograph with 'Ch. Ch. J. C. R.' at bottom. Variants: 5. stamped] pressed *CI*. 11. thereon] upon *CI*. Printed in Isherwood, 'Some Notes on Auden's Early Poetry', 4–5.

Auden's first term at Christ Church was Michaelmas 1925, which began 10 October and ended 17 December (Full Term ran from 11 October to 5 December); if the poem was actually composed in the Junior Common Room it was probably near the start of term when the location would still have seemed worthy of note. (Auden later established a habit of noting the place of composition at the foot of all of his poems.) The Fisher copy appears to be the later fair copy; it shows a revision in l. 5 from 'pressed' to 'stamped', but apparently this revision was forgotten by the time Isherwood prepared the poem for publication in 1937.

Fisher noted that Hardy's influence can still be detected in this poem ('Auden's Juvenilia', 371).

Rain

This peace can last no longer than the storm
Which started it, this shower wet and warm,
This careless striding through the clinging grass,
Perceiving nothing, these will surely pass
When heart and eardrums are no longer dinned
By shouting air; as surely as the wind
Will bring a lark song from the clouds, not rain,
Shall I know the meaning of lust again;
Nor sunshine on the weir's dull dreamless roar
Can change me from the thing I was before,   10
Imperfect body and imperfect mind
Unknowing what it is I seek to find.
I know it; yet for this brief hour or so
I am content, unthinking and aglow.
Made one with horses and with workmen, all
Who seek for shelter by a dripping wall
Or labour in the fields with mist and cloud
And slant rain hiding them as in a shroud.

[*Autumn 1925*]

CI(1), TS; CI(2), ink autograph with numerous ink and pencil autograph revisons. Variants: 15. workmen] workman *CI(2)*. Another TS of the poem, with one ink autograph revision, was sent by Auden to Cyril Connolly, possibly at Connolly's request, with the following note: 'Overleaf the Edward Thomasy poem I can't recall writing' (TLS, 18 July 1972, from Kirchstetten). The Connolly TS was probably prepared in the 1970s; I have not recorded any variants from it. It is now in the McFarlin Library, University of Tulsa, Oklahoma. Published in *Lions and Shadows*, 187.

Fisher recalls that '"Rain" was certainly written before the end of 1925' ('Auden's Juvenilia', 371). Auden included it in the list of poems he intended to preserve from those written before his visit with Isherwood to Freshwater Bay in July 1926 (see note to 'Early Morning' beginning 'Perched on a nettled stump he stands'). In a letter to Isher-

wood probably written in the winter of 1926 and mentioning several other poems writ-
ten in 1925, Auden discussed his use in the poem of the figure of the simple labourer;
as the autograph variant of the poem shows, he originally conceived of the workmen as
one workman (the letter is roughly written and I have made only one emendation,
marked by square brackets):

Now as to the labourer,
You make a mistake in suppos[ing] that I wish to idealize the labourer in any
way. Especially the damnable half educated kind. But if you have met the best sort,
as I often have, you will realise, I think, how much easier it is to preserve a truly
'simple' mind in that environment than in say Oxford.

In 'Rain' the labourer is not said to be an ideal; I only suggest that hoeing turnips
in the rain does make for peace of mind at the [?least], or rather intellectual
Nirvanah which is what one wants at that particular juncture. I

He may be sensual but he is so in a completely straightforward and animal way;
and does not [?naf] it up as so many would be seducers do in the usual Platonic
drivel. (ALS, possibly from Christ Church)

Auden included a shortened version of 'Rain' as section (d) in the first long poem in
P(28); this version is printed separately below, p. 206.

In a Country Churchyard

Nature has bought the steeple
And wears the hills around
But takes off worn-out people
And lays them underground

'Surely we have our uses,
And life is fair!' They grieve
But God with no excuses
Abruptly takes his leave.

                                        [*Autumn? 1925*]

F, ink autograph. The folio is torn in half and the rest of it is lost; a draft of the first
stanza appears on the verso with a chemical formula.

Like several poems in the Fisher collection, this perhaps dates from one of Auden's
first terms at Christ Church when he was most friendly with Fisher and when he was still
reading Natural Science. It was included in the list Auden sent to Isherwood in about
June 1927 of pieces written before July 1926 that he intended to preserve (see note to
'Early Morning' beginning 'Perched on a nettled stump he stands'), but no copy sur-
vives in the Isherwood collection. In his letter to Isherwood, Auden calls the poem 'In
a Deserted Graveyard', but it is virtually certain that he had the same poem in mind.

Fisher includes this among the poems Auden wrote in the style of Housman
('Auden's Juvenilia', 372).

The Gipsy Girl

'A penny for a poor lass with a child
Just coming, and a snowy Christmas too!
Just for the poor, Sir!'—(But her eyes were wild)—
'Maybe a pretty wife's in store for you;
We know such things as that, they're ours, the rich
Can't know of them although they've been to school—...
Ah, you're a handsome gentleman!' Words which
A step perhaps converted to 'Old Fool!'
'God send a boy,' I said and thought 'Then bring
A white day some December for your burying.'   10

Pale Cleopatra by the river bank
Once looked into those eyes and for a while
Sweet Charmian's perfume like corruption stank
Her slaves seemed corpses washed up from the Nile.
And Milton, in the chambers of whose mind
Hung gorgeous robes of purple images,
Looked downward from his tower once, half blind
With midnight reading, on some girl as this,
Whose laughter like a sheep's bell, shamed no less
Than Hagar's when she mocked at Sarah's barrenness.   20

Blessed be England for so fair a face
Drawn on the background of a leafless wood
Enchanted, menacing! With all the grace
Earth christens her own children with, she stood
Then strode away; a starling's pipe awoke
The chill remoteness of a dawn that was,
While chuckling Oberon in his scarlet cloak
Looked after her; and as he watched her pass
Giant Winter mumbled in his beard and smiled
For Youth is still undimmed and Beauty undefiled.   30

[*Autumn 1925*]

F, ink autograph. Variants: 27. cloak *this edn*] cloak. *F*.
   Fisher writes that this poem 'I think was composed during his first term at Christ
Church' ('Auden's Juvenilia', 371). Perhaps inspired by Thomas's 'The Gypsy', it al-
ludes in l. 3 to Wordsworth's 'Her Eyes Are Wild'. Other references are to Shake-

speare's *Antony and Cleopatra* and *A Midsummer Night's Dream*, Milton's 'Il Penseroso',
and the Old Testament story of Sarah and Hagar (Genesis 16–21).

Frost

The wind that blew the clouds away so silently
Has gone, leaving nothing but bright stars and the frost
These and a half moon wandering about the sky
Bewildered like a market-woman tired and lost.

To-morrow there'll be the beacon glittering beyond
The elms, and icicles to snap off from the roof
For us too, skating then perhaps on Winster Pond
If boys snowballing are not beautiful enough.

We do not notice every thing in our delight
The frozen buzzard caught upon the mill-hatch bars   10
Forget, what the farm dogs do not, this starry night
All who must walk the lanes of darkness blind to stars

[*Late 1925 or early 1926*]

CI, ink autograph, on the same folio with 'Flowers and Stationmaster'.
   In l. 10, 'mill-hatch bars' probably refers to the wooden slats on the mill-wheel itself
or some feature in the mill-dam above the mill like a floodgate or sluice. 'Frost' reflects
the continuing influence of Thomas Hardy and Edward Thomas. It is similar in tone
and theme, for instance, to Thomas's 'The Owl', and l. 9 alludes to the line 'He was a
man who used to notice such things' in Hardy's 'Afterwards', a poem Auden admired
throughout his life (see Introduction, p. xxxiv). The image of skaters who are indif-
ferent to suffering recurs in 'Musée des Beaux Arts' (1938): 'there always must be /
Children who did not specially want it to happen, skating / On a pond at the edge of
the wood' (*EA*, 237; *CP*, 170). The skaters appear again in 'Christmas Eve', probably
written in late 1925 or early 1926, which also describes suffering ignored on the eve of
the miraculous birth.
   Winster Pond may be near the village of Winster in Derbyshire, four miles west of
Matlock. In 1925 Auden wrote a number of poems on places in the Midlands ('Below
me Ticknall lay but in the light', 'The Mail-train, Crewe', 'The Canal, Froghall'); possi-
bly these are associated with visits to his paternal grandmother at Horninglow before
she died on 1 December 1925. Winster is surrounded with abandoned lead-mines,
which would explain why Auden may have gone there; however, none of the ponds
in the area is now known to bear this name. Auden may have named the pond himself,
by association with the nearby village. On the other hand, he may have had in mind
another Winster, in the Lake District, about three miles south of Windermere, where
there is also a river Winster rising nearby and flowing south to the sea.

Auden reused the image of the frozen buzzard several times: it appeared in 'Before' ('Unkempt and furtive the wind crawls'); in 'The Megalopsych'; as part (c) of the first poem sequence in *P(28)*; and later in the conclusion to the third section of the 1929 poem beginning 'It was Easter as I walked in the public gardens'.

Flowers and Stationmaster

'You like my flowers?' That woke me suddenly
From staring at the flowers I didn't see
To stare at the voice—Mountains might have dreamed him
He was tall and weatherbeaten like that
And time-worn like an old mossed water-wheel
With eyes as blue as gazing on the sky
Three hundred English seasons nearly, not
Through windows, could have made them—'Like your flowers?
Certainly'—'Look at these geraniums,
Now have you seen a finer colour, look!　　　　　　　　10
Better than those at Waterhouse, eh?'
Not knowing it, I couldn't contradict him
Nor would he have heard me, for he turned
To touch a larkspur, pushing back the hood
As if a young girl's hair lay underneath
'They want some rain, the sun has been too much
This year—' 'No, don't say that, don't blame the sun;
If God could take the sun away to-morrow
What would we do but offer everything
Wife, children all to have it back again,　　　　　　　　20
The sun's the only friend you cannot hide from'
That was all, no more of that place for me
The train came in just then, and ended it
And if the day had other things to show
They are forgotten now, I only see
Geraniums flaming in the summer heat,
The bees, the old man's quavering goodbye,
And silence biding patiently its time
Till sunshine make the blackbird tire of song
And I have passed as men have always passed.　　　　　　30

[Late 1925 or early 1926]

CI, ink autograph, on the same folio with 'Frost'. Variants: 8. windows, could *this edn*] windows could *CI*. 14. larkspur, pushing *this edn*] larkspur pushing *CI*.

This poem recalls Thomas's blank-verse pieces, although Auden may have had in mind Edmund Blunden's poem 'The Transcription', to which he alluded in 'Lead's the Best'.

Ploughing

Watching what an ant would find to do when
Stones blocked its path, and kicking now and then
The roller (lying underneath the hedge
Its long arms peering over the [?thorn] edge
Down into the road) which we sat upon
Lulled and pleased with the ring of iron on iron
I never saw him till I heard the clink
Of harness, he was well over the brink
Of the tall field and coming down the slope
The furrow behind looking like a rope   10
That lowered the plough slowly down the hill,
Larger the horses grew and nearer till
They reached the bottom of what seemed a roof
And surely now the foremost horse's hoof
Must trample us 'Fine weather for this job,
Joe,' said my friend,—'Ay we deserve it, Bob,
After last winter'—Then a syllable
The chains clanked and the horses took the pull
And soon set out on the returning climb
A rope to pay out not lean on this time. . . .   20
'He lost his wife last Fall' Bob whispered: I
Watched with new eyes his climb toward the sky
The horses reached it first and turned to gold
Then he, the ploughman, who cannot grow old
One moment stood tall, strong upon the hill,
One moment while the green world stood stock still
And he a suit of glittering armour wore.
Then he too sank and sank, the last I saw
Was his peaked hat retreating; he was gone
To his day's work and old age spent alone.   30

— — — —

We rose and walked back to the village—He
Solitary with hill and listening tree
Ploughed on but ploughing could not wake the hush
The young day felt; once from a hawthorn bush
A greenfinch sang but not loudly—the wind
Which rustled must have stroked his hair behind
Telling of life, the grave, and a new earth
The many mysteries of Death and Birth—
A hawk soared up in huge curves in the blue
Then poised outspanned and motionless—He too   40
Perhaps forgot just then his sorrowings
As I my Joy in noticing these things.
What joy or grief is there but must ere long
Return to earth in labour or in a song?

[Late 1925 or early 1926]

CI, ink autograph.
    L. 42 alludes, like 'Frost', to a line in Hardy's 'Afterwards': 'He was a man who used to notice such things.' (See Introduction, p. xxxiv, and note to 'Frost'.) 'Ploughing' is reminiscent of Thomas's 'As the Team's Head-Brass', one of the poems marked in Auden's copy of Thomas's 1920 *Collected Poems*. Auden perhaps borrowed the American term 'Fall' (21) from Robert Frost.

Helen

So this was what the day had waited for
    The sun and rain had been at war
Till now rain's scattered armies fled in rout
    Here the Helen they fought about

She was as fresh and wild from head to feet
    As charlock or as meadowsweet,
Her body sent soft ripples through her dress
    That spoke of hidden loveliness

Her eyes held all the passion of a bird
    But she passed by without a word   10
So quietly she was gone ere I could say
    'God bless you' to her or 'Good day.'

She passed within a yard of where I stood
　　To love perhaps and motherhood
Outlined against the storm-washed pane of blue
　　The moon was sweeping forward to

She took the stony track which led across
　　To farms beyond Spade Adam Moss
Three lonely farms where I had never been
　　Far-glow and Hopealone, and Seldomseen.   20

[*Late 1925 or early 1926*]

CI, ink autograph.
　　This poem recalls W. H. Davies' 'A Lovely Woman', included in his 1916 *Collected Poems*, though Auden's Helen seems more like a girl in an Edward Thomas poem than the Helen of Troy alluded to in the opening stanza. (He almost certainly knew at this time that Thomas's wife was named Helen.) An earlier poem is titled 'Farglow'.

□　□　□

At last, down in the lane
　　A cuckoo-bird
There, over and over again
　　That minor third.

So little it has of its own
　　To be content,
A blackbird might have shown
　　What real song meant

Yet silence more achieves
　　Than singing may   10
A few things every singer leaves
　　For God to say.

This bird sings now, and everything
　　All hope, all doubt
The red lips of the Spring
　　Are quite shut out.

The tears which love would weep
　　The old unrest

Are laid in earth now—go to sleep,
Silence is best   20

Dead bones will blossom to a rose
Their last song sung
While Spring leads gently those
That are with young

[*Late 1925 or early 1926*]

CI, ink autograph. Variants: 3. over and *this edn*] over, and *CI.* 11. things every *this edn*]
things, every *CI.*
Thomas's influence is evident in this poem.

Christmas Eve

The afternoon sets red and cold
And, hid by bushes, starlings scold,
Pattering over leaves and mould.

Along the wrinkled road come bands
Of shouting boys, skates in their hands.
Watching them pass, a beggar stands.

Many a toy and book and dress,
Tokens of love and friendliness,
Wait for the morrow in drawer and press.

The last sun gilds the church's wall   10
Within which women, great and small,
Pin holly sprigs on choir and stall.

The robins, on the churchyard fence
And each rime-crusted eminence,
Look as they shall look, ages hence.

[*Late 1925 or early 1926*]

U, TS on 'British Bond' with alterations in Isherwood's hand; F, ink autograph on same
folio with 'The Carter's Funeral' and 'The Canal, Froghall'; CI, ink autograph on Christ
Church letterhead, same folio as 'Trippers' and draft of '*ἥβης ἄνθος ἀπολλύμενον*'. 'Var-
iants: 4. wrinkled road] rutted lanes *F.* 9. morrow . . . drawer *this edn*] morrow . . . draw

U, CI; morning . . . draw *F*.   12. Pin] Wreathe *F*.   13. robins] robin *F, CI*. F shows 'pin' altered to 'wreathe,' suggesting as with 'The Carter's Funeral' that this fair copy is later than CI. Apparently Isherwood prepared the Upward typescript, probably from his own autograph copy which did not have the revisions; the punctuation on the Upward copy was almost certainly added by Isherwood. Possibly Isherwood posted the typescript to Upward without showing it to Auden, but if Auden did see it he may have forgotten the revisions he made on Fisher's copy. It is also possible that he tried out the revisions on Fisher's copy and decided against them.

The skaters in stanza 2, contrasted as they are with the watching beggar, may be compared to the 'skating' and 'boys snowballing' in stanza 2 of 'Frost'. Similar figures appear in l. 4 of Auden's December 1933 poem 'The earth turns over, our side feels the cold': 'The icing on the ponds waits for the boys' (*EA*, 144; later revised as 'Through the Looking Glass', *CP*, 122). See also 'Musée des Beaux Arts' (1938), where the skaters are linked as in 'Christmas Eve' to the vigil before Christ's birth.

Auden may have taken the images of winter pleasures from Hardy's 'The Prospect', which offers a prospect of the poet's coming death and of the winter scene before him:

> Iced airs wheeze through the skeletoned hedge from the north,
> > With steady snores, and a numbing that threatens snow,
> And skaters pass; and merry boys go forth
> > To look for slides. (6–9)

In the first stanza of 'The Prospect' Hardy also uses the rhyme hand/band, which Auden employs in the plural in reverse order (3–4). Auden's phrase 'wrinkled road' (4) is perhaps borrowed from Emily Dickinson's line 'The wrinkles of the road' in 'The Snow', l. 4; see *Selected Poems* (London, 1924), 150.

Trippers

> They clatter past; only the red rear light
> Shows where they travel singing through the night
> 'How vulgar!' people in the roadside houses say
> Of vanished trippers happier than they.

> [*Late 1925 or early 1926*]

CI, ink autograph on Christ Church letterhead, same folio with 'Christmas Eve' and draft of '*ἥβης ἄνθος ἀπολλύμενον*'.

This poem, or a version of it, was apparently set to music by Lennox Berkeley and sung by Cecil Day-Lewis in Oxford at the Musical Union, probably in 1926. On the same occasion Day-Lewis also sang Berkeley's settings of *The Thresher* and another unknown Auden poem. The two Auden settings are lost, but Sean Day-Lewis told Berkeley's biographer, Peter Dickinson, that Berkeley himself still remembered many years later that one of the songs 'was called "Trippers" and reflected on some people in a motor coach.' See Dickinson, *The Music of Lennox Berkeley* (London, 1988), 17–18 and 33 n. 7, and see also Cecil Day-Lewis, *The Buried Day* (London, 1960), 186. In his biography, Dickinson wrongly suggests Berkeley set Auden's 1926 'Bank Holiday', but Dickinson was not aware of the existence of this earlier poem. Auden recycled a version of 'Trippers' for

'Bank Holiday', and he mentioned the trippers again in 'Easter Monday,' written in
April 1927. Previously Auden had used the phrase 'They clattered past me' in his 1924
poem 'The Walk'; cp. l. 1.

On the same sheet, immediately above 'Trippers', is the cancelled opening of an-
other poem, 'At Birth':

> O tired wan face upon the pillow lying
> With tenderness and loving wonder eying
> The first-born son asleep beside you lying

ἥβης ἄνθος ἀπολλύμενον

The earth was certain for all that; in spite
Of cold and scarcely fattened primroses,
The babe had leaped within her womb and birds
Could not be held from singing their magnificat.
Fields full of buttercups with not one shade
Of cloud was what their songs were full of now.
Even the east wind dropped and left alone
The lovers lying underneath the hedge.
Sixteen years at most, one fair and one dark—:
The dark one nibbled at the other's ear   10
'Remember then on Monday, after school'
None else saw what that afternoon had seen
The passing of two things, Winter and Youth,
One to return again next year, the other. . . .

[*Early 1926*]

CI(1), ink autograph, on watermark 'M Ltd.'; CI(2), ink autograph with pencil title and
pencil autograph revisions on Christ Church letterhead, same folio with 'Christmas
Eve' and 'Trippers'. Variants: 3. birds] thrushes *CI(2)*. 5. with] and *CI(2)*. 8. lovers
lying] pair of lovers *CI(2)*. 11. Remember then] You'll remember *CI(2)*. 14. One to
return] The one to come *CI(2)*. In CI(2) there are also incomplete revisions and a
cancelled line following l. 11: 'Dusk fell unknowing that afternoon saw'.

The poem's Greek title, 'Hebes Anthos Apollymenon', might be translated 'The Lost
Flower of Youth'. It is from a collection of poems and fragments attributed to Theognis
of Megara, the Greek aristocrat poet who lived and wrote chiefly in the sixth century
B.C. The full sentence reads, '῎Αφρονες ἄνθρωποι καὶ νήπιοι, οἵτε θανότας / κλαίονσ᾽, οὐδ᾽
ἥβης ἄνθος ἀπολλύμενον,' which in the Loeb edition is translated as 'Fools are they and
childish who lament the dead rather than the loss of the flower of youth'; *Elegy and
Iambus: Being the Remains of All the Greek Elegiac and Iambic Poets from Callinus to Crates*, ed.
and trans. J. M. Edmonds (London, 1931), 1:354–55, ll. 1069–70. In ll. 14–15 of his
poem 'An Episode', Auden offers his own rhymed translation: 'What fools are men to
weep at death / And not Youth as it perisheth.'

Progress

A cloud rack drifts across the sun
The sparkling flywheel sobers down to dun
And women on the thresher laugh as they have done
                For years and years

A gleam of sunshine sets afire
The brass-bound engine funnel, then the byre
Milkmen and cows have splashed away to in the mire
                For years and years

The sunbeam travels on and stops
Upon the oast-house roof; the shadow drops   10
Down from its hollow cone where men have roasted hops
                For years and years

Around them; though they do not heed
Lie ghosts of flails which once threshed husk from seed
The mode their fathers found to satisfy their need
                For years and years

They think not that machines must lie
Beneath a melancholy winter sky,
They also, and their sons' sons, in the churchyard nigh
                For years and years.   20

[*Late 1925 or early 1926*]

CI, ink autograph, on the same folio with 'Waste'. Variants: 1. rack *this edn*] wrack *CI*.
This relatively unusual stanza form reflects Auden's continuing interest in Hardy.

Waste

'At last' you think—I read it in your eyes—
'Youth is too short to waste an hour of it
For one of little knowledge and less wit':
I take my leave, compelled to recognize
That hearts are wares which no one buys:

The key I moulded for you will not fit,
In other lives our names are largely writ
And nearer Acheron our Paradise.

Yet so, your wasted hour will last for me
Till I am dead and bury my own dead,   10
When learning's unripe apples harvested
With patience rot, when Age but seem to be
A Eunuch whining for old lustihead,
And life a silted, salt, and stagnant sea.

[*Early 1926*]

CI, ink autograph, on the same folio with 'Progress'.

Alone

Soundless is the Winter Darkness,
        The blood in my ears is drumming.
A cinder flickers in the grate
A step echoes past the gate
        To its fireside coming.

Why am I here in the darkness
        In solitude and desire
Walled round by loneliness and gloom
A cold and forsaken room
        A perishing fire   10

Terror leapeth out of darkness
        None knoweth the time or reason
Have I inherited an earth
Where beauty and love and mirth
        Endure for a season?

[*Late 1925 or early 1926*]

CI, ink autograph, on the same folio with 'Motherhood'.

Motherhood

The house stands just as it has always stood
      Unseen almost
Within the shadows of the lonely wood
      Half house, half ghost
    But ploughmen at the furrows turning
    See one red-curtained window burning

'She's near her time but hides, they say, for fear
      The father's name'
—'Or pride, the slut! We don't want her sort here
      To bring their shame   10
    Upon the village like her mother
    We all knew her—just such another.'

But in the dark house hunched below the trees
      A woman rests
All straight and still with nothing at her breasts
      Nor hears nor sees
    And in the silent frosty dawning
    A cry of hunger serves for mourning.

[Late 1925 or early 1926]

CI, ink autograph, on the same folio with 'Alone'.

In a letter to Isherwood in which Auden reported progress on several of his poems, he said 'I have also delivered the pregnant woman of her child' (AL, Lordswood Road letterhead). Possibly he was referring to this poem, although the letter was almost certainly written during July or August 1926, probably substantially after 'Motherhood' was completed; see note to 'Humpty Dumpty'. The only other poem that might fit this reference is 'At Birth', but this was also begun in late 1925 or early 1926, many months before the letter to Isherwood, and it was apparently abandoned without being completed. (See note to 'Trippers', where the three surviving lines of 'At Birth' are printed.)

On Receiving a Christmas Card

That you should send
Greeting to me
As to a friend,
Would seem most strange
Could we but see,
Since boyhood's end,
The world of change.

Rest we apart,
There is no need
To know Time's smart,   10
We are as when
We were friends indeed;
Strangers at heart
Should we meet again.

[Late 1925 or early 1926]

U, TS on 'British Bond'.

The Photograph of a Boy
in Costume

In hose and doublet and great ruff you stand,
    Resting one hand
Upon your hip, and through the arch of the door
Looking, as I have never seen you look before;

Stately and proud and wise,
    With sombre eyes
As of one prematurely schooled
In all that Life has ruled,

Showing to me, in face as in posed arm,
    A phantom's calm,   10
As if indeed you were
A shadow from those far days, haunting here.

[Winter or spring 1926]

U, TS on 'British Bond'.

An echo of Hardy is audible in this poem, especially in the last line, which recalls Hardy's 'Poems of 1912–1913'.

At the Maison Lyons

In exposition getting heated,
My voice attracts the stare
Of a flashily-dressed pair
Of young men opposite us seated.

My friends, you needn't hold your breath,
As if to catch an obscene jest,
Our words could give you no interest,
They are only about Death.

[*Winter or spring 1926*]

U, TS on 'British Bond'.

The title refers to a Lyons tea shop. Robert Medley recalls that Auden 'liked to write and sit in a Lyons because he liked (he said) the "anonymity."' During the 1930s, the Lyons Corner House in Coventry Street, London, was a well-known Sunday afternoon meeting place for homosexuals; Medley 'never went myself on such an expedition' on a Sunday afternoon, but he did go 'often in the 20s after a party or work for early breakfasts from about 3 am' (ALS, 29 June 1992, to Katherine Bucknell).

An Episode

The goldfinch scatters thistle-flowers
    As children used to count the hours,
And something passes that was ours.

    Skilled in the fashioning of Man,
Time sets about another plan
    And all things end where they began.

What seems so much is small, it's true,
    For I have still my work to do
And destiny its niche for you.

And always, woven through the stuff   10
Of Life's coarse blanket, seamed and rough,
   Are patterns, few but fair enough.

Shut out the blowing wind that saith:
   'What fools are men to weep at death
And not Youth as it perisheth,'

   And find, with old blind Handel, might
To say: 'Whatever is, is right.'
   We go our ways, my dear; good-night.

[Spring? 1926]

U, TS on 'British Bond' with punctuation added by hand; CI, ink autograph, on the same folio as 'Song' ('The crocus stars the border'). Variants: 13. saith: *this edn*] saith; *U*; saith *CI.*

Ll. 14–15 are Auden's own rhymed translation from a Greek passage attributed to Theognis of Megara. Auden used the last three words of the Greek, 'ἥβης ἄνθος ἀπολλύμενον' ('Hebes Anthos Apollymenon'), as the title to another, apparently earlier, poem; see p. 120 and note.

The tag in l. 16 is from Alexander Pope's *An Essay on Man* (1.294 and 4.394), but Auden may not have known this when he wrote the poem. He refers to Handel's *Jephtha*, in which Handel used the line from Pope in place of one by his own librettist.

Song

The crocus stars the border
In gardens long forlorn.
The rooks put nests in order
And helpless things are born

A single cloak o'ercovers
The sweetest thing these days
The season's pair of lovers
Who render love their praise.

[Spring 1926]

CI, ink autograph, on the same folio with 'An Episode'.

L. 2 shows the cancelled phrase 'silver struts the dawn' for 'gardens long forlorn.' This phrase made stanza 1 identical to Auden's earlier untitled quatrains beginning 'The crocus stars the border'. The second stanza is new. 'Song' is modelled on

Housman (see note to 'The crocus stars the border'), though it lacks his bitter tone. Auden was to rearrange the material again for two stanzas of his later poem 'Chloe to Daphnis in Hyde Park'.

Lead's the Best

The fells sweep upward to drag down the sun
Those great rocks shadowing a weary land
And quiet stone hamlets huddled at their feet;
No footstep loiters in the darkening road
But light streams out from inn doors left ajar,
And with it voices quavering and slow.
'I worked at Threlkeld granite quarry once,
Then coal at Wigan for a year, then back
To lead, for lead's the best'—
                       —'No, sir, not now,   10
They only keep a heading open still
At Cashwell'—
               —'Yes, the ladder broke and took him
Just like a pudding he was when they found him'—
'Rich? Why, at Greenearth Side the west vein showed
Ten feet of ore from cheek to cheek, so clean
There weren't no dressing it'—
                         steps closed the door
And stopped their mouths, the last of generations
Who 'did their business in the veins of th'earth,'   20
To place a roof on noble Gothic minsters
For the glory of God, bring wealth to buy
Some damask scarf or silken stomacher
To make a woman's body beautiful,
Some slender lady like a silver birch,
A frozen dream of a white waterfall,
Slim-waisted, and hawk-featured, for whose love
Knights sought adventure in far desert lands
And died where there was none to bury them;
Nor thought of those who built their barren farms   30
Up wind-swept northern dales, where oftentimes
The Scot swooped suddenly on winter nights

And drove their cattle back across the snow
By torchlight and the glare of blazing homes,
Where torn men lay, that clutched their wounds,
And bonnie forms face downward in the grass
As in old ballads very pitiful.
   Here speak the last of them, soon heard no more
Than sound of clarinets in country churches;
Turf covers up the huge stone heaps, green ferns   40
The dark holes opening into hollow hills
Where water drips like voices from the dead.
A pile of stone beside the stream is all
Left of the 'Shop' where miners slept at nights;
(Within, tired crowded sleepers, far from home;
Without, the torrent, darkness, and the rain);
Nor will they start again in early dawns
With bags like pillows slung across their shoulders
And watched by children enviously, who wish
Themselves grown-up to climb like that, for whom   50
Soon after it was all the other way;
Each wished himself a child again to have
More hours to sleep in.
                    All their memory fades
Like that two-headed giant slain by Jack
Who lay for years in the combe-bottom, where
Men flocked at first, then fewer came, then ceased,
And only children visited the spot to play
At hide-and-seek in the dark, cavernous skulls
Or gather berries from the thorns which hid   60
The arched ribs crumbling in the grass.
                       They go
And Hodge himself becomes a sottish bawd
Who takes his city vices secondhand
And grins, if he hears Paris mentioned. Naught
Remains but wind-sough over barren pastures
The bleak philosophy of Northern ridges
Harsh afterglow of an old country's greatness
Themes for a poet's pretty sunset thoughts.

                        [*March or April? 1926*]

The Oxford Outlook 8, no. 38 (May 1926): 119–20; CI, ink autograph, on the same folio with 'Felo de se'; F, fragment, Fisher's ink autograph transcription of the last five lines with his note 'Odd bits of Auden noted in 1926'. Variants: 4. road] street *CI.* 7. Threlkeld *CI*] Threlheld *Outlook.* 8–11. then back / To . . . sir, not now, / They only keep] but I / Came back to . . . sir. / Not now; they keep *CI.* 13. 'Yes, the] 'The *CI.* 24. a] some *CI.* 26. dream of a] thought of the *CI.* 30. those] these *CI.* 31. Up] In *CI.* 32. swooped] swept *CI.* 35. that] and *CI.* 37. old] the *CI.* 38. Here] Now *CI.* 43. stone] stones *CI.* 47. in early dawns] on Monday mornings *CI.* 55. Like that two-headed] Like Helen's face in far-off Lacedaemon / Or the two-headed *CI.* 59. skulls *CI*] stalls *Outlook.* 62–63. They go /And Hodge] And now / One word alone seems graven 'Ichabod' / For Hodge *CI.* Reprinted in Mackinnon, 49–51.

This poem is full of the names of mines and of mining terminology. Threlkeld granite quarry (7) is near Keswick in Cumberland where the Audens had a cottage; Wigan (8) is the coal-mining town in Lancashire; Cashwell mine (12) is a lead-mine just below Crossfell in Alston Moor; Greenearth Side may be part of Greenhurth in Teesdale, north-west of Middleton and not far from Alston, or it may be Greenside mine, a rich lead-silver mine near the head of Ullswater, not far from Keswick and Threlkeld. (The latter would suit the description in ll. 15–17 of the rich west vein, but see the notes to 'The Engine House' and 'Control of the Passes was, he saw, the key' for more on this name.) In ll. 15–17, the cheeks are the walls of the vein, and 'no dressing it' means that the ore required no sorting or washing before reduction. In two other poems, 'The Pumping Engine, Cashwell' and the poem beginning 'Who stands, the crux left of the watershed,' Auden described a restored pumping engine that he had admired at Cashwell. Also, he had written about a miner's death in a fall in 'The Miner's Wife'; similar accidents are the subject of 'Who stands, the crux left of the watershed.'

L. 20 is from one of Prospero's attacks on Ariel in *The Tempest*, 1.2; Auden acted the part of Caliban during his last term at Gresham's. The middle, historical section of 'Lead's the Best' (21–37) is modelled on Gordon Bottomley's 'Littleholme', which Auden probably had read in *Georgian Poetry 1918–1919* at school. 'Littleholme' describes a vanished community of weavers whose industry once connected them, like Auden's miners, to the larger world. Ll. 25–26 are revised from Auden's earlier 'Earth's Praises'. Ll. 38–39 allude to Edmund Blunden's poem 'The Transcription', another model for 'Lead's the Best'. 'The Transcription' was published in *Masks of Time* in January 1925; see especially ll. 17–25.

The 'combe-bottom' (56) perhaps represents the pit concealed with leaves and dirt into which Jack the Giant-Killer lures the Giant in the familiar childhood story, but it is also reminiscent of the dark, ancient place described in Thomas's 'The Combe', one of the many poems Auden marked in his copy of Thomas's *Collected Poems* (see note to 'To E.T.'). 'The arched ribs crumbling in the grass' (61) had appeared as l. 3 in the 'Sonnet' beginning 'April is here but when will Easter come?'

For Ichabod in the Isherwood copy of 'Lead's the Best', see 1 Samuel 4.21, though Auden may have been referring to Robert Browning's poem 'Waring', about the disappearance of a young man with unrealized literary aspirations.

Hodge, the type of the rural peasant often mentioned by Hardy, Jefferies, and Edward Thomas, is the central figure in Auden's later poem 'Hodge Looks toward London'. Auden reused the line 'The bleak philosophy of Northern ridges' in 'After' and in 'Narcissus'.

Felo de se

All knew of her as Peter's daughter;
And more than one face said 'Poor girl!' that day
The jury made her 'of an unsound mind';
They buried her, and that was ended.

No strangeness in an ancient story
A brown-eyed student on his holiday,
Long walks by moonlight to the Hangman's Stone
Blank months of waiting; then the river.

The world has grander themes to think on
They had their summer idyll anyhow   10
And he, now far away has never heard
And she already has forgotten.

[*Spring 1926*]

CI, ink autograph, on the same folio with 'Lead's the Best'.

Dethroned

Man finds himself no more omnipotent,
A little creature frightened of the dark
Cold fringes he has built his house upon,
Of walks which will not lead him anywhere,
Thought's tramlines stretching out in the unknown;
Burnt by desires he cannot act on or
Control, he crouches by his dying fire
And whimpers to his Gods 'Don't hurt me!' Yet
Sometimes, more bold, finds in him greater things,
Would strip his body of its swaddling clothes   10
Of rounded arms, red lips, and warm white buttocks
To build therefrom bleak masses bit in granite,
Gaunt shapes that know not passion or decay,
The Archetypes of an eternal Mind—
In dream would climb steel ladders down into

The wheel-pit of the soul, and see around
Pipes curving like a dead Troll's knotted fingers,
Huge cogwheels rolling irresistibly
On burnished axle-shafts, while far below
The hiss of water heaves the darkness like   20
Serpents in Eden or the voice of God.

[*Spring 1926*]

F, Fisher's ink autograph transcription and pencil note 'Spring 1926?'. Fisher records
a variant: 8. 'Don't hurt me!'] 'Have mercy!'
     Auden reused ll. 17–21 in 'The Evolution of the Dragon,' and the imagery reap-
peared in several much later pieces; see notes to 'The Engine House', 'Humpty
Dumpty', and 'The Evolution of the Dragon'.

April

Morning's breast was speckled likes a thrush's
Silent till the starlings took their places
All along the wires from here to London,
And below the eaves of countless houses,
Countless creatures, helpless, strange to sunlight
Craved a sudden entrance at the beak's point.
Yet the morning found me sullen, brooding,
Creaking door-like of one ghostly woman,
Talking to her as if still she heard me,
Scarce aware of what I grieved as lacking   10
Only 'That which once was, now it is not,
Man may whimper, but he may not alter.'
Never thinking it perhaps a strange thing
Life bareheaded under grass should worry
Like a wasp. A gate knocked loudly somewhere;
Love who sought in vain to shut the Past behind him
Left it; back she came into the sunlight
Hair unloosened, falling down her shoulders,
Fair, but with death's shadow right across them.
Yesterdays had pared the nails of sorrow,   20
Filed the angles off that bitter April,

Who could think then how that old green woman
Was to bear so many gracious children,
Smoothing out an old man's wrinkled mornings?
Laughter spurted up the hill beneath us
From the children playing in the garden
Once a graveyard and, in among the tombstones
Playing games their grandmothers once used to
Over dead bones too old now to give a shudder,
As she turned and touched me with a gesture   30
Dreams years back, but only half-forgotten,
Startling Joy, shy spring, into a fountain . . .
So the past rose up and beckoned me. I followed,
Taking one lane first and then another,
Always grass though, never larks far distant,
Nor a blackthorn in its Easter apron,
Nightingales have sung for less. I passed on
Just a little envious perhaps of
April with its summer still before it,
Tired of wondering if she slept soundly,   40
Tired of asking 'Is there balm in Gilead'
Only cuckoo had an answer ready
'Rise, go presently about your business.'

[April? 1926]

CI, ink autograph on Christ Church letterhead. Variants: 19. death's *this edn*] death *CI*.
20. sorrow, *this edn*] sorrow. *CI*.
  Easter fell on 4 April 1926; possibly Auden wrote this poem about that time. He may
have taken some Christ Church letterhead home with him during the vacation, or more
likely he sent the poem to Isherwood when he returned to Oxford some time between
7 April when Trinity Term began and 25 April when Full Term began. For l. 41, cp.
Jeremiah 8.22.

The Letter

He reads and finds the meaning plain;
It leaves no problem for the mind,
Though love he is surprised to find
So economically slain;
Acknowledging with half a smile
To each hard sentence neat and clear

That grips the pages as it were
A gift for the satiric style.

At first he looks around and hears
Huge castles toppling to the ground   10
As if the earth ceased spinning round,
The sudden panic of the years;
But trees and singing birds renew
The stablished sequence of the laws;
Creation shows no vital flaws
For God to pay attention to.

The past is vested in a sheen
His love-selected fancies weave;
It needs no woman to perceive
Just what the story might have been.   20
The spring gushed then—the causes of its
Sudden failure he cannot tell;
He loved not wisely but too well,
And Saul is not among the prophets.

He knows not, though perhaps he will,
Of much remaining to be done
When all the bitterness has gone;
Bewildered by the roads that still
Time only whispers which to take;
And he knows even less than we,   30
However casual may be
The comment that our shoulders make.

[*Spring 1926*]

Oxford Poetry 1926 (Oxford, 1926), 4–5; CI, ink autograph on Lordswood Road letter-head. Variants: 20. the] his *CI*.

Auden may have written this poem, on the stationery of his parents' home, as early as Easter vacation 1926. Term started on 7 April, Full Term on 25 April, so the poem may have been written well before the end of April. The vacation date is perhaps supported by the poem's subject, a letter, which he might have received at home from a university friend. In any case, the poem was almost certainly completed, like his other submissions to *Oxford Poetry* for that year, by the end of May.

For l. 23, see *Othello*, 5.2. For l. 24 see 1 Samuel 10.11–12 and 1 Samuel 19.24. Auden later revised ll. 3–4 for his 1927 poem 'Extract'. He used a version of l. 27 in 'Thomas Prologizes' (17), and he used the last two lines of 'The Letter' in another 1927 poem, 'Bach and the Lady'.

Chloe to Daphnis in Hyde Park

Stop fingering your tie; walk slower;
How quiet it is! A distant mower
   Is worrying a lawn,
   Where worms were slain at dawn.

So sure she seems of body-rising,
Nature, one cannot help surmising,
   Has not forgot to read
   The Apostolic creed.

The rooks now put their nests in order,
The crocus through the barren border   10
   In regiments appears,
   All brandishing their spears.

The chiff-chaff makes a curious lover,
Woos by counting his money over,
   Telling indifferent Earth
   Exactly what he's worth.

Yonder a single cloak o'ercovers
The season's pair of merry lovers,
   Who render Love their praise,
   The sweetest thing these days.   20

All journeys end in lovers meeting—
There's none so sweet as my sweet sweeting—
   Elizabethan tags
   Or conversation flags

To motor-cars and sex. Addition,
They say, can remedy Division,
   But adding me to you
   Cannot make less than two.

Stand so then up against the railing,
To watch Spring through the iron paling,   30

> Your coat-sleeve touching mine,
> And think our love divine!
>
> Easter and yearly resurrection
> We grace to-day with our inspection,
>   Delight in such and such,
>   Though we may never touch.

> [*April or May 1926*]

The Oxford Outlook, 8, no. 39 (June 1926): 209–10; CI, ink autograph on Christ Church letterhead; F, Fisher's ink autograph transcription with a note saying that a revised version of the poem appeared in the *Outlook* and thereby suggesting that the Fisher version was transcribed before the poem was published. Variants: 21. lovers *this edn*] lover's *Outlook, CI, F.* Following the final stanza, CI and F offer an additional one:

> While earth beneath us has no notion
> Of all this feverish commotion
>   Flowers and moody men
>   Silent so soon again.

F omits stanzas 4 and 5 with a note '2 bad stanzas omitted', then shows them at the end of the poem. Probably the note reflects an opinion Auden voiced at the time he dictated the poem. The Fisher collection also has another transcription copied from the *Outlook*; in l. 10 it offers the variant 'narrow' for 'barren', but this is probably just a mistake.

Easter fell on 4 April in 1926, which seems slightly early for Auden to have written this poem, although he may have begun it then, or certainly soon afterwards. The Isherwood copy is on Christ Church letterhead, which suggests a draft may not have been complete until after the Easter vacation; Auden would have returned to Oxford sometime between 7 April when Trinity Term began and 25 April, the start of Full Term.

The title points to the likelihood that the theme of 'Chloe to Daphnis in Hyde Park' was suggested by Siegfried Sassoon's 'Observations in Hyde Park,' which appeared in his *Satirical Poems*, published April 1926, around the time Auden probably wrote his poem. Beside the title on his copy, Fisher wrote '(WHA of AWP)', apparently Anthony Wyatt Parker, a Christ Church Exhibitioner in Natural Science who matriculated in 1924, the year before Auden came up with the same Exhibition. Evidently, Auden was in love with Parker before meeting William McElwee; he included 'Tony Parker' in the list he made in the early 1940s of people with whom he had fallen in love. (The list is in a notebook in the Lockwood Memorial Library at the State University of New York at Buffalo; see Introduction, p. xxxvii and n. 56.) His interest lasted at least through the summer of 1926, as he reported to Isherwood in August, 'I have a nice photo of Tony to-day.' (ALS, Lordswood Road letterhead, probably mid- to late August 1926.) Stanzas 3 and 5 are based on Auden's earlier 'Song' beginning 'The crocus stars the border', which evolved from two untitled quatrains modelled on Housman (see notes to 'Song' and to its precursor, 'The crocus stars the border'); here the imagery is sharpened, possibly by the influence of Ezra Pound's poem about spring and rebirth, 'Coitus', which begins 'The gilded phaloi of the crocuses / are thrusting at the spring air' (included in *Lustra*, 1916). The Apostolic Creed (8) taught by Christ's apostles incorporates the doctrine of the Resurrection. Beside l. 20 (in one of the two stanzas omitted from the body of his text and added at the end) Fisher wrote 'pop song'. L. 21 is from Feste's song, 'O mistress mine, where are you roaming?' in *Twelfth Night*, 2.3; Tom Driberg had used the same tag in his 'London Square,' which was first published in *The Oxford Magazine* 44, no. 15 (4 March 1926), Poetry Supplement. Driberg's influence on Auden during the spring of 1926 was pronounced (see note to 'Thomas Prologizes').

Thomas Prologizes

'Nay, an thou'lt mouth, I'll rant as well as thou.'

HAMLET

They are all gone upstairs into the world
Of candlelight. The Prodigal is left
Beneath to work his own salvation out,
Helped by the sordes of the past which taught him
Well how best to set his codpiece in order.
Have I forgot young Desmond whom I met
Behind the fives-courts every Sunday night?
Or Isobel who with her leaping breasts
Pursued me through a summer? I remember
Vases like music frozen into marble,   10
Tall nymphs callipygous who taught my soul
To lisp small lyrics which may gladden hearts
Of mistresses in elementary schools,
Limp lilies! I have bottle-fed on Art,
Life peptonised to suit a tender stomach,
Valleys of dead men's bones have been my refuge!

When all this earliness has gone, will Daddy
Tell us another and a newer story?
For Tommy is a big boy now; yes, we
Have carried Death away, and now are bringing   20
Summer into the village. As for Death,
Let the common sewer take him from distinction!
For Tommy knows a trick worth two of that;
The Fool's a conjuror as well remember!
Well, can I show you something, Madam, say?
I can wring lightning from the clouds, or get
Yon gibbous moon with child, or if you will,
I'll drag Leviathan out by the nose,

And send Behemoth sprawling on the grass.
Olympus, may I serve you, gentlemen?   30
Shall I install cold-water pipes in Hell
For Dives' sake: set automatic harps
In Heaven for the Idle Saved?

But after,
With what will you reward me? Will you bring me
Unto a land flowing with milk and honey?
Where I may burble Wagner in my bath,
Peruse the Classics in a neat edition,
Drift through the afternoon, lulled by some tale
Of Turgenev, until I fall asleep,   40
Alone on my denuded battlefield,
My reins protected by a flaccid hand,
To dream, a little surfeited perhaps,
A little stouter, of my great deeds done.

[*April or early May 1926*]

The Oxford Magazine, 46, no. 17 (3 May 1928): 467–68, unsigned; CI, ink autograph on Christ Church letterhead; F, Fisher's autograph transcription with his annotations. Variants: EPIGRAPH 'Nay . . . Hamlet'] not in *CI* or *F*. 3–4. out / Helped] out, / With midnight, gaspers, and a squalid fire / Helped *CI*, *F*. 4–5. taught him / Well how best to . . . in] taught / Him how best to . . . in *CI*; taught / Him how to . . . best *F*. 11. Tall nymphs] Nymphs *F*. 19. yes] and *F*. 20. now] we *F*. 25. Well . . . say] Say . . . yes *F*. 30. Olympus] Divines *CI*. 36. Unto] Into *CI*. 40. Turgenev] Turgenev's *F*.

Although not published until 1928, 'Thomas Prologizes' was written in the spring of 1926. Possibly Auden never intended it to be published at all, because he used a relatively long section of it in 'Thomas Epilogizes,' which he included in *Oxford Poetry 1926*. The Thomas poems might be regarded as companion pieces in which the repetition of material from the first poem in the second is deliberately meant to show a new point of view on the same themes and images, or 'Thomas Epilogizes' might be regarded as a new, revised version of 'Thomas Prologizes'. An undated, unsigned, autograph letter to Isherwood explains the poem and helps date it by referring to Auden's work in the General Strike in early May:

Re 'Thomas Prologizes' it really does seem intelligible. If my explanatory remarks seem insolent please forgive me. The idea of course is an adolescent, who feels that all his old ideas are breaking up and have taught little but lyric and lechery. Then he thinks 'let's get on to something new' and in the usual way of romantic adolescence thinks, that he is capable of doing any great and heroic thing though what he isn't quite sure of. The last part of course is obvious 'Cui Bono'. During the strike I worked for the T.U.C. and have quarrelled bitterly with certain sections of the family in consequence, which is all to the good. (On Christ Church letterhead, enclosing 'Pride', 'At Parting', and 'Portrait'.)

The poem's title perhaps alludes to Robert Browning's 'Artemis Prologizes' and links Browning's themes of death, rebirth, and mythic achievement to the aspirations and uncertainties of the adolescent in the poem. Thomas is St Thomas, the apostle who was known as Doubting Thomas because he could not believe in the risen Christ until he was invited to touch Christ's wounds and thrust his hand into Christ's side (John 20.25–28). Thomas was also called Didymus, the Greek word for twin. (The name Thomas in Aramaic also means twin.) Several times in 1942 and again in 1965 Auden signed himself 'Didymus' in pseudonymous contributions to periodicals. Perhaps the idea of the twin had some association for him not just with the second self represented by the pseudonym, but also with the idea of the Double Man. In 1926 the name Thomas apparently reflected in particular his religious doubts. It perhaps also suggests his sense of a division in himself between what he wanted to be and what others, for instance his mother, expected him to become.

In the spring of 1926, Auden came under the influence of two other Thomases, Tom Driberg and T. S. Eliot. In his autobiography *Ruling Passions* (London, 1977), Driberg recalls that he and Auden became close but chaste friends that spring and that they read *The Waste Land* for the first time together 'in a copy of the first issue of Eliot's review, *The Criterion*, read it, at first, with incredulous hilarity (the Mrs. Porter bit, for instance); read it, again and again, with growing awe' (58). Auden's own recollection tends to confirm the story: 'Tom Driberg . . . introduced me to the poetry of T. S. Eliot' ('As It Seemed to Us', *FA*, 511). But as Driberg's biographer has wondered, 'the first issue of *The Criterion*, which did indeed carry *The Waste Land*, appeared in October 1922. It was widely noticed. Could Tom, normally so alert to anything new, really have taken more than three years to discover the poem? Apparently so'; Francis Wheen, *Tom Driberg: His Life and Indiscretions* (London, 1990), 39. Possibly they became aware of Eliot when a review of his *Poems 1909–1925* appeared in *The Oxford Magazine* 44, no. 17 (29 April 1926): 414–15, but this would not have led them to *The Criterion* where they read the poem; someone may have given them a copy of the magazine before this. The poems that Driberg was publishing at this time seem to have influenced Auden; for instance, Driberg's Sitwellian 'London Square', published in *The Oxford Magazine* 44, no. 15 (4 March 1926), and reprinted by Auden and Charles Plumb in *Oxford Poetry 1926* (21) had a clear impact on Auden's Thomas poems and on other pieces like 'Cinders' and 'Chloe to Daphnis in Hyde Park'. And when Driberg took over *The Oxford Outlook* with J. N. Cameron in November 1926 he may have been responsible for the appearance there of Auden's 'Bank Holiday' and 'In Due Season'. Driberg knew the Sitwells and was instrumental in bringing about several popular public appearances by them in Oxford during this period; Edith Sitwell's influence on Auden's style during 1926 was pervasive.

Partly as a result of Auden's introduction to the work of T. S. Eliot, 'Thomas Prologizes' borrows from many new sources in Auden's reading, from Shakespeare to the Bible, and ostentatiously introduces sophisticated vocabulary and cultural references. The epigraph is from *Hamlet*, 5.1, at Ophelia's grave, when Hamlet challenges Laertes to show that the strength of his love for Ophelia matches Hamlet's own. L. 1 closely echoes the opening of Henry Vaughan's mid-seventeenth-century poem beginning 'They have all gone into the world of light'. For the prodigal son (2), see Luke 15.11–32. The 'Valleys of dead men's bones' (16) probably allude as much to *The Waste Land* as to Ezekiel 37.1, and Auden was to draw again on both of these sources in 'Cinders' and in the 1927 poem beginning 'Nor was that final, for about that time', published in *P(28)*. 'Callipygous' (11) from callipygian (of, pertaining to, or having well-shaped or finely developed buttocks) was newly in use as an adjective in the 1920s, and apparently owes its currency to Aldous Huxley's *Antic Hay* (1923). *The Oxford English Dictionary*, 2nd edn, credits Huxley with the first use of the adjective in print (chap. 4, p. 64, but see also chap. 15, p. 214, where it appears again). The Thomas poems, 'Cinders', and other contemporary pieces suggest Auden was impressed by the jazz-age attitude of cynicism and enthusiasm, boredom and excitement that Huxley depicted in his excessively learned and artistic young characters. ('Gaspers' in l. 4 of the Isherwood and Fisher copies is 1920s slang for cheap cigarettes.) Ll. 19–21 refer to the traditional European folk ceremonies of 'Carrying out Death' and 'Bringing in Summer' described by James Frazer in *The Golden Bough* and from which Auden closely imitates the phrasing of a traditional Bohemian song accompanying the ceremony; see 3rd edn, part 3 (London, 1911); the songs are on 237–38 and 246. On his copy, Fisher notes that the lines refer to Frazer's chapter on Osiris, which is wrong, although Auden perhaps drew on the Osiris chapter for another poem, 'Consequences'. L. 22 is from the final scene of Thomas Middleton's *The Changeling* (1622), when Beatrice-Joanna, mortally wounded, tells her father that he must not care about her flowing blood, which would corrupt his own; see 5.3.153. For 'Dives' (32), see Luke 16.19. Near the end of his life, Auden commented on ll. 8–9, 'had I intended it to be a caption for a Thurber cartoon, I should today be very proud of it'; see *A Certain World* (New York, 1970; London, 1971), 202.

Pride

Love's specious information,
The influence of a star
Make Saul forget his station
And grow familiar;

When God, foreseeing trouble,
Picks up a Death, a sin,
Which for this kind of bubble
Serve better than a pin.

[*May 1926*]

CI, ink autograph on Christ Church letterhead.

This poem appears on the verso of the letter to Isherwood in which Auden explains the meaning of 'Thomas Prologizes' and mentions working for the T.U.C. in the General Strike (see note to 'Thomas Prologizes'). Also enclosed with the same letter were 'Portrait' and 'At Parting'. Isherwood had apparently disliked the effect apparent in 'Thomas Prologizes' of Eliot's influence, and Auden recommended all three of the new poems with the remark 'Here are three poems which you cannot accuse of Eliotian Intellectual Bombast'. Instead, 'Pride' sounds remarkably like Emily Dickinson. Probably Saul is used here because of his rebelliousness against God's commandments; see also 'The Letter' and note.

At Parting

Though Time now tears apart
A universe, each heart,
By long-accustomed use
Will tighten up the screws.

Those hours which crept before
The opening of a door
On emptiness are all
To-morrow may recall.

Joy's subsequent increase
May still be ours, and peace   10
Not wholly vanished yet
But that hour we forget.

East finds it hard to tell
The sun to bid farewell
But even lovers' eyes
Acknowledge boundaries.

[*May 1926*]

The Cherwell, n.s. 24, no. 4 (22 May 1926): 130; CI, ink autograph on Christ Church letterhead, enclosed in the same letter with 'Pride' ('Love's specious information,') and 'Portrait'.
    See notes to 'Thomas Prologizes' and 'Pride'. This poem, like others written during the spring of 1926, reflects the influence of Emily Dickinson.

Portrait

The lips so apt for deeds of passion,
The hair to stifle a man's breath,
The symmetry of form beneath
An Irish mackintosh, the wild
Defiant pupils of a child.
The Gods, responsible for these,
Whatever else to blame one sees,
  Were artists in their fashion,

But left the signature unwritten,
Too early tired; 'twas strange to botch   10
A masterpiece, yet we who watch
Horizons to redress the wrong
See only Götterdämmerung.
Not one of us, except in dreams
Can alter by a word, it seems,
  The story that is written

Which has no happy marriage-ending;
A story which we know will fail
To turn romantic fairytale;
For neither friendliness nor tears   20
Have hands to push away the years,
We can but turn our eyes away
Before the last act of the play,
  From its unlovely ending.

           [*May 1926*]

CI, ink autograph on Christ Church letterhead, enclosed in the same letter with 'Pride' ('Love's specious information,') and 'At Parting'; *The Cherwell,* n.s. 24, no. 4 (22 May 1926): 130. Variants: 11. yet] but *Cherwell.* 24. From] And *Cherwell.* The punctuation in the *Cherwell* copy is less successful than that in CI. Auden could have sent the poem to Isherwood after having submitted it to *The Cherwell,* or the editors may have altered it, or Auden may simply have forgotten how he punctuated the better CI version. 'At Parting' and 'Portrait' were sent to Isherwood together, and also probably to *The Cherwell* together (the two poems were published side by side); nevertheless, in the case of 'At Parting' I have used the better *Cherwell* version as the copy text, as it seems at least possible that the two poems were not handled in the same way by the editors or by their author even though they appear on the same page. Reprinted from *The Cherwell* in *The Best Poems of 1926,* ed. L. A. G. Strong (New York, 1926), 9.

 For more on 'Portrait', see notes to 'Thomas Prologizes' and 'Pride'.

Amor Vincit Omnia

Six feet from One to One.
Yet what change would have been
Were you upon the sun
Or epochs in between?

Antipodes his plan,
Love tauts his rigging, but
Can sail no further than
The shores of Occiput.

Behind which great sea wall
Love, impotent in deed,   10
In words sends forth his all
Which you will never need.

'Tis strange no love nor Art
Six feet of space can tread;
No more than sets apart
The daylight from the dead.

[*Spring 1926*]

The Oxford Outlook 8, no. 39 (June 1926): 180; F, Fisher's ink autograph transcription, which appears to have been prepared from the *Outlook* text. F shows no variants except that stanza 3 is enclosed in square brackets; possibly Fisher marked it in the 1960s while preparing his essay 'Auden's Juvenilia', in which he printed the poem without stanza 3. It is not clear when he made his transcription, though he says the poem was written 'at the beginning of 1926' ('Auden's Juvenilia', 372).

Fisher detects an echo of Emily Dickinson's voice, and he recalls that Auden discovered her work around the time he went up to Oxford when Cape had published her *Selected Poems* ('Auden's Juvenilia', 372); this edition of Dickinson, edited by Conrad Aiken, appeared in September 1924. On his own copy Fisher notes 'Marvell' opposite the first stanza, also a likely influence; see for instance Marvell's 'The Definition of Love'.

Yes and No

Together, passing by
The dead gull on the heath
The Two kiss and deny
The quality of death.

Parted, they cannot touch.
The pressure of strange knees
Shivers in Two at such
Smell of mortalities

But when the crowd has gone
They embrace, out of reach   10
Of the tide, in the sun,
On the crestfallen beach.

And very properly may:
Since, like them, sceptical we
Shall lie in earth and say
That there is no more sea.

[*Spring 1926*]

CI, ink autograph.
   The phrase 'pressure of strange knees' (6) also appears in 'Cinders', first published
3 June 1926.

Cinders

Four walls are drawn tight round the crew of us,
Like passengers in the last omnibus,
Companions, never chosen, loath to stay,
The last survivors of a working day.

We draw our squares about the Universe
To make the habit of it suit our purse,
As out of place and as uncommented
As gramophones would be among the dead.

Expound our neat cigar-philosophies,
With God above, as harmless as you please,   10
The keeper of a Paradise for fools,
A dear Arch-Monad in horn spectacles.

Our love as pure as the Symposium,
We give fair hearing to the life to come,
Breathe, propagate, and with a sour face
Do our eugenic duty by the race;

In chaster moods love all the nicer things,
A swallow chasing flies, or Saturn's rings,
Or sun, straddled across a wounded hill,
With spear poised for the last down thrusting kill;   20

Gods, poets almost, till some harlot bliss
Shall make us mortal with a Judas kiss,
Distort the earth until our sogged eyes see
A phallic symbol in a cypress tree.

Sweet lust runs softly by. Dissolute man
Thinks 'Dare I drink it?' and decides he can,
Forsakes phlegmatic company of stars
For pressure of strange knees at cinemas.

But, after sporting thus a little, he
Turns back to lyric, tired of lechery,   30
To his celestial manoeuverings,
Cherub a trifle damaged in the wings.

The great are gathered and gone by together
With Jezebel and others of her feather,
And love was put away at evenfall
Shamefacedly behind the stable wall.

Troy Town is burning; its despairing ashes
Flame from the shores the Everlasting washes,
But there remain, when all are dead and gone,
The candle-litten miles to Babylon,   40

The Dark Tower, the Azores, though Chanticleer
Query both Advent and Platonic year.
Are nought reserved for Gentiles save the lowest
Places? Can these bones live? O Lord, Thou knowest!

[*May 1926*]

Oxford Poetry 1926, ed. Charles Plumb and W. H. Auden (Oxford, 1926), 6–7; *The Oxford University Review* 1, no. 8 (3 June 1926): 284; U, ink autograph on watermark 'Library Parchment'; F, ink autograph signed 'Wystan Auden. May 28th 1925' at the foot (the date is wrong by a year) and with Fisher's pencil note 'written out and signed for me'. Variants: 5. about] across *Oxford University Review*. 10. harmless] handsome *Oxford University Review*. 17. moods love] moments loving *Oxford University Review, F*. 27. phlegmatic] the wordless *F*. 40. candle-litten miles] candle-litter rides *F*. 43. Are . . . the] Is . . . the *Oxford University Review*, Shall these go higher up who took the *F*.

Auden's reference to the 'Symposium' hints as broadly as the Thomas poems that the love in 'Cinders' is at least partly homosexual, and it reintroduces the conventional notion of a natural progression—embodied in the Thomas poems by the succession of the figures Desmond and Isobel—from homosexual to heterosexual love. The 'Platonic year' (42)—derived from Plato's *Timaeus* (39d) where it is called the Great Year—suggests his ironic doubt of Plato's doctrines. But the poem doubts equally Christianity and all other philosophical systems. The 'Arch-Monad' (12) refers to Leibniz's notion of God as the supreme monad. In 1925 or 1926 Auden inscribed and presented what was apparently his own copy of Leibniz's *Monadology* to his undergraduate friend Rex Warner. Auden may have learned about Leibniz and other Enlightenment philosophers at Gresham's from his friend and schoolmaster Frank McEachran; see John Bridgen, 'Frank McEachran (1900–1975): An Unrecognized Influence on W. H. Auden', *AS1*, 125. Auden's father referred to H. Wildon Carr, *A Theory of Monads* (London, 1922) in an article published a few months before 'Cinders', and Auden possibly drew in 'Cinders' on his father's discussion of consciousness as a continuum of changing individual states; see George A. Auden, 'On Endogenous and Exogenous Factors in Character Formation', *The Journal of Mental Science* 72, no. 296 (January 1926): 18–19.

'Sweet lust runs softly by' (25) alludes to the refrain of Spenser's 'Prothalamion', 'Sweet Themmes runne softly, till I end my Song,' which Eliot had used in the third section of *The Waste Land*. And the 'Dare I' of l. 26 echoes the repeated question of Eliot's Prufrock, 'Do I dare?' Auden recycled the image of the 'pressure of strange knees' (28) from 'Yes and No'.

For the theme of lyric and lechery in stanza 8, see note to 'Thomas Prologizes'. For Jezebel (34), see 1 Kings 16.31 to 2 Kings 9. For 'The Dark Tower' (41), see Browning's 'Childe Roland to the Dark Tower Came', and *King Lear*, 3.4; Auden referred to the Dark Tower again in later poems. Advent (42) marks the first and second coming of Christ, the first to redeem and the second to judge the world; the Platonic year (42) is its classical counterpart: both refer to a millennium. Auden rewrote ll. 41–42 for 'The Megalopsych' and for section (h) of the first poem sequence in *P(28)*. 'Can these bones live? O Lord, Thou knowest!' (44), loosely quoted from Ezekiel 37.3, is also alluded to in *The Waste Land*. Auden drew on both texts for 'Thomas Prologizes' and again on this passage from Ezekiel in his 1927 poem 'Nor was that final, for about that time'.

In a 1927 letter to Isherwood discussing revisions to 'The Megalopsych', Auden said: 'I have scrapped Cinders. That type of cleverness wont do' (AL, on Christ Church letterhead, probably written late May or early June 1927).

Thomas Epilogizes

(For C.I.)

'The bells that are the same are not stirring.'

GERTRUDE STEIN

Inexorable Rembrandt rays, which stab
Through clouds as through a rotting factory floor,
Make chiaroscuro in a day now over,
And cart-ruts bloody as if Grendel lately
Had shambled dripping back into his marshes.
The train runs on, while in the sagging West
Gasometers heave Brobdingnagian flanks
Like dragons with their bat-wings furled for sleep.
(No rock nor twisted thorn was there to fill
Uneasy silences, save once a poplar   10
Wrung its bewildered leaves, and once a mill
Raised heavy hands and dropped them to its side.)
I, Thomas, the disappointed lover,
My reins protected by one flaccid hand,
Trace thumb-nail sketches on the sweaty pane,
Sole audience for the coach-wheels chattering,
(Οἴκαδέ, οἴκαδέ, οἴκαδέ, Home!)
For thoughts of you and of the growth of love,
A sigmoid curve, that dwindled suddenly
As love grew hungry, but the diet stale.   20
Love mutual has reached its first eutectic,
And we must separate. The train runs, pushing
The spirit into undiscovered lands,
Far from the sirens calling in the Park
For Ulysses, dressed up like a sore finger,
To roll like Nebuchadnezzar in the grass;
From wattled parsons gabbling over graves;
From sunken acreage of basement kitchens,
The thousand rustling pages of Romance,
As floury cooks await Apocalypse.   30
So I forget young Desmond, whom I met
Behind the fives courts every Sunday night,
And Isobel, who with her leaping breasts

Pursued me through a Summer; the train
Runs swiftly on through stranger continents,
Like Mozart arias which cast no shadows,
Or sailors' tales, in leafy lanes, in June,
Of crazy forests like a giant's hair,
And slant-eyed fawns sprawling with profuse locks
In moonlight splashed on ruined water gardens.   40

Lights!
The train shies, throws its rider. There's an end
Of our pathetic search for difference.
We are embraced by lichenous desires,
The poodle has returned to her old vomit,
We to our model homes like crouched Ophelias,
Where Job squats awkwardly upon his ashpit,
Scraping himself with blunted occam razors,
He sharpened once to shave the Absolute.
A cold wind clutches at his scraggy knees,   50
The mindless wind, the trumpeter of April,
Thrusting the grass blades into their America,
Like bowler hats before a passing hearse,
As April, that Byronic lover, comes,
His 'gurdy coughing through the afternoon.
Eliphaz, Zophar, Bildad, rise together,
Begin to creak a wooden sarabande,
'Glory to God,' they cry, and praise His name
In epigrams that trail off in a stammer.
Suave Death comes, final as a Handel cadence,   60
And snaps their limbs like twigs across his knees;
Silenus nods, his finger to his nose.

[*May or June 1926*]

McElwee's copy of *Oxford Poetry 1926* (private American collection), 1–3, with Auden's ink autograph revisions; *Oxford Poetry 1926*, 1–3; U, fragment, ink autograph on watermark 'Library Parchment', l. 47 to end. *Oxford Poetry* spelled the title 'Epilogises', presumably following the publisher's house style, but Auden spelled it with a 'z'. Variants: 5. his] her *Oxford Poetry*. 34–35. the train / Runs . . . through stranger continents] nor remember / Vases like music frozen into marble, / Tall nymphs callipygous, who taught my soul / To lisp small lyrics which may gladden hearts / Of mistresses in elementary schools. / The train runs . . . through continents *Oxford Poetry*. 38–39. hair, /And] hair, / With pterodactyls clashing in the twilight, / And *Oxford Poetry*. 44–45. desires, / The] desires, / Change Wanderlüst to Weltschmerz in the Underground. /

The *Oxford Poetry*. 46. model homes] cottages *Oxford Poetry*. 47–48. ashpit, / Scraping]
ashpit, / Alone on his denuded battlefield, / Scraping *U*.

Oxford Poetry appeared in November 1926; this poem was almost certainly completed
between mid-May and the end of June. Upward recalls receiving his first letter enclosing
poems from Auden just after the General Strike, which began on 4 May and ended on
12 May, and he believes 'the figure of Grendel came into one of them' (ALS, from
Sandown, Isle of Wight, 13 November 1989, to Katherine Bucknell). 'Thomas Epilo-
gizes' quarries from 'Thomas Prologizes' l. 14 and another long passage beginning at
l. 31, but Auden cancelled about half of the latter in McElwee's copy, as the variants
show. ('Thomas Prologizes' does not mention Grendel, so it is not the poem Upward
remembers.) 'Thomas Epilogizes' would have been completed in time to be submitted
to *Oxford Poetry*, before the end of Summer Term 1926 (Term ended 10 July; Full Term
ended 18 June), though Auden would not have written the revisions in McElwee's copy
until the volume appeared in November.

The dedication to Isherwood is perhaps a joke, as Isherwood criticized the poem
ruthlessly. The Thomas of the title refers to the apostle St Thomas, known as Doubting
Thomas, and the poem also reflects the influence of two other Thomases, Thomas
Driberg and Thomas Stearns Eliot; see note to 'Thomas Prologizes'. Among other
things, Driberg introduced Auden to Gertrude Stein's work; she appeared with the
Sitwells in Christ Church on 7 June 1926 (advance notices from Harold Acton appeared
in several undergraduate magazines, and there were reviews afterwards). Her talk was
later published as one of the Hogarth Essays, *Composition as Explanation*. The epigraph
is unidentified.

In addition to what 'Thomas Epilogizes' borrows from 'Thomas Prologizes', its open-
ing image of the sun's rays shining through clouds 'as through a rotting factory floor'
(2) derives from the final stanza of Auden's March 1925 poem 'A Visit'. Here Auden
rather melodramatically heightens the effect with the word 'stab', probably imitating
the similar image with which Driberg opens his 'London Square' (first published in
March 1926): 'Swift needles from the sun pierce down / Indigo clouds to London
town'. Auden was to use the image again, without the reference to Rembrandt, in ll.
9–10 of the 1929 poem beginning 'Which of you waking early and watching daybreak'.
The four lines in parentheses (9–12) are combined from the earlier poems 'Landscape'
and 'November at Weybourne'. 'Landscape' draws on images reaching back to some of
Auden's earliest work, and from 'November at Weybourne' Auden reuses the phrase
'bewildered leaves' that he had first used in a letter to his parents written in October
1923 (see notes to 'Landscape' and 'November at Weybourne'). The penultimate line
of 'Thomas Epilogizes' also draws on earlier work: it has its original in the untitled
poem beginning 'Now from far eastern wolds, the bay' which concludes, 'though God
ere long / Break your back across his knees.'

The Greek in l. 17, *oikathe*, means home, as the line suggests; cp. l. 9 in Driberg's
'London Square', 'Those delicate bulb-sides cried 'Home!'' Probably Auden, and per-
haps Driberg, borrowed it from the same passage in *The Odyssey* (book 5, ll. 219–20),
which Auden was to use in his 'Letter to William Coldstream, Esq.', in *Letters from Iceland*
(1937)—on p. 226 Auden misquotes from Odysseus's farewell to Calypso. The Loeb
edition has: 'ἀλλὰ καὶ ὣς ἐθέλω καὶ ἐέλδομαι ἤματα πάντα / οἴκαδέ τ᾽ ἐλθέμεναι καὶ νόστιμον
ἦμαρ ἰδέσθαι,' (226), or 'But even so I wish and long day by day to reach my home, and
to see the day of my return,' trans. A. T. Murray, (London; New York, 1919), 184–85.

A sigmoid curve (19) is either like the uncial sigma (c) or like an s. In a notebook he
began using about 1929, Auden made a notation: 'The course of every natural desire is
that of the orgasm. Being satisfied they desire their own death. (The sigmoid curve of
autocatalytic reactions)' (Garland Notebook, British Library, Add.MS.52430, fo. 11).

'Eutectic' is a physics term for a mixture whose constituents are in such proportions as to melt and solidify at one temperature like a pure substance. Both these terms probably reflect that Auden was still studying Natural Science, as he was required to pass his first year exams before being allowed to change his School.

The figure of Job squatting upon his ashpit (47) probably alludes to Eliot's 'Gerontion' as much as it does to Job 2.8. For Eliphaz, Zophar, and Bildad (56), see Job 2.11ff. Silenus (62) is the garden deity and companion to Bacchus; near the end of Plato's *Sym'posium* Alcibiades compares Socrates to Silenus, a squat little statue carved to hold shepherds' pipes, but which, when opened, has images of the gods inside (see note to 'Cinders').

'Thomas Epilogizes' appeared at the height of Auden's activity as a published undergraduate poet. His work attracted the attention of undergraduate reviewers, who were either wildly enthusiastic or morally and aesthetically outraged. Those who liked poems like 'The Sunken Lane' were unable to appreciate Auden's modernist phase. Even though he edited *Oxford Poetry* again in 1927, fewer of Auden's own poems appeared after his first year in Oxford; he was beginning already to husband his best work for his first volume.

Humpty Dumpty

Dawn rose for hunting, trampling on the hills,
Pushing the shadows down from lower ridges,
Till one stood up and bared itself for glory,
A clear horizon, and a single tree
With dancing ring of children who would carry
May to the village underneath them soon.
Above them were the fells, the unused day,
Cloaked shepherds motionless among their sheep
Like Monoliths amid a ring of boulders,
Below a world about to stretch itself. . . .   10
Noon followed in the valley presently,
Where trees were darkly cool as under water,
And Lovers in the shadow of stone idols
Stirred not till evening touched them, and they saw
Flushed necks of waterfalls far-off, that spouted
From hanging valleys; Death seemed no more than
The echo of an axe, and life so lovely
Time's snarl sank in his throat to leave him staring,
And Change froze with his mattock in the air.

— — — —

'Let the day perish wherein I was born.'   20
(Some derelict had found the shady wall
A comfortable spot to curse his day in)

Words made the Watcher face about and turn
On Wonderland the backside of indifference,
To scrutinize a world of slag-tips, chimneys
More eloquent of Death than cypresses.
Kilns, truncated cones expressive of
Endeavour and the throwing up of hands,
Squat tenements in streets that imitate
Infinity but never get so far.   30
Houses were dumb till wind blew doors away,
Displaying fragments fitted into frames;
Bald heads like bloated spiders chasing crowns
And pennies with the pubic furtiveness
Of small boys' conversation in latrines:
A poet prattling prettily of love,
Indulging his plush insincerity,
His gulping courage, and his sexual day-dreams,
And all his facile armament of tears.
Soon there were lights in many windows; of   40
Cathedrals where a choirister's sweet treble
Brought moisture to a curate's nether lip,
Of village churches mouldering by the sea
Where gentlewomen and a North-East wind
Piped tunes to set a devil capering,
Of colleges where intellectuals
Oped magic casements with Columbus tales
Of Alfred Douglas and the Prince of Wales.

— — — —

'All the king's horses and all the king's men
Could not—' His head fell forward and he dreamed   50
Of equilibrium and a noiseless fall
Which shattered and said nothing till the grass
Had spelled forgetfulness upon the spot.
The merchants and the hairpin kings forsook
Their palaces; There were no pipes in doorways,
Cranks stiffened like the clenched fist of a corpse,
And sheds were silent save when a cinder
Dripped through the bars of furnaces and sizzled.
The kings went crawling on their hands and knees

(Their top hats lost on brambles long ago   60
  Their tethered motors rusting under trees,)
  Calling—'Sing us one of the songs of Sion—'
—'What's one and one and one and one and one?'
  And making Tom o' Bedlam at the edge of Things
  Turn back his face from the Abyss and gibber.
  Some found the wall but cut their fingers on it,
  For there was bottle glass along the top
  And they were lost and it was growing dark,
  The trickling laugh of water seemed a sneer.
  Death touched them in the pressure of a leaf   70
  And dug them nearer their Antipodes;
  Some with carved water jugs and scrolls upon them
  To keep them in the verger's memory,
  And some there were had no memorial
  But hearts and arrows cut in trees and stones,
  And marks in books of Public Libraries.
  No dog barked in the lampless valleys now,
  In the silent valleys of broken chimneys
  Where water-wheels had lost the use of hands.
  There was no gateway now into the valleys   80
  But crazy tramlines and a choked canal.
  A moon sailed skyward, frailly sad, to look
  Upon a world that guttered and went out.

— — — —

  He woke and rubbed his eyelids puzzled by
  Persistent questions pines and chimneys ask,
  These tautomeric changes in the mind,
  Our palimpsests upon reality,
  These worlds which we already knit the shrouds for
  To be replaced, till one day or the next
  There comes an end of worlds and an Eternity   90
  Goes with them, but not yet; while crocuses
  And waltzes still have something to recall
  Of Adam's brow, and of the wounded heel.

                                    [*July–August 1926*]

CI, ink autograph on Lordswood Road letterhead. Variants: 5. carry *this edn*] carry. *CI.* In l. 41 Auden wrote 'Choirester', apparently his misspelling of the obsolete form 'choirister'. Auden appears to have worked on the poem during the summer of 1926, not in the autumn and winter of 1926–27 as I suggested in *The W. H. Auden Society Newsletter* 4 (October 1989): 1. He mentions it in two letters to Isherwood. The first, possibly sent not long after he visited Isherwood at Freshwater Bay in July 1926, says, 'I am quietly stewing over Humpty Dumpty and will let you see the result when it comes' (AL, Lordswood Road letterhead, [July or August 1926]). The second letter says, 'I enclose Humpty Dumpty which is even more illegible than usual' (ALS, Lordswood Road letterhead but with 'Allenheads, Northumberland' added by hand, [August or September 1926]), and it probably enclosed the surviving copy of 'Humpty Dumpty', as Auden had apparently taken some of his parents' letterhead with him. In the first letter Auden also mentions revisions to two other poems that I have not been able to trace, the first, entitled 'The Unrequited Lover', which included the lines 'Uncircumnavigated, and as odd / To me as torsion in the Gastropod', the second about a pregnant woman and her child (see note to 'Motherhood'). Probably he had shown these poems to Isherwood at Freshwater Bay and never sent him copies.

Ll. 5–6 refer, as in 'Thomas Prologizes', to the traditional folk ceremony of 'Carrying out Death' and 'Bringing in Summer', described by James Frazer in *The Golden Bough*. Frazer explicitly links the ceremony of 'Carrying in the May' to 'Carrying in Summer' (see note to 'Thomas Prologizes').

For l. 20ff., see Job 3.3 and 3.1. Ll. 20–32 also carry echoes of Eliot's 'Gerontion' and 'The Love Song of J. Alfred Prufrock'. The nursery-rhyme theme underpinning the poem may have been suggested in part by 'The Hollow Men', which Auden and Isherwood both admired (see note to 'Bank Holiday'), and Auden also learned such techniques from the Edith Sitwell of *Clown's Houses* (1918), *Façade* (1922), and *Troy Park* (1923).

'The Watcher' (23) is Auden's version of 'the Watcher in Spanish', a Mortmere creation of Upward and Isherwood described by Isherwood in *Lions and Shadows*, 'The phrase came, I believe, from a line in a poem about: "The Watcher in Spanish Cape. . . ." We imagined him as a macabre but semi-comic figure, not unlike Guy Fawkes, or a human personification of Poe's raven. He appeared to us, we said, at moments when our behaviour was particularly insincere. . . . he warned us never to betray ourselves by word or deed. He was our familiar, our imaginary mascot, our guardian spirit' (53–54). In an earlier, unpublished piece on which this passage in *Lions and Shadows* was based, Isherwood also described him as 'a presence representing our combined personalities. A bogey to whom we appealed or whom we tried to deceive. The sneering umpire of our lives' ('Mortmere Introductory Dialogue', TS prepared by Upward, British Library). Isherwood and Upward also drew on their memories of *Alice in Wonderland* in creating Mortmere (*Lions and Shadows*, 68); cp. l. 24.

Auden's description of the kilns as 'truncated cones expressive of / Endeavour' (27–28) reaches forward to the 'Enormous cones of myth and art' in his mature evocation of this symbolic landscape in 'New Year Letter' (*CP*, 227). The 'throwing up of hands' (28) and the water-wheels which 'had lost the use of hands' (79) both recall the mill which 'Raised heavy hands and dropped them to its side' in 'Thomas Epilogizes' and earlier poems. The imagery in ll. 55–57 of pipes, cranks, and sheds appears in several other poems, including 'Dethroned', 'The Evolution of the Dragon', and 'I chose this lean country'; in the last of these it is presented, as in 'Humpty Dumpty', as dream material prefaced by an intense sensation of falling (see 'I chose this lean country', ll. 34ff.). The phrase 'frailly sad' (82) had previously appeared in the 1922 poem 'A Moment' and had been used again in 'The Dark Fiddler', written, probably, in 1925.

The 'magic casements' (47) from Keats's 'Ode to a Nightingale' (69) are alluded to by Auden and Charles Plumb in their preface to *Oxford Poetry 1926*, written probably in June 1926 not long before 'Humpty Dumpty': 'If it is a natural preference to inhabit a room with casements opening upon Fairyland, one at least of them should open upon the Waste Land' (v). In 'Humpty Dumpty' the 'magic casements' open on to a homosexual underworld exposed by public scandal: Oscar Wilde was imprisoned in 1895 as a result of his friendship with Alfred Douglas, and the Cleveland Street Affair, surrounding a male brothel at that address, caused a sensation in 1889. The Prince of Wales (later Edward VII) suppressed the role of his eldest son, Prince Albert Victor, but Albert Victor's close friend implicated with him, Lord Arthur Somerset, was threatened with prosecution and lived permanently abroad. Possibly Auden labels these stories 'Columbus tales' (47) because they describe a New World of homosexual activity previously unknown to the naïve undergraduate and perhaps somehow sanctioned in being presented by intellectuals in, presumably, Oxford colleges (46).

For l. 62, see Psalms 137.3. For l. 74, see Ecclesiasticus (Apocrypha), 44.9. 'Tautomeric' (86) is used in chemistry to describe organic compounds which can behave in different reactions as if they possessed different constitutions; that is, as if their atoms were arranged in at least two different ways. The term is particularly applied where the differences in behaviour are due to the reversible migration of an atom or group within a molecule, especially hydrogen; see *The Oxford English Dictionary*, 2nd edn.

L. 17 reappeared in *Paid on Both Sides* (*EA*, 14; *Plays*, 30). Auden revised the two final lines of 'Humpty Dumpty' for the conclusion to the poem beginning 'Nor was that final, for about that time', poem 7 in *P(28)*. L. 12 is echoed in part 3 of the 1929 poem beginning 'It was Easter as I walked in the public gardens': 'Air between stems as under water' (*EA*, 39; titled '1929' in *CP*, 48). Auden eventually abandoned 'Humpty Dumpty', but it was for a time the repository for a number of seminal themes and images.

Lovers' Lane

I

Few roads grassen quicker than Lovers' Lane.
Choked up with blackberry where beardless Time
In hollow antres oversleeps himself,
And tapestried with all a lover's flowers,
Lad's Love, and Love-in-idleness, nor yet
Excepting nightshade, medicine for lovesick
Maids, or nettles to ditch love decently
With elder-scent for memory.

          Now England
Has conquered Wales, until eclipsing clouds   10
Pass, and the moon joins Severn to the Dee,
Making two islands that look up to watch
A solemn poplar bowing at a star

And down the hill where lighted windows seem
The pennon-flames of tapers pointing them
To bed as they cluck home remembering
A mother's knitting eye, but blinded to
The smirking Past, the bone hands of To-morrow.

II

'They're burying young Dick—'
                                        Outside the pane
A woman crouches, tugging at a grave
Which fangs itself on the defeated lover.
A man that looks on glass may see sometimes
No further than his heart: I only see
The spot behind me where perspectives meet,
('A pity isn't it?—') imagining
I viced your hips between my palms, or hung
Upon one corner of the crooked moon   10
Awaiting your 'Go now!' when I should drop
Headlong to crack the bottom of the sky.
I dredge through fathoms of a queasy soul
For phrases barnacled until your voice
Flares like a hand raised sideways suddenly,
To indicate a spiritual turning—
'You haven't seen my roses—' but your eyes
Signal 'No nearer' as I hold the door:
I follow, keeping my circumference

III

I squelch through mire past sodden ricks. Behind
The sunken day; before me now a land
Stretched out like a dead weasel, lean and stark,
With here an ashamed willow with its hair down,
And there an ivy-strangled oak, one branch
Protruding like a blackened tongue, a gasp
That came to nothing. As I pass a thorn
Quavers a withered claw at me—'Scut home,

Your tail between your legs: the road's your place.'
      O heigho it is most jolly   10
      Walking the valley with silent melancholy.
But the swift hunted look of summer lightning
Chokes music. Shadows stoop at me. Strange stones
Loom up ahead like monstrous tusks before
Gigantic darkness of a rising storm
Which soon will set its itching fingers on
The windpipe of the world. The doors are shut
Upon my father's house There was a star
Once in a Tower. Now I do not see it.
Where am I now? Echo . . . Echo . . .   20

IV

The oboe notes
Of the chipped egg
The winter leaves
Quickened to a gigue
The cherry-eye of a bird.

The bulb pillow
Raising the skull
Thrusting a crocus through clenched teeth.

The flickered shadow
Of an early swallow   10
And at your dress
The first shy fumbling of a lover's hand
'Rapunzel, Rapunzel, let down your hair!'

[August 1926]

CI, ink autograph, on small watermarked sheet. (The paper appears to be the same as that used for 'Bank Holiday', 'Last Bus, Saturday Night', and the 'Song' beginning 'Relation seemed ordained for us', though the watermark is not fully visible. Probably a larger sheet was cut in halves or quarters; the full watermark may have been 'Papyrus Westbourne'.) Variants: 1.15. them *this edn*] them. *CI.*

Auden mentioned this poem in the letter he sent to Isherwood around June 1927 in which he divided some of his poems into those written before and those written after his July 1926 visit to Freshwater Bay; see note to 'Early Morning' ('Perched on a nettled stump he stands'). 'Lovers' Lane' was listed with those written afterwards, and he told Isherwood that he had scrapped 'the other three parts of Lovers' Lane', by which he meant that by this time he wished to preserve only the final section of this poem; he used most of this final section in 'The Megalopsych' and later just three lines of it in section (c) of the first poem series in *P(28)*. In the Ansen notebook, a partial draft of 'The Megalopsych' gives further evidence of the date of 'Lovers' Lane'. Opposite a torn-out page (9 in the facsimile reproduction of the notebook) is the notation, on p. 8: 'Written August 1926. "Daffodil bulbs instead of eyes" Eliot. Intimations of Mortality'. The passage from 'Lovers' Lane' does not appear in the notebook, probably because it was written with other missing passages on one of the torn-out pages, but most likely it was opposite this date. Auden's note suggests that the three lines he preserved, 'The bulb pillow / Raising the skull / Thrusting a crocus through clenched teeth', were inspired by a play of allusion among three poems: Eliot's 'Whispers of Immortality' (Auden had first written 'Whispers' and then changed it to 'Intimations'), Words-worth's 'Ode: Intimations of Immortality from Recollections of Early Childhood', and Wordsworth's 'I Wandered Lonely as a Cloud'. In the last poem, the 'host, of golden daffodils' (4) seen by the lake later 'flash upon that inward eye' (21). Turned by Eliot's lines, 'Daffodil bulbs instead of balls / Stared from the sockets of the eyes!' (5–6), Auden debunks Wordsworth's moment of vision with the macabre image of the eye of the rotting corpse actually replaced by the flower.

'Lovers' Lane' is an almost chaotic miscellany of stylistic influences, and presents, along with a handful of other contemporary pieces, a critical phase of disarray in Auden's transition towards the apparently unified style of his earliest mature work; in the shorter run, it is a precursor of 'The Megalopsych' and thus, eventually, of the first untitled sequence of poems in *P(28)* in which Auden was to record more carefully and discretely many of the styles he had practised throughout his adolescence. 'Lovers' Lane' begins in the style of Edward Thomas, but as early as l. 3 in part 1 the poetic and unusual word 'antres' is probably borrowed from *Othello*—in the journal he kept during 1929 in Berlin, Auden was to cite the line, 'Antars vast and Desarts idle' (*Othello*, 1.3) as an example of the kind of 'verbal dexterity' that he found by then 'exhibitionistic, and Society for pure English'. Auden soon introduces the strains of Eliot's *The Waste Land*, especially with the first line of part 2, 'They're burying young Dick—'. Part 3 of 'Lovers' Lane' draws on Auden's own earlier work in the style of both Thomas and Hardy, quarrying 'A Visit', 'Landscape', and 'The Road's Your Place'. Ll. 2–3, 'before me now a land / Stretched out like a dead weasel, lean and stark,' echo ll. 9–10 of Hardy's 'The Darkling Thrush': 'The land's sharp features seemed to be / The Century's corpse outleant'.

Bank Holiday

The Princes run downward on to the shore,
But their pilgrim shadows bravely explore,
Founding their colonies first that these
May sit all the day by domestic seas.

The Kings stand stork-like on pebbles and beg
The green waves to cover each shining leg,

Or slumber in deck-chair thrones and implore
The waves to lie down with a royal snore.

But Royal Families sooner or later
Visit Madam Zana, delineator   10
Of soiled palms and fortunes. Now one and all
With a trembling heart reach her Delphic stall.

— — — —

—'You meet a lady in September;
   A Cleopatra, so, remember!'
      Coo, I says, ain't she lovly
—'Nor think that you have there a stone
   To turn all gold, the only one'—
      Mummy, I want to do big!
—'But hear behind her door, the groans,
   The snarl, the crunching of old bones.'   20
      Come on, don't lose your nerve, girl.

—'Lest you should be surprised to note
   The heavy arms about the throat.'
      Which way do you like it best, dearie?
—'And you inhabit too like those,
   The Spirit's equatorial snows.'

— — — —

The clapper in the old church-tower nearby
(Which ever pushes at the tidal sky)
   Clangs like a rusty gate to scourge Doom on
To lead away the idiotic sun   30

And with the mop of darkness in his hands
To sponge the Princes from the dirty sands.
But wind already flits about their ears,
And fills them with a thousand sudden fears.

— — — —

They rattle home; only the red rear light
Shows where they travel singing through the night.
'How vulgar!' irritated villas say
Of vanished princes happier than they.

At last the kings most gorgeously march down
With picture cards in triumph through the town,   40
And crying 'We will go no more, for we
Have passed away and there is no more sea.'

Only the old queen's sunken-breasted chatter
On thresholds, like a window frame's loose clatter,
And bars where ancient kings have stared all day
Down pewter mugs to puff their fate away.

The squeezing of a lover's arm, the meet
Of children's cold toes underneath the sheet
Token a few things unforgotten by
The keepers of the royal memory.   50

On that dismantled and crestfallen shore
Where kings are not remembered any more,
Wind shuffles by, that scavenger in rags,
Collecting souls from vacant paper bags.

Earth crawls down its knife-edge, far from the sun,
'Neath yawning skies, another gesture done.

[*August or September 1926*]

The Oxford Outlook 8, no. 40 (November 1926): 242–44; CI, ink autograph on small sheet watermarked 'Papyrus', probably part of a watermark which may have been 'Papyrus Westbourne' (see note to 'Lovers' Lane'); David Ayerst (Auden's Christ Church friend), ink autograph on Lordswood Road letterhead, signed 'W. H. Auden'. Variants: In Ayerst, two additional stanzas precede the first; these are also shown in CI, where they are cancelled:

The Queen's hand on the king's cold shoulder falling
Bids him awaken to the Siren's calling
The shaving-mirror bids him never fail
To pay his visit to the Holy Grail

Their coaches run swiftly as their desires
Scattering birds from the telegraph wires.

> Their straw-crowns rocking on torrid scalps
> Like Hannibal's army over the Alps (*CI*)

1. run ... on to] rush ... onto *Ayerst*. 2. But their ... shadows bravely] Their ... shadows now bravely *CI*; Their shadows like pilgrim fathers explore *Ayerst*. 4. domestic] enchanted *Ayerst*. 12. heart] hearts *Ayerst*. 23. heavy] hairy *CI*. 28. the] a *CI*. The format of the poem's second section was rearranged; in CI it is presented in alternating groups of two- and three-line stanzas, beginning with two, and in Ayerst it is presented in alternating groups of two lines and one line each, beginning with two. Following stanza 7, Ayerst offers two other additional stanzas, also shown (with minor differences) and cancelled in CI:

> London Bridge is broken down
> London Town is falling down
> The Towers left to hold the sky
> Are crumbling, there is no one by
> And London Town is burning, burning
> And all the Towers turning.
>
> Hold the Fort for we are coming.
> Ride a cock Horse
> To Banbury Cross
> To Banbury Cross
> To Banbury Cross
> To
> Banbury
> Banbury
> Banbury
> Banbury
> Cross! *CI*

'Bank Holiday' is listed among the poems Auden wrote after his July 1926 visit to Freshwater Bay; by the late spring of 1927 it was rejected even though it had already been published (see notes to 'Lovers' Lane' and 'Early Morning' beginning 'Perched on a nettled stump he stands'). The title is apparently taken from Katherine Mansfield's story 'Bank Holiday', which presents an analogous crowd of characters and the diverse idioms of their mingled voices. The poem is reminiscent of *The Waste Land*, and the additional passages in CI and Ayerst reveal some borrowing from 'The Hollow Men' as well. In a letter to Isherwood roughly contemporary with the poem, Auden mentioned the latter among his particular likes: 'I am so glad about Eliot. Your choice is entirely mine with the emphasis on the Hollow Men, and with the exception of parts of Portrait of a Lady which has fine lines in it. eg. 'Recalling things that other people have desired' [.] Bits in Preludes are good too. The rest of course are vers de société' (ALS, on Lordswood Road letterhead from Allenheads, Northumberland, [August–September 1926]). The work of Edith Sitwell also influenced the poem; see, for instance, 'Minstrels' in *Clowns' Houses* (1918), poem 6 (called 'Hornpipe' when it was reprinted in *Bucolic Comedies*) in the second part of *Façade* (1922), and 'Perrine' (the first part of 'Country Cousin') and 'Clown's Luck' in *Troy Park* (1925). Stanza 8 is recycled from Auden's own earlier piece 'Trippers', which was later abbreviated and reused again in 'Easter Monday', written in April 1927. L. 29 reappeared in 'Hodge Looks toward London', and l. 30 in the poem beginning 'I chose this lean country', published in *P(28)*.

In *The Music of Lennox Berkeley*, Peter Dickinson suggests that Berkeley set 'Bank Holiday' in about 1926, but probably the poem was 'Trippers'; see note to 'Trippers'.

Last Bus, Saturday Night

The bus jolts on defunctive gasoline,
A Tumbril rattling to the Guillotine.

The clucking market women would appease
The Furies with the price of cabbages.

A quavering voice and hand would make so bold
To offer the Moon something for the cold.

Fat sleep has taken to her vulgar heart
The drowsy down-lipped Samuel set apart.

The Lovers huddle closer hand in hand
Like strangers from a far enchanted land.   10

Two shadows from two worlds they seem to be
'O do not hurt us, for we will not see.'

The gibbous moon above who cannot bless
The uncomplaining benedictionless

The virgin stars dragged through the streets of sky
By Time who walks out with all, by and by.

Leaves shaken by the owl's outrageous cry
'The world is weary, but it cannot die!'

[*Summer or autumn 1926*]

CI, ink autograph on small sheet watermarked 'Papyrus', the same folio as 'Song' ('Re-
lation seemed ordained for us'). Probably this is only part of a watermark which may
have read 'Papyrus Westbourne' (see note to 'Lovers' Lane').

Auden's description of Samuel as 'down-lipped' (8) suggests he is adolescent, al-
though it may also be intended as a reference to the vow made by Samuel's mother,
Hannah, that if God would give her 'a man child, then I will give him unto the Lord all
the days of his life, and there shall no razor come upon his head' (1 Samuel 1.11). The
'gibbous moon' in stanza 7 had previously appeared in 'Thomas Prologizes', and the
stanza may be compared to two lines in Auden's 1937 ballad 'As I walked out one
evening': 'Life remains a blessing / Although you cannot bless' (*EA*, 228; *CP*, 135).

Song

Relation seemed ordained for us
    I turned my face to run
To my Atomic Nucleus,
    My Positive, my Sun.

To be your satellite possession
    For you were to control
My Equinoxial procession
    Each nodding of a Pole.

But passion's waywardness has spoiled
    The motions I began   10
A lover's eagerness has foiled
    Love's mathematic plan.

Love's calculating eye divines
    What yet no watchers know,
The intersection of our lines,
    The flash, the bidding 'Go'.

When I spin rapidly afar
    Till I am burnt away,
No planet, but a shooting star
    Decline my Bedlam way.   20

[*Summer or autumn 1926*]

CI, ink autograph on verso of 'Last Bus, Saturday Night' (see notes to 'Last Bus, Satur-day Night' and 'Lovers' Lane'). Variants: 14. know, *this edn*] know. *CI.* 18. away, *this edn*] away. *CI.*

Like other poems of 1926, the clipped style of 'Song' owes something to the *Songs and Sonets* of John Donne; l. 16 echoes the conclusion to Donne's 'The Expiration': 'Being double dead, going, and bidding, goe.' Auden's solar system metaphor may derive from his father's 1926 article on character formation: 'Now in the earliest years of his life the child is essentially individualist. He feels himself the centre of a universe of his own, round which the various planets of his little solar system revolve. But, as he grows, the experience of reality ere long teaches him that there are other solar systems besides his own, the orbits of whose planets cross and recross his own.' George A. Auden, 'On Endogenous and Exogenous Factors in Character Formation', *The Journal of Mental Science* 72, no. 296 (January 1926): 11.

First Meeting

A wind felt for the breastbone,
    A leaf slid down the road,
And drops of rain flung savage
    From corners of abode.

A face looked through the window,
    It will not pucker much
At orgulous encounters,
    Though soul squawk to the touch.

[*Autumn 1926*]

P(M), ink autograph on 'Shell Brand'.

In the late spring or early summer of 1927, Auden apparently copied out for John Pudney a number of poems written during the previous year; the watermark suggests this poem is one of that group (see note to 'Consequences'). Its style, reminiscent of Emily Dickinson, places it roughly in the second half of 1926, though it could have been written later.

Consequences

'Was it for this the clay grew tall?'

WILFRED OWEN

She said 'How tiring the lights are!'
I said 'How noisy it is!' So up we scrambled
Into the loft which smelt of hay.
'Supper!' They said, all too soon. We were young
                            then and walked,
Past the engine to the wood
Where the dog hurt its paw. Under such pines
I gave a penny for his thoughts. He sent
A photograph signed; but spiders crawled across it
Obscuring the face.

'What does it mean?'   10
After the hymn we sat, wiped sticky fingers,
Thinking of home. 'What does it mean
To us, here, now?'

□

What does it mean
To us who were not born in Egypt?
These memories beguiled us coming up;
Now we have heard conclusion on this matter,
See only worn-down gubber tusks,
Denuded stumps of larger systems, waiting
The last transgression of the sea.   20

A cock crowed, starting tears:
Almost at dawn
Water rose suddenly to greet him
'I did not make him, nor know why he was born.'
The sun drives on,
Bestowing not a glance
Where once was arrogance

[*Autumn 1926*]

P(B), ink autograph on ['Shell Brand']; *The Oxford University Review* 2, no. 5 (18 November 1926), 177; CI, ink autograph on the same folio as 'Early Morning' ('Earth rolls these houses out into the sun') and 'Tea in November'. Variants: EPIGRAPH Wilfred Owen] not in *Oxford University Review* or *CI*. 15. Egypt] Egypt* *Oxford University Review*, *CI*. The asterisk refers to a note at the foot of the poem: *'Born in Egypt' a corruption of 'Corn in Egypt'; signifying 'lucky' *Oxford University Review*, *A colloquial phrase in the midlands meaning 'lucky.' A corruption of 'corn in Egypt' *CI*. 19. larger] large *Oxford University Review*. 24. nor] or *Oxford University Review*.

'Consequences' was possibly written near its November 1926 publication date, and in any case almost certainly after the July visit to Freshwater Bay. I have used P(B) as the copy text because I believe Auden may have copied out the poem for Pudney in the late spring of 1927, well after its publication. The paper and watermark match two letters Auden sent to Isherwood during the Summer Term of 1927, probably in May or June. The first of these letters mentions that Sacheverell Sitwell 'has made me send my things to Eliot which I did to-day' (ALS, Christ Church); this apparently contributed to Auden's undertaking a general sorting through his work around this time, which would in all likelihood have included copying out to send to his old school-friend, Pudney, some of the poems written and published during the previous year. Pudney's copies of 'First Meeting', 'In Due Season', 'Pride' ('When Little Claus meets Big Claus in the road'), 'Hodge Looks toward London', 'Aware', and 'Extract' (titled on his copy 'The Seekers') are also on Shell Brand. Auden used paper unpredictably, so the matching watermarks on the letter and the poems do not conclusively show they were written at the same time, but other features also suggest the Pudney version of 'Consequences' was written out later than the published one: it usefully attributes the epigraph to Owen, omits the joky *Waste Land*–like footnote to l. 15, and generally seems to take itself a little more seriously than what appear to be the earlier copies. The Owen epigraph is from 'Futility'. The lines to which the asterisk and note were attached, beginning 'What does it mean', reappeared combined with the similar material from the preceding stanza as the opening of 'Address for a Prize Day' in *The Orators* (*EA*, 61). This passage parodies the sermons given by the headmaster at St Edmund's, Cyril Morgan Brown;

the theme given in *The Orators* is 'Commemoration'. In *Lions and Shadows*, Isherwood describes 'Weston' as being 'brilliant at doing one of Pa's sermons' on the meaning of St Edmund's Day (184).

In his unfinished 1930s epic, Auden again linked the images of the engine and the hurt dog as in ll. 5–6; see Lucy McDiarmid, 'W. H. Auden's "In the year of my youth"', *The Review of English Studies*, n.s. 29, no. 115 (August 1978): 289, ll 334–60. Possibly both passages refer to an incident which may also lie behind the lines in 'Letter to Lord Byron': 'My earliest recollection to stay put / Is of a white stone doorstep and a spot /Of pus where father lanced the terrier's foot' (*EA*, 191; *CP*, 106).

'Coming up' (16) is in the sense of coming up to start university. 'Gubber tusks' (18) is probably Auden's approximation of 'gubber-tushes', large projecting teeth. 'Systems' (19) is apparently meant in the geological sense, as in systems of mountains or other geological formations. Ll. 19–20 reappeared in the poem beginning 'The houses rolled into the sun,' which was at one time intended for publication in *P(28)* (see note to 'Deemed this an outpost, I'), and eventually the lines were incorporated into *Paid on Both Sides* (*EA*, 3; *Plays*, 16).

A parody of Auden's work—'Rotation' by 'Mystan Baudom'—appeared in *The Oxford University Review* 2, no. 6 (25 November 1926): 210. It seems to have been inspired partly by 'Consequences', both by the style of the dialogue in stanza 1 and by the pedantic footnote to l. 15; see Appendix, where 'Rotation' is printed with a note.

In Due Season

In Spring we waited. Princes felt
Through darkness for unwoken queens;
The itching lover weighed himself
At stations on august machines;

And Jacob fled down passages
Before those shambling feet, which came
Still nearer, splintering doors. They fought,
Rucked hams before he told his name.

Then Summer hid the grass. We sang
Our descant until love one day,   10
That pedal-entry in the fugue,
Roared in, swept soul and knees away.

October had its casuistry.
The robin on the fallen spade,
Saw eyelashes upon close flesh,
The nice distinctions lust had made.

Pockets, not hair, glue fingers now.
To lovers trespassing alone,
The rusty chains of creaking gates
Cry in the hand, the cool of bone.   20

The sunset pours contempt upon
The choking sticks. Was Cressid fair?
Shall pages lose their meaning now
For steps approaching on the stair?

[*Autumn 1926*]

P(B), ink autograph on 'Shell Brand' (see note to 'Consequences'); *The Oxford Outlook*
8, no. 41 (December 1926): 298; *Oxford Poetry 1928*, ed. Clere Parsons and B.B. (Oxford,
1928), 2. Fisher transcribed a version of ll. 11–12: 'Till love that pedal entry in the fugue
/ Sweep soul and knees away' with a note: 'Odd bits of Auden noted 1926'. The text in
Oxford Poetry 1928 may have been pirated from *The Oxford Outlook*; Auden wrote to
Spender from Berlin probably in late 1928, 'The awful poem of mine in O.P[.] was
taken without permission and against my express wishes' (ALS on watermark 'WHS'
[presumably letter paper from W. H. Smith's that Auden had carried with him to Ger-
many], Berg).
    For the lover weighing himself (3–4), see Stephen Spender, *World within World* (Lon-
don, 1951), 48, where Spender describes such an experiment by a friend. The obser-
vant 'robin on the fallen spade' (14) recalls 'The robin on the churchyard fence' in
Auden's earlier poem 'Christmas Eve'. The shortened name 'Cressid' (22) can be
found in Shakespeare's version of the story, *Troilus and Cressida*; in the summer of 1926,
Auden told Isherwood he was reading this for the first time (ALS, Lordswood Road
letterhead, [August 1926]). In 1968, Auden wrote another poem titled 'In Due Season'
(*CP*, 801–2), but the two have no connection other than their titles.

Early Morning

Earth rolls these houses out into the sun
That dazzles housemaids on their knees before
Ashes which battled longer with the dark
Than men. In gardens the wet bushes creak
The trees shake hands, mean nothing more. A bird
Fingering a note no louder than peace
Asked no more questions than his country cousins;
The cart horse stamping just to emphasise
Infinite preference for hay to words,

The kestrel perched upon a splintered oak   10
Rubbing his left eye with a sleepy lid
A sentinel, dark, motionless, at dawn.

[*Autumn 1926*]

CI, ink autograph, on the same folio as 'Consequences' and 'Tea-time in November' (entitled 'Tea in November' on Isherwood's copy).

Auden had previously used the title 'Early Morning' for the poem beginning 'Perched on a nettled stump he stands.' The phrase 'trees shake hands' first appeared in his early poem 'Woods in Rain' (9), printed in *Public School Verse 1923–1924*. Ll. 10 and 12 are taken nearly intact from the 1925 sonnet 'Richard Jefferies', and a faint echo of Edward Thomas competes in 'Early Morning' with the T. S. Eliot of 'Morning at the Window' (the housemaids) and 'Preludes' (the cart horse). In his 1926 letter to Isherwood describing which of Eliot's early poems he most liked, Auden mentioned 'Bits in Preludes are good too' (see note to 'Bank Holiday'). The opening line of 'Early Morning' was revised for the poem beginning 'The houses rolled into the sun,' which Auden initially intended to include in *P(28)*.

Tea-time in November

Milk flounces upward in the tea like smoke:
So bonfires blossomed in a garden; through
Unconscious leaf, sun advertised a hand;
Touch yearned, but separation said 'Not you!'

Cold shakes, cries 'Home!' Look back once to these walls,
The lichen-stain soaks imperceptibly;
The tower stands, a side slipped half away,
Ruin hooked over by an angry sky.

Narcissus faces broken window-panes.
Nose at the door, she'll come, with dugs slopped over,   10
Splay-footed, warty, lave-eared, platter-cheeked;
You shall not flinch who used to be her lover.

Time passes. 'Take, O take, those lips away'
Sighed Mariana in her moated grange.
We see them now, and not as they were seen,
But they were barren, and there was no change

[*November? 1926*]

P(B), ink autograph on ['Shell Brand']; CI, ink autograph on the same folio as 'Conse-
quences' and 'Early Morning' ('Earth rolls these houses out into the sun'). Variants:
TITLE Tea-time] Tea *CI.* 5. back once to] backward on *CI.* 7. The . . . away, *this edn*]
The . . . away. *P(B)*; This . . . away *CI.* 8. Ruin] Ruins *CI.* 10. the] this *CI.*

'Home!' (5) recalls 'Thomas Epilogizes', l. 17, with its allusion to *The Odyssey*; see note
to 'Thomas Epilogizes'. Auden devoted a whole poem to 'Narcissus' in the spring of
1927. For ll. 13–14, see Shakespeare, *Measure for Measure*, 4.1, and Tennyson's 'Mariana'.

The Happy Tree

The blossoms burgeon sumptuously,
No salt reminder at their feast
Of leaves once likewise entertained
Until the personal interest ceased,
Of piteous pummelling at doors,
The final slinking in despair
To stain a cistern or to kiss
A foot, impatient far from here.

A driver in a cart obscures
My sunshine on my tree, not his.   10
No tongue grows taut, prepared to speak
Of vegetable images;
His eyes bulge no astonished 'You!'
I would have said his tree was lying,
But who applauds the sleeping dancer,
Since when have cats known kings were dying?

A dazzled penitent, from church
I walked away, threw sixpence in
A beggar's greasy cap, absolved
From all but seven minutes' sin.   20
The lever in my hands, I kept
The engine waiting. Once at Ryde
We played duets, she turned the page,
More quavers on the other side,

Dispassionate pressure of the Past
Makes Thisness ponderable. Was dew

A chill last night; were touching hands
In error when they thought they knew?
The doors are shut on passing feet
That took an individual way;   30
Their voices echo from a valley,
Mocking across the break of day.

[*November? 1926*]

P(B), TS on 'WHS Voucher Bond' with ink autograph revisions; The Poetry/Rare
Books Collection, State University of New York at Buffalo, ink autograph on 'Shell
Brand' with signature 'W. H. Auden'. Variants: 10. tree] wall *Buffalo.*

Ll. 22–24 probably refer to Auden's childhood pastime of playing piano duets with
his mother. Ryde (22) is a resort town on the north-east coast of the Isle of Wight.
During the Easter holidays in 1917, Mrs Auden took all three of her sons to stay at
Totland Bay in the Isle of Wight, about twenty miles from Ryde. Carpenter records that
in a diary the boys kept of their trip, one entry describes an evening when Auden gave
'a "Grand Concert" of piano solos and duets with his mother' (20), but there is no
evidence that any of the family visited Ryde during the holiday. Possibly the lines recol-
lect another, similar occasion, or perhaps Auden used 'Ryde' for the rhyme. Auden
reused ll. 23–24 in poem 12 in *P(28)*, beginning 'The four sat on in the bare room',
written in December 1927. Ll. 23–24 also gave inspiration to the parodist who wrote
'Rotation' by 'Mystan Baudom'; *Oxford University Review* 2, no. 6 (25 November 1926).
Intriguingly, the exact version of the lines in the parody survives only in the 1927 poem
'The four sat on in the bare room', written after the parody was published; see Appen-
dix and note.

Winter Afternoon

The office sunlight, edging back, protrudes
Lean fingers to discover stains upon
Excellent hands; the window-tapper looks
Down railways tending to uncertain bournes,
And soiled with snow in fribbled messes waiting
A drizzle's rapture. Boys on bicycles
Toil steep streets dazzled out into the sun:
There slippery stone shames fuddled senile knees,
Colin and Phyllis move to an encounter,
Anticipation hung on other sleeves.   10
They pass, each hopeless for a thrush's titter,
Dunged boots, a harvest-moon capitulation:
Intending along street of lacquered gold,
Colin is homesick, zany, was deceived.

[*Autumn or winter 1926–27*]

P(M), TS on 'WHS Voucher Bond'; CI, ink autograph.

About a year after writing this poem, Auden told Isherwood 'I have destroyed the excellent hands poem' (ALS, Christ Church, about 1 December 1927); he did, how-ever, resurrect the phrase he mentioned for the Yeatsian line, 'How excellent hands have turned to commonness,' in the poem beginning 'Taller to-day, we remember similar evenings', published in *P(28)*. Moreover he used it again in his 1928 epitha-lamium for Cecil Day-Lewis beginning 'This morning any touch is possible' (see note to 'Punchard').

Say Yes!

They climbed a mountain in the afternoon:
He found sufficiently appealing
The eager hair about the face, but then
Decided to withstand the feeling.

The glow of evening spurred 'Say yes, say yes!'
He said; but she withstood the trial.
'Under the circumstance, it must amuse?'
He sniggered, trembling for denial.

[*Autumn or winter 1926–27*]

P(B), TS on 'WHS Voucher Bond' with ink autograph revision; CI, purple autograph (possibly a carbon) with black ink autograph revisions. Variants: TITLE Say Yes!] Per-sonal Relations *CI*. 3. face, but] eyes, and *CI*.

Ballad

He offered her his paucity;
Refusal checked the plan.
He turned, laughed wryly, went abroad
A disappointed man.

A tilted profile on the snow,
Designs for an Ascension,
Served in some measure to relieve
The spiritual tension.

His thoughts went riding, borne upon
The bubbles in a stream;   10

'Elektrizitätswerk streng verboten'
Lay shadowed on his dream.

A Prince ruled in a golden age
For an obedient land;
He found her starving in the street
And took her by the hand.

In pearls, in silk magnificence
Equipped the royal bride;
At middle of the night she came
All naked to his side.   20

In later sunlight, on the steps
They met, good friends again;
They chattered, eyes were frank, the new
Relationship was plain.

The case at least was rubicund,
Laughed savagely 'Tee hee!'
'If spirit pules, control is brave'
I laughed to laughing Me.

[*Winter 1926–27*]

P(M), TS with one ink autograph revision on 'WHS Voucher Bond'; CI, ink autograph.
Variants: TITLE Ballad] A Tale of Love *CI.* 9–10. His thoughts went riding, borne . . .
/bubbles in] He wandered, crucified . . . / . . . border of *CI.*

The influence of Edith Sitwell lends the poem, like many from this period, its whim-
sical eccentricity. The German in l. 11 can be translated 'Power-plant strictly forbid-
den', though a more usual way of putting this might be 'Elektrizitätswerk: Eintritt streng
verboten' or 'Power-plant: entrance strictly forbidden'. Auden travelled to Austria with
William McElwee during the Christmas vacation in 1926–27; the snow (5) and this
prohibiting sign perhaps refer to experiences during their trip. L. 16 was slightly revised
for l. 37 of 'Hodge Looks toward London', which has a long series of stanzas similar to
these in style and theme.

The Last of the Old Year

My latest love appeared to me,
Convex and satisfactory.

The carpet grovelled on the floor;
Aunt Edith tried the closet door.

The 9.10 Up passed the 9.10 Down;
Both cried 'The other way to Town'

The grass looked upward at the flower
Through lenses of a fallen shower.

Here scowled at There; the Now and This
Enjoyed at last connubial bliss.   10

Out of the tensor $G\mu\nu$
Hamilton built the world anew.

The photograph upon my shelf
Beat Time—'Physician heal thyself.'

[*Winter 1926–27*]

P(M), TS on 'WHS Voucher Bond' with Greek letters added in Auden's hand.

In a late 1927 letter to Isherwood, Auden mentioned that he had 'destroyed' this poem (along with 'Winter Afternoon'), saving only the fourth and fifth couplets, which he incorporated into 'The Megalopsych' (ALS, Christ Church, around 1 December 1927). Of these two couplets, only the fourth survived his subsequent revisions to appear in section (h) of the first poem in *P(28)*; see notes to 'Winter Afternoon' and the long poem in parts beginning 'The sprinkler on the lawn'.

Ll. 11–12 refer to William Rowan Hamilton (1805–65), the Irish mathematician who invented quaternions, an extension of Cartesian geometry. However, the tensor $G\mu\nu$ is familiar not from Hamilton's quaternions but from Einstein's theory of general relativity, where it describes the notion that space is curved and that objects do not move in straight lines. Hamilton would not have understood relativity. Although until 1916 quaternions might have been thought to be the building blocks of the physical universe, the language of quaternions was not sufficient for relativity. It is not clear why Auden used Hamilton and not Einstein in the poem, because in the mid-1920s Einstein was at the height of his spectacular public position. It may be a deliberate piece of nonsense playing on a theme, hinted at by the title, of outmoded systems of thought; otherwise Auden may have wrongly understood Hamilton to have pre-empted Einstein in his understanding of the tensor $G\mu\nu$. Nevertheless, it is true that in a general sense,

Hamilton's quaternions foreshadowed the four-dimensional world (three dimensions of space, one of time) which Einstein's general relativity revealed. See C. Lanczos, 'William Rowan Hamilton—An Appreciation', *American Scientist* 55, no. 2 (1967): 128–43.
  For l. 14, see Luke 4.23.

Before

Unkempt and furtive the wind crawls
Round houses stupid in the rain;
The drops unwinding down the glass inspect
Clouds spawning in a nasty sky.

The Spring saw snowdrops
Brown paper smoked behind the bushes
A frozen buzzard
Flipped down the weir and carried out to sea,
Before the trees threw shadows down in challenge
To snoring midges;   10
Before the Autumn came
To focus stars more sharply in the sky
Bringing your bare body
A clenched fist cuffed with darkness

We have passed face to face
And have not known each other.
Passing the other way we could not speak
As midnight whispered to a pillow

Unatrophied have borne
The bruise of words   20
The footsteps on the glass above us
Evening sermons and the eyes of boys
The shadows of returning girls

The stone falls down
The stem grows up
To answer Pilate's question
And flesh
Says 'yes' to contact

□

Passing the other side we hear
The unconcluded cry   30
The snap of leaves.
No wasp shall writhe inside the core
No drowned hair crease the pond again

[*Winter 1926–27*]

P(B), ink autograph on ['Shell Brand']; CI (1), ink autograph on letterhead of the
Classical Association, c/o the Triangle Offices, 1 South Molton Street, London W1;
CI(2), ink autograph on Lordswood Road letterhead. Variants: 1. Unkempt and furtive
the wind] With furtive innuendos Winter *CI(1)*, *CI(2)*. 7–10. buzzard / Flipped . . . weir
and . . . out to sea, / Before . . . down in challenge / To] buzzard, flipped . . . weir / And
. . . out / To sea. / Before . . . down / In challenge to *CI(1)*. 15–23. not in *CI(2)*. 16–17.
other. / Passing . . . could not] other. / Under the shadow of gasometers / Passing . . .
cannot *CI(1)*. 18. whispered] whispers *CI(1)*. 19. Unatrophied have] We have not lost
/ Our morale. We have *CI(1)*. 21. above us] above *CI(1)*. 22–23. Evening sermons and
the eyes of boys / The shadows of returning girls] {The shadows of returning girls / or
Known evening sermons and the eyes of boys} which do you prefer? *CI(1)* (Auden was
asking Isherwood to choose between these lines, but in the end he included both).
24–28. The . . . down / The . . . up / To answer Pilate's question / And flesh / Says] The
. . . down, the . . . up to answer / Pilate's question and flesh says; *CI(2)*. 29–31. Passing
the other side we hear / The unconcluded cry / The snap of leaves.] Till Death has
scribbled on the sun, and graves / Close over it with a contemptuous snap *CI(2)*.
Auden added glosses in brackets beside the last two lines of CI(1): indicating the
penultimate line with an arrow, he wrote 'no more life'; indicating the last line, 'No
resurrection'. This suggests that the line looks forward to the conclusion of his 1929
poem beginning 'It was Easter as I walked in the public gardens', where the line also
connects drowning with the failure of resurrection, 'The lolling bridegroom, beautiful
there' (*EA*, 40; '1929', *CP*, 49). CI(1) also has Auden's sketch of a clenched fist emerg-
ing from a shirt cuff inside a coat sleeve (cp. ll. 13–14); the fist is labelled 'your body'
and the cuff is labelled 'Darkness'. Both Isherwood copies are accompanied by ink
autograph notes referring to a visit that apparently could not be arranged and, in the
second copy, to the revised version of the poem. Auden may have been in London and
trying to see Isherwood during Christmas vacation 1926–27 or Easter vacation 1927.
The Classical Association letterhead was outdated; it names at the top the 'President for
1924' and was probably available as scrap paper in the London office, or perhaps even
in Auden's father's study at home. Dr Auden was a long-time member of the association.
Some images in this poem are central in Auden's development. In addition to the
image of drowning, the frozen buzzard first appeared in 'Frost', written probably while
Auden was still at Gresham's, and reappeared, loosened by spring's thaw, with ll. 7–12
of 'Before', in part (c) of the first long poem in *P(28)*. These lines, in turn, were incor-
porated into part 3 of the 1929 poem 'It was Easter as I walked in the public gardens'
(*EA*, 39–40; *CP*, 47–48). Auden reused ll. 21 and 23 in poem 12 of *P(28)*, 'The four sat
on in the bare room', where a slight revision makes clear that the 'glass above' is glass
laid in the pavement as above the basement windows of many London houses. Pilate
asked a number of questions; see John 18.33–40. One question, put to the Jews, asking
whether he should release Jesus to them, Auden answered in his 1925 'Sonnet' ('April

is here but when will Easter come?'): 'Not this man but Barabbas.' In 'Before' Auden
refers to 'What is truth?' He used this question again in the 'Commentary' to *Journey to
a War* (1938), 292. The ghost of early Eliot haunts numerous lines in 'Before'.

Encounter

'Nothing will come of nothing'

LEAR

Dark struggles broken westward. Men blink out
With eyes like unwashed jewels at the dawn,
Stale from a night of joy. Rain falls for miles
To dash itself against a stone.—To-day!

Now thoughts begin to piece themselves together
Like window-breaking on a film run backwards,
Between the earth's legs mind throws back the sun,
Grows roots again to watch dusk go, and you.

The bald fells crested with a hopeless sunset
See no two atomies whose paths cross but   10
Who do not stop. Day goes its road to ruin;
It makes no comment on the eyes of men,

It sees that nothing happens. No expectation
Died slowly of exposure on a dial;
No courage gulped, no looks averted from
The ragged ends of overdrawn farewells.

No mutual consciousness whipped pulses up,
Till creeping fingers touched, wrenched limbs together.
So Love was stifled 'twixt a pair of sheets
And thrust out like a bottle turned stone-cold.   20

Heroes have fallen into vats and stewed
And men drunk up their beer unknowing. Birds
Stir orchestras to rhythm. Unsleeved arms lend

Stone precision. None speak to them about it.
Nor shall a sign be given you that once
You made a day less mortal than its fellows.

[*Winter 1926–27*]

CI, ink autograph.

For the epigraph, see *King Lear*, 1.1. Ll. 1–2 of 'Encounter' allude to Cordelia's fare-well to her sisters, 'The jewels of our father, with washed eyes / Cordelia leaves you' (1.1). In a letter to his brother, John, written at the beginning of Christmas vacation in 1926 (ALS, Lordswood Road letterhead), Auden mentions that he has to do all of Shakespeare criticism over the holidays. In mid-February, Auden probably went with Isherwood to see the Oxford University Dramatic Society production of *Lear*. In a letter also from Lordswood Road at the end of Christmas vacation, he mentions that he will be happy to put up Isherwood at the time of the play (ALS). Performances were on 15–19 February 1927.

Like several poems from this period, 'Encounter' is a resting place for lines and images in transit from earlier work to later. A version of the first stanza appears as the last stanza in 'After'; it is not clear which poem was written first. From this first stanza, ll. 1–2, with the allusion to *Lear*, were reused in 'Aware', which later became section (b) of the long first poem in *P(28)*; section (b) subsequently appeared separately in *P(30)*. Part of l. 3, and the surrounding imagery of dawn, reappeared in the final stanza of poem 10 in *P(28)*, 'The mind to body spoke the whole night through'. Ll. 21–22 also appear, slightly altered, in 'After'.

After

After the train meandering through August
Had slowed up shivering in rain-swept November;
(The bleak philosophy of Northern ridges)
When soaked twigs scratched the panes instead of leaves
        They rested.

After the hopeless beauty of the sunset
Upon denuded snow roofs streets away;
After the soiled house with the purple blinds
        They rested.

Heroes have fallen into vats and stewed   10
And men drink up their beer unknowing. Death's
Pale flag is not advancéd here—'Red 'ot

Ole man—no heel-taps gentlemen!—' They sprawled
Inert across the tablecloth, or hung
Head-downwards in their damaged chairs to drain.
Dreams of a face that looked unkindly in,
Abominable contacts in a slype
Or sewer, startled occasional screams
Which bubbled down through undistinguished mutters
To stertorous silences. Wrists dropped again. . . .   20

Dark struggled broken westward. Men blinked out
With eyes like unwashed jewels at the Day,
Stale from a night of joy. A cock in scorn
Upon a sodden dunghill crowed. Rain fell
For miles to dash itself against a stone.

[*Winter 1926–27*]

CI, ink autograph on Lordswood Road letterhead.

Ll. 11–12 slightly misquote *Romeo and Juliet*, 5.3, when Romeo looks on Juliet in the tomb, thinking her dead. A heel-tap (13) is liquor left in the bottom of a glass after drinking. A slype (17) is a covered passage from a cathedral or church transept into the chapter house or deanery.

'After' is a miscellany of lines quarried from earlier work and quarried for later work. A phrase from l. 1 reappears in the poem beginning 'Out of sight assuredly, not out of mind'. L. 3 had been used in 'Lead's the Best' and was later used again in 'Narcissus'. Some lines used here also appear in 'Encounter' (probably written around the same time, though it is uncertain which is the earlier poem), and these were incorporated in several poems in *P(28)* and *P(30)* (see note to 'Encounter'). 'Encounter' and 'After' both may refer to Auden's platonic affair with William McElwee, with whom he travelled to Austria for three weeks during the Christmas vacation of 1926–27.

Day-dreams of a Tourist

Across the Waste to Northward, go
Telegraph-posts through shifting snow,
A corrugated-iron shed
Signs an exhausted road ahead.

Thus eye perpetually restocks
The soul's mnemonic treasure-box.
Preliminary rummage yields
A print of flooded football-fields.

The box exposes its inside,
Becomes a stage. Forms gesture pride   10
For groundlings' mirth: ear notes as well
A tolling disillusioned bell.

Perspective wavers; these become
Mere purple dots, mere pulse's drum:
The stage collapses; splinters throw
Diffraction colours as they go.

The point in focus moves away,
A few strides back, to yesterday,
When eyes agreed to notice you,
And travel was no aim in view.   20

[*Winter? 1926–27*]

P(B), ink autograph on 'Shell Brand'. Published with a photographic reproduction of
the manuscript in W. H. Auden, *Three Unpublished Poems* (New York, 1986).
   The opening lines perhaps echo the opening of Edith Sitwell's 'By the Lake': 'Across
the thick and pastel snow / Two people go'; 'Spleen', *Bucolic Comedies* (London, 1923).
L. 12, which echoes the line 'Tolling reminiscent bells' in section 5 of *The Waste Land*
(l. 384), reappears in the second stanza of the poem beginning 'The mind to body
spoke the whole night through', poem 10 in *P(28)*.

The Evolution of the Dragon

Your shoulder stiffens to my kiss,
A point upon the outside of the world.
Lines on a spherical surface, denizens of Flatland, are
In unperceived Depth, we in Time.

'No pandering with the second best
No looking backward, no cowardice,' said the Preacher.
Eyeballs wrenched backward see
Fells where we lost our way, talking of inns,
Stumbling along the beck to the mine-buildings.
'This is the turbine' said the Manager, and opened a door.   10
We watched
Pipes curving like a dead troll's knotted fingers

Huge cog wheels rolling irresistibly
On burnished axleshafts, while far below
The hiss of water heaved the darkness like
Serpents in Eden or the voice of God.
Back we stepped into the yard to face the birds.
The quiet gave us room to speak. Standing on broken quartz
You were entrusted with a discrete sky.

Rich Argonauts from Colchis row   20
And spin behind a wake of stars;
Medea and Jason walk the deck,
Who gaze at moonlit mountain scars.

Such, dead, in camp-fire tales become
Receivers of heroic souls,
Send rain upon the earth, direct
The Equinox, the nodding poles

But terror tufts the chest with hair,
Contracts the forehead, draws the stride;
Shaking a beam, a giant stalks   30
Tall-shadowed on the mountain side.

Metempsychosis has no end;
Toe-nails uncut soon turn to claws,
Sebaceous belly drags in dust,
Scales glitter now above the paws,

Creased armpits leather, sprouting vanes;
From marshes in the Land of Spleen,
Flattened on gold, a dragon roars
All night for daughters of the queen.

The final cadence ended, clapping soon lost heart.   40
After the week-end the two friends parted,
Spilt hot tea in their saucers in the third-class waiting room,
Scraping back chairs for the wrong train.
When we face life only
From undusted mantelpieces, it may be so and so:
Avoiding puddles on the cinderpath,

Or tapping railings in the winter garden, sleeves may brush.
'Dis! Qu'as-tu fait, toi que voilà?' Once upon a time
What happened, did happen.

[*Winter? 1926–27*]

P(B), ink autograph on [?'Shell Brand']. Variants: 20. row *this edn*] row. *P(B)*. Published
with a photographic reproduction of the manuscript in W. H. Auden, *Three Unpublished
Poems* (New York, 1986).

The title is taken from G. Elliot Smith's *The Evolution of the Dragon* (Manchester and
London, 1919), in which Smith presents the thesis that the dragon is a personification
of the life-giving and life-destroying powers of water. He traces the evolution of dragon
mythology throughout the history of civilization, comparing its development with the
building up of a dream story, though the dragon myth is 'vastly more complex than any
dream, because mankind as a whole has taken a hand in the process of shaping it' (77).

L. 10 recalls Auden's earlier poem 'The Engine House', in which he describes being
shown a large turbine, and which has the similar line 'He opened a small wooden door'.
Ll. 12–16 are taken from another, early poem, 'Dethroned' (ll. 17–21), and the figure
of the manager and the imagery of machinery and moving water look back to 'The
Engine House'. Auden described a similar setting in stanza 3 of the 1927 poem begin-
ning 'I chose this lean country', published in *P(28)*, and a passage in the last will and
testament of his lost 1930 play *The Fronny* suggests that the images derive from an expe-
rience which was a persistent subject of his dreams:

> Item, to Cushy, the unshaven Scot
> Who showed us the engine at Hackwood Pit
> The cranks of which still menace me in dreams
> A weekly pint at the Miner's Arms. . . . (*Plays*, 479)

Some of the images appeared again in ll. 330ff. of the epic beginning 'In the year of my
youth when yoyos came in', where in l. 336 Auden called the turbines 'dragons of metal'
(see note to 'The Engine House'). Auden apparently had the material in mind again
when he wrote Quant's first speech in *The Age of Anxiety* (*CP*, 466).

Metempsychosis (32) is Pythagoras's doctrine of the transmigration of souls, which
influenced Plato, among others; Auden referred to Plato in 'Cinders' and he mentioned
Pythagoras in a draft of the poem beginning 'Out of sight assuredly, not out of mind'. He
apparently studied these philosophers during the brief interlude in which he thought of
changing his course to Philosophy, Politics, and Economics. Ll. 41–43 were revised and
combined with material from 'The Happy Tree' for poem 12, beginning 'The four sat
on in the bare room', in *P(28)*, and l. 43 was reused again as ll. 16–17 in the 1930 poem
beginning 'Between attention and attention' (*EA*, 53; titled 'Easy Knowledge' in *CP*, 37).

L. 49 is borrowed from Verlaine's *Sagesse* (1881), and reemphasizes the theme of
anxious guilt underlying 'The Evolution of the Dragon':

> —Qu'as-tu fait, ô toi que voilà
>   Pleurant sans cesse,
>   Dis, qu'as-tu fait, toi que voilà,
>   De ta Jeunesse? (Part 6, ll. 13–16)

This may be roughly translated as 'What are you doing, oh you there crying unceasingly,
say, what are you doing, you there with your youth?'

Pride

When Little Claus meets Big Claus in the road
The shadow dwarfs him, and he sidles by;
Then, recollecting later, thinks—'Of course!
For he was further from the light than I'.

Alone on mountains, in the Underground,
He folds his arms, is set apart, secure;
Watching the animals at play, he feels
Aesthetic pleasure, sublimated, pure.

At restaurants, disarmed by violins,
Sometimes the soul is jostled, and he stares;   10
Lowers the glances to the saucer, but
Through finger-chinks the sentiment declares.

Artistic temperament revolts, divines
A Circe. He congratulates himself;
Indulges in approved embraces now,
His own physician to his mental health.

'—So Absalom was lifted from his horse,
Swung by his dead hair from the swaying bough,
While David wept—' speech slept in Babylon,
But handcuffs clanked 'What price pricked bladders now?'   20

[*Winter? 1926–27*]

P(B), ink autograph on 'Shell Brand'. Published in *The Yale Review* 71, no. 1 (Winter 1982): 172.
    This poem combines nursery, biblical, and mythological sources in the style of Edith Sitwell. Little Claus and Big Claus are characters from the tale by Hans Christian Andersen. Auden had known Andersen's stories since childhood (see Carpenter, 9). (Wilfred Owen's blank verse rendering of 'Little Claus and Big Claus' was not published until 1931.) For ll. 17–19, see 1 Samuel 18.9–15 and 32–33, although Auden may have had another, later source.

Quique Amavit

'Amo!' Four walls constrict great purposes
To vex themselves, Halve the halved moment, keen
To rap out 'Hold!' (The tune congeals) display
Amo not yet complete Amavit, fresh
Amo condensing out of silence. Tune
On unstopped ears bursts frantically again;
Horizon marches, Future is coming You,
Your cheek's arisen overwhelming arc,
And You a nailbreadth or a pulsebeat hence

You here? Which you? As lids unclose, the You   10
Crushing a cigarette-end in a saucer,
You in a kitchen, drinking, wet with snow,
Confound the present You. Past is not yours:
Alone I found the sheep skull in the grass,
Alone, amazed by death, life passes like
The flashing train, thaws Time to evening thoughts————
I said 'Good-night!' and hid them. This and This,
Once alien, are acquainted, lacking You.

Good-night, good-night! Desire has lost its way,
Aimless for faces rather there than here,   20
And vows are episodes; what is, is I.
As listless as a child, playing alone
On darkened afternoons, I hear the wind
Driven across the ignorant sea, the ground,
To hurt itself on panes, on bark of elm,
Where sap unbaffled rises, being Spring.
'Quique amavit cras amet'—So thoughts
Draw circles round a name, worshipping air,
Divine the world's end round the corner, breast
The hill 'θάλασσα' ready on the tongue,   30
Snap at the dragon's tail, astonished yelp.

[*March? 1927*]

P(B), TS on 'WHS Voucher Bond' with ink autograph corrections; M, ink autograph on Christ Church letterhead, signed 'Wystan Auden'. Variants: 1–2. constrict great purposes / To vex themselves] constrict the enlarging soul / Which muttered name on name, worshipping air, / To vex itself *M.* 3. congeals) display] congeals) exhibit *M.* 5–7. of silence. Tune / On unstopped ears bursts frantically again; / Horizon marches] of time—On ears / Unstopped the tune bursts suddenly again: / Limit marches *M.* 9. pulsebeat] heartbeat *M.* 14–15. Alone I found the . . . grass, / Alone] Finding the . . . grass, I stood / Alone *M.* 19–22. Good-night, good-night! Desire has lost its way, / Aimless for faces . . . / And . . . / As listless] You go. Desire is lost, aimless for faces; / As listless *M.* 23–25. I hear the wind / Driven across the ignorant sea, the ground, / To hurt . . . elm,] I watch the flies / Doomed, sluggish on the ceiling, hear the wind /Driven across the ignorant sea, the earth / To . . . elms, *M.* 27–29. thoughts / Draw circles round a name, worshipping air, / Divine the . . . breast] thought / Foresees the . . . breasts *M.* 30. on the tongue] on its tongue *M.* 31. Snap . . . yelp] Snaps . . . yelps *M.*

Across a corner of M Auden wrote 'To the onlie begetter Mr W.L.', a slightly disguised dedication to William McElwee (his first two initials were W. L.), which points up the poem's debt to Shakespeare's *Sonnets.* Auden was immersed in Shakespeare that winter (see note to 'Encounter'), and evidently equated his unrequited love for McElwee with Shakespeare's presumed love for the young man of the *Sonnets.* He quoted sonnet 121 in a later letter to McElwee, probably written in September 1927 (ALS, Dalbuich, Carrbridge, Aviemore, Inverness), and about nine years after that he borrowed the same lines from Shakespeare's sonnet 121 in part 4 of 'Letter to Lord Byron': 'No, I am that I am, and those that level / At my abuses reckon up their own. / I may be straight though they, themselves, are bevel' (*EA*, 190; the lines were later dropped).

The poem's title and the related lines are based on the refrain of the anonymous late Latin poem *Pervigilium Veneris,* which is set during the evening or vigil before the festival of Venus and looks forward to the coming of love the next day. The poem is included as the third section of *Catullus Tibullus and Pervigilium Veneris,* the 1925 Loeb edition that Auden owned all his life (now at HRHRC; see notes to 'Truly our fathers had the gout' and 'Easter Monday'). In the Loeb edition the title is translated as 'The Eve of St Venus' and the opening line, which serves as the refrain, 'Cras amet qui nunquam amavit quique amavit cras amet,' is translated as 'To-morrow shall be love for the loveless, and for the lover to-morrow shall be love' (348–49). In the closing lines of *The Waste Land* Eliot alludes to the final stanza of *Pervigilium Veneris,* but Auden uses the poem differently than Eliot does. Although he touches like Eliot on the theme of spring—and some of his other poems, for instance 'Easter Monday', also make clear he was interested in the rituals associated with Venus and in myths of death and rebirth—his wordplay is cerebral and Shakespearean.

Auden reused ll. 20 and 23–26 in the second stanza of his 1927 poem beginning 'Who stands, the crux left of the watershed,' was which included in *P(28)* and reprinted thereafter. He also revised the closing lines of 'Quique Amavit' for the last stanza of the poem beginning 'The crowing of the cock', written in September 1927, which was included in *P(28)* and again, slightly altered, in *P(30).* The Greek in the penultimate line, 'Thalassa', means 'the sea' and alludes to Xenophon's account of how his soldiers, on their return from Persia, reached the summit of the mountains and, catching sight at last of the sea, cried out 'Thalassa Thalassa' (*Anabasis,* 4.7) Auden glossed these closing lines in a 1932 letter to Naomi Mitchison; see note to 'The crowing of the cock' for his reference to *Anabasis* and for his letter to Naomi Mitchison.

Easter Monday

Spring, a toy trumpet to her lips
Unsettles sleeping partnerships;
Eyes, meeting of a sudden, raise
Associations with the phrase.

Tits sharpening their saws, behold
Umbrellas creeping on the mould
Through crocuses; Now one or two
Crawl out into the avenue,

Down which inexorable groove
In singular possession move.   10
The Lady Venus in her carriage
Stiffly ignores a canine marriage

Jeunesse dorée with his mama
Trips nervous; the κινημα-star,
Fluttering down implores the nod,
The stone smile of a garden god.

On green canals the barges pass
The tow-rope swishing through the grass,
The ripple jangling ere it dies,
The wet inverted factories.   20

The sunset on the flooded streets
Lends majesty to paper fleets;
Behind the wall an engine stutters,
The navies flounder in the gutters

The trippers rattling homeward shout
Their holiday-excursion out;
Although across the parting stile
The lovers fidget for a while;

Rooks cawing to a naked nest
By farms in the sharp-featured west,   30

The frightened scurry of a leaf,
Make syntax in an echoed grief.

Though 'neath our witticisms drone
The vulgar platitudes of bone,
And thunder-riven branches bring
Tidings of the eunuch king

[*April 1927*]

P(B), ink autograph on unwatermarked small grey letter paper matching Pudney copy
of 'Narcissus'; CI, ink autograph on Lordswood Road letterhead with additional non-
matching sheets attached; M, ink autograph on Lordswood Road letterhead. Probably
written just after Easter, 17 April 1927. Variants: 1. to] at *CI, M.* Stanzas 2 and 3 are not
in *M.* 13–14. Jeunesse . . . with . . . / Trips nervous] The jeunesse . . . walks with . . .
/Embarrassed *M.* Stanzas 5 and 6 appear in reverse order in *M.* 19. jangling] jostling
M. 36. king] king* *CI, M*; on both copies the note indicated by this asterisk says 'Attis'.
At the top of M Auden wrote 'I am afraid this poem did not turn out as conventional as
I thought[. T]his is the first draught.' Published in *Oxford Poetry Now* 2 (Michaelmas
1976): 2–3.
    Ll. 1–2 were condensed into the first line of the 1928 poem beginning 'The Spring
unsettles sleeping partnerships', which Auden later included in *Paid on Both Sides.* L. 4
quotes almost exactly from a prose description of spring that Auden had written in a
letter to McElwee, probably in late March 1927 around the start of the Easter vacation:
'Tits sharpen their saws, the spider spins across the broken eggshell in the dustbin, the
crocuses are breaking their necks, for spring does not forget even the gardens of the
middle class' (ALS, Lordswood Road letterhead, British Library, Add.MS.59618). He
wrote virtually the same passage in a letter to Isherwood (ALS, Lordswood Road letter-
head) around the same time, but without the first phrase that he used in 'Easter Monday',
and he later drew on these matching passages for two lines in 'Narcissus'. The crocuses
on the mould in stanza 2 and the rooks in stanza 8 appear in several earlier spring poems;
see the quatrains beginning 'The crocus stars the border', 'Song' (also beginning 'The
crocus stars the border'), and 'Chloe to Daphnis in Hyde Park'. The last of these is also
an Easter poem which shares other similarities with 'Easter Monday'. Stanza 5 reworks
several lines from 'The Canal (Froghall)'. The trippers in stanza 7 first appeared in an
earlier individual quatrain entitled 'Trippers' and then in 'Bank Holiday'.
    The tone and characterization in 'Easter Monday' recall Edith Sitwell's *Façade*
(1922), especially 'The Doll' (in the section titled 'Winter'), from which Auden echoes
lines and phrases such as 'Madame A . . . the élégante, / With Madame X . . . the ele-
phant, / / Walked down the lengthy avenue' (9–11), and 'The angels and myself be-
tween us / We break their doll the Lady Venus' (21–22). The influence of T. S. Eliot
also emerges in 'Easter Monday', especially in the poem's final stanza, but by eliminat-
ing the note 'Attis' as a gloss for 'the eunuch king' Auden made this debt somewhat less
obvious. Dropping the note also partially concealed his borrowings from James Frazer's
The Golden Bough; see 3rd edn, part 4 (London, 1914), vol. I, book 2, chap. 1. According
to Frazer, Attis is the Phrygian god of vegetation whose death and resurrection were
mourned and rejoiced at an annual spring festival. Some accounts say he was killed by
a boar, like the Syrian vegetation god Adonis; others say he castrated himself and bled
to death underneath a pine tree. Afterwards he was turned into a pine tree. His priests

also castrated themselves when they entered into the service of the fertility goddess who loved him, Cybele. The 'toy trumpet' in the poem (1) perhaps alludes to the 'blowing of trumpets' (268), which was the chief ceremony of the second day of the festival of Cybele and Attis as it was practised in Rome. Frazer notes that because Astarte, the divine lover of Adonis, was identified with the planet Venus, the festival of Adonis in Syria 'was regularly timed to coincide with the appearance of Venus as the Morning or Evening Star' (258–59). Auden satirizes his Venus as a prudish lady of fashion (11), not unlike Pound's 'Lady Valentine' in *Hugh Selwyn Mauberly*, part 12. The Greek in the poem (14) is 'kinēma', to make 'cinema-star', but it is not clear from the syntax whether Auden's Lady Venus *is* the cinema-star or somehow associated with her. Auden might have come across the Greek word in Pound's phrase 'prose kinema' in *Mauberly*, part 2, l. 11. The phrase 'fluttering down' (15) refers to Frazer's account of how at one temple of Astarte in Syria, a meteor, Aphaca, fell like a star from the top of Mount Lebanon into the river Adonis, signalling the start of the rites; the meteor was thought to be Astarte herself falling into the arms of her lover. The 'stone smile' implored in the poem (16) probably alludes to the stone images of the gods worshipped in the festivals and the phrase 'garden god' in the same line refers to the presumed power of these gods over vegetation. Frazer takes some pains to draw parallels between these spring festivals and the commemoration of the death and resurrection of Christ at Easter, and even suggests that it was the Morning Star, associated with Venus, which guided the three wise men to Bethlehem for the birth of Christ (259). Auden clearly wished to amplify this comparison in his poem. Auden also knew the story of Attis from Catullus, poem 68, which begins 'Super alta vectus Attis celeri rate maria' ('Borne in his swift bark over deep seas, Attis'). The poem abruptly describes Attis's maddened self-castration and subsequently dwells at length on his desperate regret and the fury of Cybele. Several letters to Isherwood mention Auden's enthusiasm for Catullus during the spring of 1927, and in his own copy of *Catullus Tibullus and Pervigilium Veneris*, Auden made scansion marks across the bottom of the page, 91, on which the English translation of the Attis poem begins. See the Loeb edition (London and New York, 1925), 90–91. Auden's copy is now in HRHRC; see also note to 'Truly our fathers had the gout'.

Narcissus

'Volentes enim gaudere forinsecus facile vanescunt, et
effunduntur in ea, quae videntur et temporalia sunt,
et imagines eorum famelica cogitatione lambiunt.'

S. AUGUSTINE'S *CONFESSIONS* IX.4.

I shall sit here through the evening,
Hour when the fisherman at the inn
Stares at the window, his boots off, waiting for the lamp;
When frogs protrude their muzzles from the pond,
Exhale in the dusk.
The pond was large till reeds invaded it,
Deep under the bank where the may falls,

Where I shall sit, continue sitting,
Hear the mud squeaking in the reeds, frighten the otter
Wrinkling the taut-stretched surface with its snout,   10
Dull at the end of a diminished world. . . . .

It was you or I, Narcissus
Who laced his boots up on the stairs,
Who cracked the wind on an embittered cliff, beheld
The bleak philosophy of Northern ridges,
Heard, flushed by April rain
A linnet piping in a sunken lane.
But where are Basley who won the Ten,
Dicken so tarted by the House,
Thomas who kept a sparrow-hawk?   20
Day led down peeling corridors, and drew aside
A wretched arras
Where in corroded mirrors dismantled princes
Haggle for kingdoms.
The words we stuck together on the nursery floor
Broke in our jammy fingers. We rose as the clock struck,
Our tongues ashamed, deceived by a shake of the hand. . . .

Let the dry leaf fall, the spider spin
On egg-shells in the rubbish-bin,
Leave me alone   30
With you, my sterilised left-handed lover.
I know you now, see well what you are doing.
Bend, asymptotic to our unity.
We meet at last, this film between us,
Between the perception and the noun,
The desire, and the assurance, I and AM.

                    Distant sawing
Rumours an old touch. I touch the pool,
Engine of your becoming—Distortion? Grief? Disgust?
Your calmed lips murmur my prevented question,   40
The stone gleams white again behind the eyes.

                    [*Late April or May 1927*]

CI, TS, with ink autograph revisions on 'Croxley Extra Strong'; P(B), ink autograph on small grey letter paper matching 'Easter Monday'. Probably written not long after Easter (which fell on 17 April in 1927), and certainly before the end of May. Auden mentioned the poem to McElwee in a letter apparently written on Good Friday 1927 (ALS, Wildboar Clough, Derbyshire, dated 'Jesus died today'). He sent the typescript to Isherwood enclosed in a letter along with 'Aware', 'Bach and the Lady', and 'Extract' (entitled 'The Seekers' on the Isherwood copy) sometime after the beginning of term, 1 May, and then mentioned the poem in another letter about 7 June (2 ALS on 'Shell Brand'). There are no substantive variants between the two copies of the poem, only incidental and typographical differences; in fact, both copies show similar revisions, apparently made after they were completed. Possibly Auden made fair copies for a typist of this and the three other poems that he sent Isherwood with it; then probably once the typescript was ready he sent the fair copies to Pudney and the corrected typescripts to Isherwood. The poem was published in *Oxford Poetry* 1, no. 3 (Spring 1984): 87–89, where it was wrongly dated July.

An earlier poem, 'Tea-time in November', also mentions the figure of Narcissus. For the epigraph, the Loeb edition of St Augustine's *Confessions* gives the 1631 translation of William Watt: 'seeing they that take joy in anything without themselves, do easily become vain, and spill themselves upon those things which are seen and are but temporal; yea, and with their hunger-starved thoughts lick their very shadows' (London, 1912), 2:20–21. The passage describes the way in which St Augustine's just anger with his former self led to his determination not to sin in the future, but it is difficult to interpret in the context in which Auden quotes it, since the passage seems to justify narcissism as a way of preserving the self from being wasted on outward, temporal things. In his letter to McElwee mentioning that he was working on the poem, Auden quoted another passage from St Augustine that further underlined how hard he was struggling to achieve, or perhaps maintain, asceticism, and he emphasized his hope for spiritual regeneration through physical purity: 'iam liber erat animus meus a curis mordacibus ambiendi et adquirendi et volutandi atque scalpendi scabiem libidinum'; Loeb translation: 'Now became my soul free from those biting cares of aspiring, and getting, and weltering in filth, and scratching off that itch of lust' (*Confessions* 9.1, pp. 4–5). 'Narcissus' seems to have grown out of a fit of depression which Auden described in his Good Friday letter to McElwee, where he made a clear link between the poem and what he called his melancholia: 'I am just recovering from a week of abject depression which culminated in my getting flu[.] I staggered up here more dead than alive but have now flapped to the surface, disturbing the green squirt of melancholia. Narcissus gathers but so slowly, but I feel now that it will come to a head in the end.' Perhaps Auden was already familiar with the psychological relation traced in Freud's work between melancholia and narcissism; he was to explore this more thoroughly in *The Orators*.

The setting of pond and mill are based on a favourite haunt near Gresham's which Auden described in his 1925 poem 'The Mill (Hempstead)'; ll. 6 and 9–10 and also the image of the pool as a mirror are borrowed from the earlier poem. L. 15 had been used previously in 'Lead's the Best' and in 'After'. Ll. 16–17 are quarried from 'The Sunken Lane'. As Nicholas Jenkins has pointed out in a note to the poem in *Oxford Poetry*, 'The Ten was a cross-country race at Sedbergh, Gabriel Carritt's old school'. Auden went round the course with his Oxford friend Carritt and another boy, named Wallace, when he visited the school in December 1927, but he had been told about the race before this, probably by McElwee. Christ Church is known as 'the House' (19), but probably Auden was referring to one of the houses that he or his friends lived in at public school or prep school. 'Basley' (18), 'Dicken' (19; Auden elsewhere wrote 'Dickon'), and 'Thomas' (20) are unidentified, and Gabriel Carritt has the impression that Auden made up these names for boys at Sedbergh whom he had heard about through, presumably, William or Patrick McElwee. In the novel he was working on at the time, Isherwood used the name 'Basley' for the object of a schoolboy crush recalled by one of his characters, Victor Page; see *All the Conspirators* (London, 1928), 117. Ll. 23–26 once again draw on the nursery idiom of Edith Sitwell. Ll. 28–29 are taken nearly verbatim from the prose description of spring which Auden had written in letters to McElwee and to Isherwood (from the McElwee letter he had also taken a few other lines for 'Easter Monday'; see note to 'Easter Monday' where the passage is quoted, p. 184). The third stanza recalls Eliot's 'The Hollow Men', both in atmosphere and in the phrasing of the first and the last three lines. The auto-erotic theme of 'Narcissus' confirms that the remembered 'old touch' (38) is the poet's own. In his 7 June letter to Isherwood, Auden included a sketch which serves as a gloss to the poem and which bawdily emphasizes the theme of schoolboy masturbation. It shows the pond with the bush of May, ducks, mill and mill-wheel, and the pine woods with music emanating from the hidden sawmill. Everything in the sketch is labelled. Narcissus sits beside the pond and a bubble connected to his head says, 'the touch of memory / the copulatory movement / splendid obscurity'.

Although Auden eventually discarded 'Narcissus', he resurrected a version of ll. 4–5 for the second line of the 1929 poem 'It was Easter as I walked in the public gardens' (*EA*, 37; *CP*, 45), and he used a substantial part of stanza 2 in 'The spring will come,' printed as poem 17 in *P(28)* and later as part of *Paid on Both Sides* (*EA*, 414–15 and 15; *Plays*, 11 and 31).

Hodge Looks toward London

Black sticks poke out of the back-garden
To hold patched linen to the light; torn wire-netting
Waits for grimed arms to prick. What? Shall I do it now,
Or run indoors
To read my letter, splash through flooded fields
Crippling unreal fences,
Hasten, eager for the turn in the valley
To pant with greasy Jane?
A smoke-ring begs the question, dangles a loop
To haul me skyward.   10

William lived at Wellington,
    (None stronger, faster, were than he)
Darned his socks, and kissed his wench,
    So William ran away to sea

Under Southern stars he sailed;
    His wrists were cable-chafed, his hairs

Icicles; he reached a land
  Of Unicorns and millionaires;

Passed the Withered Tree, and crossed
  The Desert of the Overwise,   20
Who in mushroom-shadow sit,
  And rub the sand into their eyes;

Famished, thirsty, came upon
  The Palace of the Open Doors;
Clutching bricks behind him, he
  Repulsed a regiment of whores.

For a year and for a day
  He stretched himself on Glasscock Hill,
Found the waterchute and slid
  Down fathoms to the Giant's Mill.   30

How he blew the castle horn
  All the stories written tell
Fought the ogre, threw his head
  To the bottom of his well;

How he found a maiden there
  Awakened her and held her fast,
Led her by the hand, but then
  Just grazed the lintel as they passed,

So he lost her, wandered by
  A lonely penitential year,   40
Found her playing by a pool,
  Embraced her then, and lay with her.

So to London in the end
  Came William and a slender bride.
'Way, make way for the Lord Mayor!
  Hurrah for Willy,' London cried.

London. Gold. There's cash in Town
Gives life a spaniel sleekness

Rung on zinc will buy elixirs,
To sway the structure of the world, or fluttered   50
Will conjure ten lascivious Helens. I'll go,
Do it, do what I'll do.
When dynamos and boilers lie
In tickling silence,
I'll burn a midnight oil, writing my name in books,
Being better,
Or with strange algebras, (let AB differ from BA)
Axioms applicable to a cheek-surface,
Unriddle Woman.
So working out my days, conclude   60
In peace with honour—wheeled into the garden,
Like a bird on a wet road watching
Children (catch me! catch me! I've won)
Or under an abject willow
To rumour greatness, ideal moments. . . .
                      Champagne at the lip, sniffing mortality
Whispers from the bed
Interrupted the beating heart. . . . . .
                      The Clock
Clangs like a rusty gate to scourge on Time   70
To sponge away this people, lead
Hermits to mildewed dormitories: the wind
Snuffles and shuffles on a lost battlefield.
Broken jam pots, abandoned canisters.

                                                [*May 1927*]

P(B), ink autograph on 'Shell Brand'; CI, TS with ink autograph revisions. P(B) appears to be a fair copy of CI. Variants: TITLE toward] towards *CI*. 3–4. prick. What? Shall . . . now, / Or] pick. What / Shall . . . now? Or *CI*. 12. faster, were than] faster, than *CI*. 36. held] caught *CI*. 37. but] and *CI*. 45. way, make] way! A make *CI*. 49. zinc] bars *CI*. 50. of the world] of a world *CI*. 68–69. heart. . . . . . / The] heart. . . . . . The *CI*.

This poem is mentioned in three letters written to Isherwood in the summer of 1927. In the earliest, the letter listing work as written before and after the 1926 visit to Freshwater Bay (see note to 'Early Morning' beginning 'Perched on a nettled stump he stands'), Auden defended the poem: 'I shall be unyielding about Hodge; I resent the imputation of Edith Sitwell there, because I believe it to be untrue. If anyone R. Graves in the middle section, Tourneur + Eliot in the others.' The next letter shows that he has begun to relent: 'Hodge and London is more the effect of too many Elizabethan plays than Edith Sitwell I think, about whom I think I have come to agree with you' (ALS on 'Shell Brand', about 7 June; see note to 'Narcissus'). Finally, at the beginning of July he wrote 'Hodge is scrapped' (ALS, Lordswood Road letterhead, [between 30 June and 13 July 1927]).

Auden had previously used Hodge in 'Lead's the Best'. Part of ll. 4–5 reappeared in ll. 4–5 of 'On the frontier at dawn, getting down', poem 5 in *P(28)*. He probably took the name Glasscock (28) from William Francis Glasscock, a Christ Church Exhibitioner in Natural Science who was two years ahead of him. The Giant's Mill (30) and the slaying of the ogre (33–34) hark back to the tale of Jack the Giant-Killer referred to in 'Lead's the Best'. The blowing of the castle horn (31) alludes to Childe Roland blowing the slug horn when he arrives at the Dark Tower in Browning's poem; probably Auden linked it with the theme of the giant because in Edgar's mad song in *King Lear*—which inspired Browning's poem—Childe Roland's words are the traditional ones of the giant: 'Fie, foh, and fum, / I smell the blood of a British Man' (3.4). Auden had previously alluded to the story of Childe Roland in 'Cinders' and he was to do so again in the poem beginning 'The mind to body spoke the whole night through', published in *P(28)*. The conjuring of Helen in l. 51 is borrowed from Marlowe's *Doctor Faustus*, where Mephistopheles conjures up Helen of Troy (5.2). Ll. 53–54 are recycled from 'Dethroned' and were to be used again in the poem beginning 'I chose this lean country', poem 2 in *P(28)*. Auden also used l. 64 in the last part of the poem beginning 'I chose this lean country' and then again, nearly a decade later, in the song for Benjamin Britten beginning 'Underneath the abject willow' written March 1936 (*EA*, 160; revised as 'Underneath an abject willow', *CP*, 140). L. 71 had been used in 'Bank Holiday', and ll. 72–73 reappeared in the poem beginning 'I chose this lean country'.

Aware

'Happiness makes us base'

MARSTON. *SOPHONISBA.*

Bones wrenched, weak whimper, lids wrinkled, first dazzle known,
World-wonder hardens as bigness, years; brings knowledge, you.
Rank presence-smell a rich mould augurs for roots urged,
Eased by mucous tenderness, to absorb the Word
Which was before began; flesh-dough suffills to spilling
Concave of spirit—so you here I have: but gone,
The soul is tetanous; gun-barrel burnishing
In summer grass, mind lies to tarnish, untouched, undoing,
Though body stir, hand hold a spade, leg lever ground,
Sweat trickle down to loin; these, squat as idols, brood   10
Infuriate the fire with bellows, blank till sleep
And two-faced dream—'I want' voiced treble as once

Crudely through flowers till dunghill cock-crow, crack at East.
Eyes, unwashed jewels, the glass-floor slipping, feel, know Day,
Life, stripped to girders, monochrome. Deceit of instinct,
Figure, feature, form, irrelevant, dismissed,
Ought passes through points fair plotted; and you conform,
Seen yes or no. Before which argument my buts are impudent.

[*May 1927*]

CI, TS on 'Croxley Extra Strong' with ink autograph corrections; P(B), ink autograph
on 'Shell Brand'. The changes to CI are to correct mistyped words that are difficult to
read in P(B), rather than slips of the finger. They make clear that this poem—along
with the others enclosed in the same letter to Isherwood, 'Narcissus', 'Bach and the
Lady', and 'Extract' (entitled 'The Seekers' on Isherwood's copy)—was prepared from
the Pudney fair copy by a typist (see note to 'Narcissus').

This Hopkinsian poem is the earliest piece by Auden to survive virtually intact in his
mature published work. He revised it for *P(28)* (the revised version is printed separately
in this edition as section (b) of the long first poem beginning 'The sprinkler on the
lawn'), and it was reprinted separately in *P(30)*. The epigraph from William Marston's
The Wonder of Women; or, Sophonisba (1606), 5.3.92, occurs in the play's climactic scene
when Sophonisba, preferring to preserve her husband's honour than to consummate
their marriage, prepares to commit suicide. 'Suffills' (5) is Auden's neologism, which
apparently means fills up with air or wind like dough rising or, by analogy with the
French, like a soufflé. 'Tetanous' (7), also a new word, is a made-up adjectival form of
'tetanus', usually 'tetanic' or 'tetanoid'. Here the sense seems to be that when the lover
departs, the poet's soul is wounded and poisoned, and becomes spasmodic or rigid—as
with the disease, tetanus or lockjaw—ceasing to grow according to the prevailing meta-
phor of the poem's opening lines. Ll. 13–14, with their allusion to *King Lear*, had al-
ready been used in 'Encounter' and 'After'.

Bach and the Lady

Do not sneer, stranger, if one by one,
The crowd who followed her are gone
To strangle their own shadows, or lie
Bitterly with a harlot. I
Have heard in a Bach fugue some phrase,
Perplexed with flowers and sunlight, wake
The green-leaved morning to her praise;
More generous, pitiful than we
However casual may be
The comment that her shoulders make.   10

[*May 1927*]

CI, TS on 'Croxley Extra Strong' with ink autograph revisions.

'Bach and the Lady' was enclosed in the same letter to Isherwood with 'Narcissus', 'Aware', and 'Extract' (entitled 'The Seekers' on Isherwood's copy); in a later letter Auden said the poem was 'the effect of too much whiskey' (ALS, 7 June 1927; for both letters, see note to 'Narcissus'). In another letter, the one in which he listed work to be preserved from before and after his 1926 visit to Freshwater Bay, he said 'Bach and the Lady' was scrapped; see note to 'Early Morning' ('Perched on a nettled stump he stands'). The last two lines of the poem served as the conclusion to the 1926 poem 'The Letter' ('He reads and finds the meaning plain').

Extract

(For J.B.A.)

Consider, if you will, how lovers lie
In brief adherence, straining to preserve
The glabrous suction of good-bye; others,
Less clinically-minded, will admire
An evening like a coloured photograph,
A music stultified across the water.
The desert opens here, and if, though we
Have ligatured the ends of a farewell,
Sporadic heartburn show in evidence
Of love uneconomically slain,   10
It is for the last time, the last look back,
The heel upon the finishing blade of grass,
To dazzling cities of the plain where lust
Threatened a sinister rod, and we shall turn
To our study of stones, to split Eve's apple,
Content if we can say 'because'; absorbed
Slouch on to our prodigious welcome; die
Unanswerable like any other pedant,
Like Solomon and Sheba, wrong for years.

May 1927

Oxford Poetry 1927, ed. W. H. Auden and C. Day-Lewis (Oxford, 1927), 1; CI, TS on 'Croxley Extra Strong' with ink autograph corrections, enclosed in same letter with 'Narcissus', 'Aware', and 'Bach and the Lady'; P(M), ink autograph on 'Shell Brand'; J. B. Auden, ink autograph on the flyleaf of Robert Graves, *Whipperginny* (London, 1923), signed and dated 'Wystan. May 1927.' Variants: TITLE AND DEDICATION Extract / (For J.B.A.)] The Seekers *CI, P(M)*; The Seekers. (For J.B.A.) *J. B. Auden.* 16. if we can *CI, P(M), J. B. Auden*] if can, *Oxford Poetry*. Auden incorporated a revised version of 'Extract' into 'The Megalopsych', which became the first untitled poem sequence in *P(28)*; the revised version was printed separately by Isherwood in 'Some Notes on Auden's Early Poetry', 6–7.

Auden wrote to his brother John, then in India, 'I am sending you a volume of Graves' poetry, one of the best of the younger men. I have just bought his collected works hence this generosity. At the end I have added one of his best poems not in this book, at the beginning a poem of my own stimulated by and dedicated to yourself' (ALS, Christ Church, [May 1927]). The 'study of stones' (15) refers to John Auden's being a geologist. In the back of the volume Auden had copied out Graves's 'Essay on Knowledge'. Around the same time, he also wrote to Isherwood 'Glad you like the seekers which was my attempt at classical gravity. . . . The seekers is a thrust at my attitude and perhaps yours too,' and he glossed 'sporadic heartburn' as 'Attacks of the iodoform feeling' (ALS, [late May 1927]; see note to 'Narcissus'). He had previously explained the latter to McElwee: 'I am suffering badly from the 'waking alone' sensation, a sick slightly medical feeling like the smell of iodoform' (ALS, Hill Cottage, Sawbridgeworth, [Easter vacation 1927]). In the May letter to Isherwood, Auden also provided two sketches following the one for 'Narcissus'. One, labelled 'Sinister Rod', looks like a penis with the stick figure of a person inside one end. The other, labelled 'Prodigious welcome', shows a church and graveyard with bodies rising out of the graves, arms raised in welcome; two slouching figures approach across a flat landscape, a path stretching out behind them; the sun is half visible on the horizon.

For the 'cities of the plain' (13), see Genesis 19.24–29. 'Slouch' (17) invokes the apocalyptic conclusion to Yeats's 'The Second Coming' (1919): 'And what rough beast, its hour come round at last / Slouches towards Bethlehem to be born?' For Solomon and Sheba, see 1 Kings 10.1–13 and 2 Chronicles 9.1–12, although Auden apparently has in mind Yeats's poems about Solomon and Sheba in *The Wild Swans at Coole* (1919) and *Michael Robartes and the Dancer* (1921). In 'On Woman' Yeats associated the pair with the transfer of wisdom rather than the pedantry that Auden suggests:

> Though pedantry denies,
> It's plain the Bible means
> That Solomon grew wise
> While talking with his queens. (9–12)

A version of l. 10 had appeared previously in Auden's 1926 poem 'The Letter' ('He reads and finds the meaning plain'). L. 12 reappeared in the final stanza of the four-part 1929 poem 'It was Easter as I walked in the public garden'.

□   □   □

> Out of sight assuredly, not out of mind
> Which cranes above your shoulder to regard
> Foreshortened carriages and mimic engine
> Chasing through fields, to register each pause,
> The junction stop, the train meandering
> Through nearer stations, homologues you have
> For scarps of shale mist-hackle and stone wall

Wherein I recognize approach to home:
Till these are crowded out by memories
Acceptable in such a house—of wrist   10
Chafed red by a wet leash and scarred by claws,
The first hand bent into the swaying nest,
The corner turned upon the summer day
Surprised by rolling and the smell of tar.
But mind sheers off like gull from granite, mind
Must build a house or blush for it, denying
The right of objects not to be considered.

So, leaning on a gate, biting a straw,
Between the chuckle of a woodpecker
And a sawmill's outrageous cry, I drew   20
Some nugatory conclusions. After,
Being alone, I wrote them out for you
Against to-morrow and your soon return
No better than to-day but different.

A bus ran homeward, on the public ground
Lay fallen bicycles like huddled corpses.
No chattering valves of laughter emphasized
Nor the swept gown-ends of a gesture stirred
The sessile hush: until a sudden shower
Fell willing into grass and closed the day,   30
Making choice seem a necessary error.

[*Late May or early June 1927*]

S, ink autograph on watermark 'H. P. Pope / Stationers Printers / Birmingham'; CI, ink autograph extensively revised in four pieces of correspondence to Isherwood: ALS, from Christ Church, June 1927; AP, from Christ Church, '9.6.27'; ALS, from Christ Church, [November 1927]; AN, [January 1928]. The heavily revised version of this poem that Auden sent to Spender in the summer of 1928 may have been completed a year or even more after the Isherwood draft. S appears on the back of a letter in which Auden advises Spender which poems he may drop from *P(28)* if he runs out of space (ALS, [August 1928]; see Textual Note, p. lxix, and note to 'Deemed this an outpost, I'). In the variants listed below, the readings from the first draft are included alongside the later revisions, and each variant is labelled according to whether it appeared in the draft (CI) or in one of the items of subsequent correspondence (ALS or AP, etc., with date). Variants: CI has a title, 'Letter to a Friend Upon His Week-end Visit to His Home'. 4. pause] step *CI.* 5. stop] pause *CI.* 6. Through nearer stations,

homologues you] Through stations sharpening in significance, / Whatever homo-
logues they are you *CI.*   9. Till these are crowded out by] Till such retreat in face of *AN*
[January 1928]; But these are crowded out by *CI.* For ll. 15–17, CI has a long additional
middle section:

> Apotheosis was childish then; now,
> More hirsute grown, the shrill incessant bicker
> Of owl and nightingale exasperates.
> The nightingale nostalgic for the womb—
> 'Concept and object, builder and stone were one,
> And is not life an interlude between
> This first placental, that last coffin kiss?
> What's foolish but a pursy mouth? . . .' Owl in-
> -terrupts—'Mathematicians get a curve,
> The jovial ellipse, the mystical
> Hyperbole, or sad parabola,
> And take more pleasure from a formula
> Than from the nape of Helen's neck, not waking
> To a charred city, nor dragged out heel-first
> As Hector was, that bold bad pugilist. . . .'
> Each screams the other down. 'Choose me'—'Choose me'.
> Till mind sheers off, like gull from granite, suspects
> The hoof beneath the antinomian shoe.
> 'The fool may bang his bladder on the king,
> The knave, or scullion, as best pleases
> His foolishness, yet pays for his porridge
> By playing as the king pleases. Who's the fool?' *CI*

Auden revised this by letter from the end of the third line onwards:

> . . . exasperate.

> *Nightingale*

> To footsteps wandered in the meadow brass
> Cool rising wood
> A fortress is. We saw
> Spring's green preliminary giggle. Later,
> On a blind afternoon
> The clammy ankle-brush of fern
> Remarked a separation, yet we rest, assured
> By squeezing of an arm, the meet
> Of cold toes underneath the sheet.

> The pressure of uneven ground
> Is comfort; salt air cracks the lip,
> But union comes.
> Hook wicked thumb in fur; the scream,
> The bulging eye
> Homage the willing God, though the sclerotic mind
> Would twist its rat's tail harder
> Pythagoras in cap and gown
> Redraw the figure upside down.

Owl

Expresses pass
Discoloured waggons, frayed tarpaulins, relics
Of shunting in the Autumn. Mouths essay
To cure nostalgia
To forget the womb,
But reflex images dissolve;
And are not heard
Voices behind the door, the feet
Reiterated on the [?heart]

Catchpennies to tickle gudgeons!
Though gravel snarl
At a pretentious serenade, tossed syncopation mock
The pledging cup.
Now melt their focus to an even haze
And breed no fever; stilled
The jabber of the blood. In this unlittered room
Smooth forehead, brilliance streaming down
Pronounce the Tetragrammaton.

The lobes are flattered twice. No tertium quid.
Till mind sheers off, like gull from granite, suspects
The hoof beneath the antinomian shoe.
'Must I then swallow this preposterous bolus,
Then build a house or blush for it, denying
The right of objects, not to be considered?' *ALS, June 1927*

(This passage might be compared to the two lines shown as cancelled between 14 and
15 in S: 'But now, when grown too big for whipping and / Now hirsute grown, choice
assumes authority.') 18. So] Thus *CI.* 21. Some] These *CI.* 25. ran homeward] ran
home then *AP, 9.6.27*; runs home now *CI.* 26. Lay] Lie *CI.* 27. emphasized] empha-
size, *CI.* 28. stirred] moved *AP, 9.6.27*; move *CI.* 29. until a sudden shower] and noth-
ing more is left *CI.* 30–31. Fell . . . into . . . day, / Making . . . error.] fell . . . to the . . .
day, / Making . . . error. *AP, 9.6.27*; To send but a traditional expression / Of an affec-
tion also traditional *CI.* S was printed in *Oxford Poetry* 1, no. 3 (Spring 1984): 86–87.

When he sent Isherwood the first draft of this poem, Auden wrote: 'I think you will
probably dislike the enclosed poem; it is partly a deliberate experiment in the letter as
a verse form, with the slight pompousness which should be associated therewith. You
may (Please forgive my assumptions) criticize the remarks of the owl and the nightin-
gale as too literary. I have tried deliberately to make them so, make them accord to a
convention, as being suitable to the Owl and the Nightingale Symbolism. Please let me
know about it sometime, as I can't judge it myself' (ALS, Christ Church, [late May or
early June]). Apart from 'The Megalopsych', this poem is the last of the pedantic mis-
cellanies Auden wrote in his pseudo–high modernist phase, and his instinct to trim and
simplify it began to emerge even before the ink was dry. His many subsequent verse
letters are anything but pompous; in fact, he usually turned to the form when he wished
to speak with colloquial informality or even to write light verse.

The poem, or verse letter, is addressed to William McElwee, the 'Friend' of the title
in the Isherwood version. It is significantly influenced by the prescribed Middle English
texts in the Oxford syllabus, not only *The Owl and the Nightingale*, but also, for instance,

Sir Gawain and the Green Knight. The Oxford English Dictionary's only recorded use of 'mist-hackle' (7), for a cloak of mist, is in *Gawain* (with the spelling myst-hakel, 2nd edn), from which Auden must have borrowed it. On the versos of the first draft are Auden's notes for some Middle English translations.

A phrase in ll. 5–6 is borrowed from the opening line of 'After'. Ll. 18–20 recall the setting of 'Narcissus', 'The Mill (Hempstead)', and other earlier poems. Auden revised ll. 3–4 for l. 14 of his unfinished 1932 epic 'In the year of my youth when yoyos came in'. The images in ll. 10–12 of the wrist chafed by the leash and the hand reaching into the nest and also the image of the gull in l. 15 were all reused in his 1929 poem 'Under boughs between our tentative endearments' (*EA*, 29). The hand reaching into the nest perhaps refers to an outing during a visit to McElwee's home early in 1927, as Auden wrote to him 'Do let me know if you have the time about the nests we found. Was the one in the single tree a crow's?' (ALS, Wildboar Clough, Derbyshire, 15 April 1927). A line in one of the abandoned passages sent to Isherwood, 'the meet / Of cold toes underneath the sheet', appeared previously in 'Bank Holiday', and several phrases from superseded sections were to reappear in *P(28)*: 'Spring's green preliminary giggle' and 'shunting in the autumn' were used in poem 11 ('From the very first coming down'), and 'the jabber of the blood' was used in poem 10 ('The mind to body spoke the whole night through'), which also preserves from the abandoned middle section the structuring conception of a dialogue between opposites.

Auden's final stanza was to become the conclusion to part 1 of the 1929 poem 'It was Easter as I walked in the public garden'. L. 26, striking for its introduction of war imagery onto 'the public ground' (perhaps a park or playing field), seems to allude to Siegfried Sassoon's 1918 poem 'The Dug-Out', which begins, 'Why do you lie with your legs ungainly huddled'; 'The Dug-Out' had been printed in de la Mare's anthology *Come Hither!* which Auden owned at school, and Auden had become interested again in Sassoon's work in early 1926 (see note to 'Chloe to Daphnis in Hyde Park'). The 'sudden shower' (29) is borrowed from the third section of Yeats's 'The Tower', which Auden had read in the June *Criterion* and which he praised highly to Isherwood in his letter enclosing the first draft of this poem.

The phrase 'Apotheosis was childish then', in the first line of the abandoned middle section, also appears in the parody 'Rotation' by 'Mystan Baudom' published in November 1926. This raises three possibilities: that Auden had previously used the line and perhaps others from this poem in a much earlier work now lost, that he borrowed it from his parodist, or that he himself wrote the parody; see Appendix and note.

The Megalopsych

Im Winkel König Fahrenheit
hat still sein Mus gegessen.
—„*Ach Gott, sie war doch schön, die Zeit,*
die man nach mir gemessen!"

I

The sprinkler on the lawn
Breeds a cool vertigo and stumps are drawn:
The last boy vanishes,
A blazer half-on, through the rigid trees.

Upon a balcony
Among the mountains and a violet sky,
In sessile habit men
Behind cigars anatomize women.

II

'The Megalopsych,' says Aristotle,
'Never runs swinging his arms.'
So when I saw
The Reverend Bythesea Bubb,
The customary fine for paucity was inflicted;
But when I was drunk; 'Goo Goo,' I said,
'Lovely men!'
You, my tragomaschulous* wench, my flatulent snake,
Lean on my shoulder after a gift,
But do not think   10
Your unwashed navel escapes me. Are you conceited
Because the pathic day
From our tumescent folly refused to look away?

*with armpits smelling like a goat. Aristophanes.

III

'Buzzards!' I heard you say,
And both of us stood still
As they swept down the sky
 Behind the hill.

I, though a watcher too,
Saw little what they did.
Who could have dreamed that you
 Would turn your head?

IV

Squatting Euclid drew in sand
 And forced the sky to answer.
Stupidly the hour-glass leaked—
 —Salomé was a dancer.

'I,' said God, 'by nature must
 Limit the chosen few;
Coincidence and copula'
 —Spinoza was a Jew.

Francis preached before the birds
 About the Mystic Union: 10
His wonderful complexion showed
 The Ideal Companion.

Love will speechlessly accept
 The perfume of a kiss;
Dung disturbs—'I wish to know
 The meaning of all this.'

V

The oboe notes
Of the chipped egg,
The winter leaves
Quickened to a gigue,
The cherry eye of a bird.

The bulb-pillow
Raising the skull,
Thrusting a crocus through clenched teeth.

The flickered shadow
Of an early swallow,   10
And at your dress
The first shy fumbling of a lover's hand—
'Rapunzel, Rapunzel, let down your hair.'

VI

Consider, if you will, how lovers lie
In brief adherence, straining to preserve
The glabrous suction of good-bye; others,
Less clinically-minded, will admire
An evening like a coloured photograph,
A music stultified across the water.
The desert opens here, and if, though we
Have ligatured the ends of a farewell,
Sporadic heartburn show in evidence
Of love uneconomically slain,   10
It is for the last time, the last look back,
The heel upon the finishing blade of grass,
To dazzling cities of the Plain where lust
Threatened a sinister rod, and we shall turn
To our study of stones, to split Eve's apple,
Content if we can say 'Because'; absorbed
Slouch on to our prodigious welcome, die
Unanswerable like any other pedant,
Like Solomon and Sheba, wrong for years

VII

Amoeba in the running water
Lives afresh in son and daughter
'The sword above the valley'
Said the Worm to the Penny.
Dirty thoughts in a green wood.

VIII

Upon the ridge the mill-sails glow
Irrelevant to Quixote now.

The dew-wet fur of the dead hare
Smokes as light sparkles on the snare.

Wind chills the wet uplifted thumb.
'Change seats. The King's come;

He has the key.' But Chanticleer
Questions the Platonic year.

Snotty Eulenspiegel stands
Snooks or smirks behind the hands.   10

Gargantua—the race is run—
Kicks the view over, pisses at the sun.

IX

I wake with a dry mouth,
Something, important once, on the tip of my tongue.

[Assembled late May or June 1927]

CI, ink autograph on 'Shell Brand'. Variants: EPIGRAPH Punctuation and capitalization
have been normalized following the original German text. The parts of this poem series
were written over a period of years, beginning as early as October 1924 with section 3
(the lyric about the buzzards), section 5 in August 1926, section 2 in the autumn of
1926, and culminating in May or perhaps early June 1927, by which time all the remain-

ing sections had been written. Auden began rearranging and revising 'The Megalo-psych' almost as soon as he had assembled it, and he continued to do so intermittently until the publication of *P(28)*. Revisions which he described in letters to Isherwood are not incorporated into this text, but almost all of them are described in the relevant place in the notes. In the end, the Isherwood version of 'The Megalopsych' might be seen as a draft for the first poem sequence in *P(28)*, but it stood separately for a number of months, and it includes material of significant interest that did not survive in the later piece. The two poems call for close comparison.

'The Megalopsych' is the Great-souled or Great-minded man in Aristotle's *Nicomach-ean Ethics*, into which Auden may have first dipped when he was thinking of studying Philosophy, Politics, and Economics in 1926. The claim in section 2, l. 2, that the mega-lopsych 'never runs swinging his arms' refers to *Nicomachean Ethics* 4.3: 'One cannot imagine the great-souled man running at full speed when retreating in battle,' or, in a more literal translation, 'fleeing swinging his arms at his side'; for both translations, see H. Rackham, Loeb Classical Library (London, 1926), 216–17. Rackham suggests that this characterization of the megalopsych may recall 'by contrast the leisurely retirement of Socrates from the stricken field of Delium (Plato, *Symposium*, 221 A).' In one letter to McElwee, written in late June or early July from Appletreewick, Auden referred to the megalopsych in terms that suggest it represented to him the intellectual overkill of pretentious undergraduates: 'Cecil and I had a megalopsych journey culminating in my asking the station master at Skipton "Do you know the geography of the station?' " (a euphemistic request for the toilet). Auden may have been making fun in the poem of his own literary ambitions, but however satiric his aims, the work is also partly an earnest attempt to preserve some of the best of his own early work.

The epigraph, from the second stanza of 'Kronprätendenten' ('Pretenders to the Crown') in Christian Morgenstern's *Galgenlieder*, or *Gallows Songs*, (Berlin, 1905), part 3, may be translated 'In the corner, King Fahrenheit / Quietly consumed his pap. / "Ah, God, what happy times those were / That were measured by me!"' (Germany had begun to go over to metric and centigrade measurement by the end of the nineteenth century.) Auden and Day-Lewis quoted the same passage from Morgenstern in their preface to *Oxford Poetry 1927*, using it as an example of 'that acedia and unabashed glorification of the subjective so prominent in the world since the Reformation.' They explained that the lack of homogeneity among the undergraduate poems in the vol-ume was due to their generation's being surrounded not by any 'standardization of thought'—such as the standardization of measurement in Germany—but by a 'chaos of values'; thus, they argued, 'All genuine poetry is in a sense the formation of private spheres out of a public chaos' (v). 'The Megalopsych' presents a series of such private spheres, formally and thematically discrete, some of them not even internally unified; and yet the poem as a whole prepares the way for a new uniformity in Auden's work. In the commentary to *Journey to a War* (1938), Auden again alluded to the passage from Morgenstern (see 297).

In a version of 'The Megalopsych' in the Ansen notebook, section 1 is dedicated to John Auden, and it probably recalls a scene from the brothers' shared experience at prep school; on the facing page of the notebook, p. 6, is the notation 'S Edmunds' heavily crossed out. 'Stumps are drawn' (2) refers to the removal of the wickets after a game of cricket. Auden told Isherwood the second stanza of this section would be dropped: 'I shall scrap the second verse. All I want really is a pianissimo roll on a buggers' gong' (AL, Christ Church letterhead, [June 1927]).

In the same letter, Auden explained to Isherwood about section 2: 'I know this is no excuse for if it sounds literary it is literary, but incidently the tirade is about a joy-boy and a very real experience, or rather amalgam of experiences (you may recognize one of them).' He also said that he would alter 'wench' to 'friend'. 'Paucity' (5) recalls 'He offered her his paucity' in 'Ballad', and may have had a bawdy second meaning; yet in the version of the poem written in the Ansen notebook, Auden made a note facing this line: '"Paucity that never was simplicity" Owen. Insensibility', thus explicitly referring to the effect of battle on the imagination. The passage in Owen's poem reads:

> But cursed are dullards whom no cannon stuns,
> That they should be as stones.
> Wretched are they, and mean
> With paucity that never was simplicity.
> By choice they made themselves immune
> To pity . . . (50–55)

This sombre allusion contrasts with the crude comedy of the rest of the passage in the same manner as the allusion mentioned above to Socrates retiring from the field at Delium; a rampant lack of decorum hallmarks 'The Megalopsych'. Auden later used the phrase 'Goo Goo' (6) in a letter to McElwee expressing his excitement on first visiting Sedbergh School, which had long since captured his romantic and sexual imagination: 'O Boy this is my lucky day. Goo Goo lovely cigars. My visit to Sedbergh is much too significant to explain other than personally' (ALS, Lordswood Road letterhead, [mid-December 1927]). 'Tragomaschulous' (8), for which Auden's note gives the correct meaning, is borrowed from Aristophanes' *Peace* (l. 811), where it describes some foul-smelling gorgons to whom in a passage of comic abuse Aristophanes compares several lesser tragedians.

Section 3 is printed and annotated separately as 'Buzzards', p. 64.

A version of section 4 was probably completed in the autumn of 1926; its first three lines figure in the parody 'Rotation' by 'Mystan Baudom' published that November in *The Oxford University Review* (see Appendix and note). Isherwood did not like this section and Auden replaced it with 'Aware': 'but I don't promise to scrap this poem. I am I am afraid incorrigible about that sort of thing' (AL, Christ Church letterhead, [June 1927]). For Salomé (4), see Matthew 14.6–11. The 'Mystic Union' (10) is the interior possession of God, best described by St Teresa of Avila or by her confessor, St John of the Cross; it is originally realized in the union of Godhead and manhood in Christ. The 'Ideal Companion' (12) possibly refers to Christ, who told his apostles he would be with them always, or to the Holy Spirit, which 'showed' as a saintly or holy radiance emanating from the face of St Francis. The term also describes an early stage of psychic development that is free of any internal conflict; see George A. Auden, 'On Endogenous and Exogenous Factors in Character Formation', *The Journal of Mental Science* 72, no. 296 (January 1926): 23.

Section 5 is wholly composed of the fourth part of Auden's earlier poem 'Lovers' Lane', though in his [June] letter, Auden promised Isherwood he would drop the last line, mentioning Rapunzel. Opposite a missing page in the Ansen notebook, which probably had on it a version of section 5, Auden wrote 'Written August 1926' and '"Daffodil bulbs instead of eyes" Eliot. Intimations of Mortality'; see note to 'Lovers' Lane', for this allusion to Eliot and Wordsworth.

Section 6 is printed and annotated separately as 'Extract', p. 193.

Section 7 recalls Housman's quatrain poems, which Auden had begun imitating early in 1925. In his first letter to Isherwood about revising 'The Megalopsych', Auden explained that this section 'doesn't mean anything but seemed emotive to me and as you like it I suppose communication is adequate. The connection in my mind between "the sword above the valley" and the coming of the Warriors into Archaic civilization, with the destruction (worm) of the miners (penny) need not worry you' (AL, Christ Church letterhead, [June 1927]). He later included the first four lines—as published in *P(28)*— among the group of case histories written out in the Garland notebook in 1929 or 1930 (British Library, Add.MS.52430). The fifth line perhaps alludes to Marvell's 'a green thought in a green shade' in 'The Garden'.

Auden mentions lines from section 8 in a letter to Isherwood apparently written in June 1927, so the poem may have been composed around this time. Another 1927 letter makes clear that material for this section was quarried from earlier work well after 'The Megalopsych' had first been assembled; see 'The sprinkler on the lawn', section (h), where these lines appear, and note, p. 209. The themes and idioms of *The Waste Land* inform this and other sections of 'The Megalopsych', especially section 9. Chanticleer and the Platonic year (8.9–10) are taken from the conclusion to 'Cinders' (see 'Cinders' and note, p. 145).

□   □   □

(a)

The sprinkler on the lawn
Weaves a cool vertigo, and stumps are drawn;
The last boy vanishes,
A blazer half-on, through the rigid trees.

(b)

Bones wrenched, weak whimper, lids wrinkled, first dazzle known,
World-wonder hardened as bigness, years, brought knowledge, you,
Presence a rich mould augured for roots urged, but gone,
The soul is tetanous: gun-barrel burnishing
In summer grass, mind lies to tarnish, untouched, undoing,
Though body stir to sweat, or, squat as idol, brood,
Infuriate the fire with bellows, blank till sleep,
And two-faced dream—'I want' voiced treble as once
Crudely through flowers till dunghill cockcrow, crack at East.
Eyes, unwashed jewels, the glass floor slipping, feel, know Day,   10
    Life stripped to girders, monochrome. Deceit of instinct,
    Figure, feature, form, irrelevant, dismissed,
    Ought passes through points fair plotted, and you conform,
    Seen yes or no. Too just for weeping argument.

(c)

We saw in Spring
The frozen buzzard
Flipped down the weir and carried out to sea,
Before the trees threw shadows down in challenge
To snoring midges.
Before the autumn came
To focus stars more sharply in the sky
In Spring we saw
The bulb pillow
Raising the skull,   10
Thrusting a crocus through clenched teeth.

(d)

This peace can last no longer than the storm
Which started it; the shower wet and warm,
The careless striding through the clinging grass
Perceiving nothing, these will surely pass
When heart and ear-drums are no longer dinned
By shouting air. As surely as the wind
Will bring a lark song from the cloud, not rain,
Shall I know the meaning of lust again;
Nor sunshine on the weir's unconscious roar
Can change whatever I might be before.   10
I know it, yet for this brief hour or so
I am content, unthinking and aglow;
Made one with horses and with workmen, all
Who seek for shelter by a dripping wall,
Or labour in the fields with mist and cloud
And slant rain hiding them as in a shroud.

(e)

'Buzzards' I heard you say,
And both of us stood still
As they swept down the sky
    Behind the hill.

I, though a watcher too,
Saw little where they sped.
Who could have dreamed that you
    Would turn your head?

(f)

Consider if you will how lovers stand
In brief adherence, straining to preserve
Too long the suction of good-bye: others,
Less clinically-minded, will admire
An evening like a coloured photograph,
A music stultified across the water.
The desert opens here, and if, though we
Have ligatured the ends of a farewell,
Sporadic heartburn show in evidence
Of love uneconomically slain,   10
It is for the last time, the last look back,
The heel upon the finishing blade of grass,
To dazzling cities of the plain where lust
Threatened a sinister rod, and we shall turn
To our study of stones, to split Eve's apple,
Absorbed, content if we can say 'because':
Unanswerable like any other pedant,
Like Solomon and Sheba, wrong for years.

(g)

Amoeba in the running water
Lives afresh in son and daughter
'The sword above the valley'
Said the Worm to the Penny.

(h)

Upon the ridge the mill-sails glow
Irrelevant to Quixote now.

The dew-wet fur of the dead hare
Smokes as light sparkles on the snare.

The grass looks upward at the flower
Through lenses of a fallen shower.

Wind chills the wet uplifted thumb.
'Change seats. The King's come.

'He has the key.' But Chanticleer
Questions the Platonic year.   10

Snotty Eulenspiegel stands
To snook and smirk behind the hands.

Gargantua—the race is run—
Kicks the view over, pisses at the sun.

[*Revised 1927 and 1928*]

P(28), poem 1, 3–7; S, TS (carbon) on 'Croxley Extra Strong' with ink autograph revisions and further pencil revisions in Isherwood's hand, Spender's printer's copy; AA, 6–8, fragment, ink autograph with pencil autograph revisions, heavily marked and with many pages excised; F, fragment, Fisher's ink autograph transcription of sections (a), (f), and (g). This poem sequence is a heavily revised version of 'The Megalopsych', and it incorporates other individual poems written between 1924 and 1927. Earlier versions of the sequence and parts of it are printed and annotated separately in this edition and are not listed among the following variants (see 'The Megalopsych', 'Aware', 'Rain', 'Buzzards', 'Extract', and respective notes). Variants: (a): AA offers the same text as

P(28), but shows it as cancelled. Beside the stanza is a dedication to Auden's brother, '(For J.BA)', and opposite is a note 'S Edmunds', also cancelled, discussed above in the note to 'The Megalopsych'. (b) 12. Figure, feature] Feature, figure *AA*. (b) 14. Too just for weeping argument] Before which argument my buts are impudent *AA*. (c) AA has the first six lines of the section which in 'The Megalopsych' appears as section 2 ('"The Megalopsych," says Aristotle,'), but these lines are cancelled and the title 'Rain' is written beside them, indicating the planned substitute. The remainder of AA is missing, although a version of (g) is written out separately on the facing page, p. 6, as if it were a note to (b) ('Bones wrenched, weak whimper, lids wrinkled, first dazzle known') rather than part of the poem; it offers the following variant: (g) 2. in] as *AA*. (h) does not appear in S, and in *P(28)* it is printed on an erratum slip with the words 'Erratum. Please read also after g:—'. After the publication of *P(28)*, Auden reprinted only section (b) as an individual poem—*P(30)* and thereafter—although individual lines from other parts of the series were reused in his later work. Section (f) was reprinted by Isherwood in 'Some Notes on Auden's Early Poetry', 6–7.

Most of the revisions made to 'The Megalopsych' during the year leading up to the printing of *P(28)* are described in letters to Isherwood. In what appears to be the earliest of these letters, Auden writes: 'Since I know that I have no taste about my own work I shall adopt all your suggestions'; he lists at least one for each section of the poem (AL, Christ Church letterhead, probably June 1927). These changes are detailed in the note to 'The Megalopsych'. Later letters describe further intermediate revisions and rearrangements, all earlier than the published text; some are mentioned above, a few others are also described in the note to 'The Megalopsych'. These letters show that Auden continued to refer to the poem as 'The Megalopsych' at least as late as January 1928 (see AL, on verso of 'The weeks of blizzard over', probably January 1928).

The poems used here underwent numerous metamorphoses before finding their final shape. As mentioned above, much of the material in this poem is printed and annotated separately. Section (c) combines just three lines from part 4 of 'Lovers' Lane' ('The Megalopsych' used the whole section) with the image of the frozen buzzard recycled from Auden's earlier poem 'Frost'; this image survived, with several other lines from (c), in part 2 of Auden's 1929 poem beginning 'It was Easter as I walked in the public gardens', and the skull and bulbs were recycled in *The Orators* (*EA*, 64). Auden mentions lines from section (h) in a letter to Isherwood apparently written in June 1927, so the poem may have been composed around this time. Another 1927 letter makes clear that material for this section was quarried from earlier work well after 'The Megalopsych' had first been assembled: 'I have destroyed the excellent hands poem, and the "my latest love appeared to me" though the couplets "the grass looked upward"—and "here scowled at there" are incorporated in the penultimate section of the Megalopsych' (ALS, Christ Church, [around 1 December 1927]). Nothing from the 'excellent hands' poem (almost certainly 'Winter Afternoon', where the phrase occurs) appears in 'The Megalopsych,' but stanzas 4 and 5 of 'The Last of the Old Year', which begins 'My latest love appeared to me', were apparently added to what was then still the penultimate section of the poem; stanza 5 of 'The Last of the Old Year' was subsequently dropped, for only stanza 4 appeared in *P(28)*. The phrase 'excellent hands' was used later in 'Taller to-day, we remember similar evenings', published in *P(28)*. Ll. 4–7 of section (h) reappeared in *The Orators* (*EA*, 65).

The evolution of 'The Megalopsych' illuminates more fully than that of perhaps any other poem the nature of the working relation between Auden and Isherwood and the impact Isherwood as a critic had on Auden's early work.

□   □   □

I chose this lean country
For seven day content,
To satisfy the want
Of eye and ear, to see
The slow fastidious line
That disciplines the fell,
A curlew's creaking call
From angles unforeseen,
The drumming of a snipe,
Surprise where driven sleet   10
Had scalded to the bone
And streams were acrid yet
To an unaccustomed lip.

So stepping yesterday
To climb a crooked valley,
I scrambled in a hurry
To twist the bend and see
Sheds crumbling stone by stone,
The awkward waterwheel
Of a deserted mine;   20
And sitting by the fall
Spoke with a poet there
Of Margaret the brazen leech,
And that severe Christopher,
Of such and such and such
Till talk tripped over love,
And both dropped silent in
The contemplation of
A singular vision
And sceptical beholder,   30
While a defiant bird
Fell down and scolding stood
Upon a sun-white boulder.

Last night, sucked giddy down
The funnel of my dream,
I saw myself within

A buried engine-room.
Dynamos, boilers, lay
In tickling silence; I
Gripping an oily rail,   40
Talked feverishly to one
Professional listener
Who puckered mouth and brow
In ecstasy of pain
I know I know I know
And reached his hand for mine.

Now in a brown study
At the water-logged quarry,
I think how everyman
Shall strain and be undone,   50
Sit, querulous and sallow
Under the abject willow,
Turning a stoic shoulder
On a Saint Martin's summer,
Till death shall sponge away
The idiotic sun,
And lead this people to
A mildewed dormitory.
But as I see them go,
A blackbird's sudden scurry   60
Lets broken treetwigs fall
To shake the torpid pool;
And, breaking from the copse,
I climb the hill, my corpse
Already wept, and pass
Alive into the house.

[Late June or early July 1927]

P(28), poem 2, 8–11; S, TS (carbon) on 'Croxley Extra Strong' with ink autograph revisions, Spender's printer's copy; CI, ink autograph, revised in subsequent correspondence. Variants: CI is titled 'Appletreewick' and has the dedication '(For C. D-L.)'. 4. eye and ear] the five wits *CI*. 11. Had] Has *CI*. 12. were] are *CI*. 18–19. Sheds . . . / . . . waterwheel] The awkward waterwheel, / Sheds crumbling stone by stone *CI*. 20. a] the *CI*. 27. And both] For each *CI*. 30–31. And sceptical beholder, / While] And I in envy bit / Upon the stem of my pipe / Exasperated at / The folly of my hope, or The inaptitude of hope. / That trusted gerry builder; / While *CI*. 39. tickling] ticking *uncorrected copies of P(28)*. 40–46. Gripping . . . / Talked . . . / Professional . . . / Who . . . /

In . . . / I know I know I know / And . . . mine.] Gripping . . . / Talked . . . / Professional
. . . / I know old boy, I know / And . . . mine. *uncorrected copies of P(28)*; Talked feverishly
to an / Insane philosopher / Who spluttered 'Is that all' / And winked a lecher's eye
/ 'In love and chaste! There are . . .' / And laughed himself away. *CI.* 49–50. everyman
/ . . . undone,] everyman / From the morning of his birth / Shall strain a sinew with
/ Himself, with that brash booby, / And both shall be undone *CI.* Reprinted in Carpen-
ter, 71–72.

The title and dedication of the Isherwood version refer to a week that Auden and
Cecil Day-Lewis spent in Appletreewick, where they went at the end of June 1927 to
write the preface to *Oxford Poetry 1927*. (In a letter to McElwee, Auden mentions plans
to get up for an eclipse which occurred during their visit. This helps date the trip as
starting before 29 June, when there was an eclipse of the sun; see ALS, pencil, The New
Inn, Appletreewick, Skipton, Yorkshire, [late June 1927]). Appletreewick is the village
in the Yorkshire dales where Auden had spent an intensely happy week with Robert
Medley and his family in August 1923, and about which he had written the earlier poem
'Appletreewick' and perhaps some others, including possibly 'Buzzards' and the Har-
dyesque poem beginning 'Whenever I see for the first time'. Auden may have written
this new poem in Appletreewick or on his return to Harborne, from where he appar-
ently sent it to Isherwood (enclosed in an ALS, Lordswood Road letterhead). By 13 July
he was already sending Isherwood revisions to the poem, especially to one passage that
he revised repeatedly before the poem was printed. The earliest interim solution he
offered for ll.42ff. was:

> —Hare-lipped philosopher
> Who spluttered 'Is that all?'
> And winked a lecher's eye
> 'My heart, my Very Dear'   (from Coventry Patmore)
> And laughed himself away.
>   (API, 42 Lordswood Road, postmarked 13 July)

The Patmore tag is derived from the opening of 'A Farewell'. Spender's printer's copy
shows another version of the troublesome passage, also cancelled, in which the line
from Patmore is replaced with a phrase from Catullus, poem 41, 'Puella defututa';
Auden told Isherwood this meant 'drab fucked to the wide' (ALS on 'Shell Brand',
[about 7 June 1927]). In a 1928 letter Auden revised the passage again to the version
that appears in the uncorrected text of *P(28)*. In *P(28)*, ll. 43–44 were added by hand,
and l. 45 was altered from 'I know old boy I know'. The final version of the passage
seems to allude to the psychoanalysis that Auden began probably in early 1928, well
after he first drafted the poem. He wrote to Isherwood not long after sending him the
poem: 'I am going to be psycho-analyzed probably next vac, by the Margaret referred to
by your side, one of those pleasant pornographic women' (ALS, probably from Har-
borne, before 20 July). Margaret Marshall, 'the brazen leech' or doctor (23), was a
trained psychoanalyst and a close friend of Day-Lewis who introduced her to Auden; see
Cecil Day-Lewis, *The Buried Day* (London, 1960), 149–52. She eventually numbered
among her four husbands Auden's brother John, though the marriage (John's first of
two) was brief and unhappy. The 'poet' (22) is Day-Lewis and 'that severe Christopher'
(24) is Isherwood. Because the 'professional listener' (42) is sexed as male by the
phrase 'his hand' (46), the label may refer to another analyst, possibly practising in Spa,
Belgium, where Auden visited in the summer of 1928. (See notes to 'The spring will
come', 'Grow thin by walking and go inland', and 'To throw away the key and walk
away'.) Another passage appears on Spender's printer's copy as cancelled, a longer

version of ll. 49–50: 'I think how everyman / Supported by the earth / Shall strain a sinew with / Himself, with that brash booby, / And both shall be undone'.

Auden may have borrowed l. 9 from Wilfred Gibson's dramatic dialogue 'The Scar' in his 1907 volume *The Stonefolds* (31). Many of Gibson's poems and plays (with Audenesque titles such as 'Borderlands' and 'Kestrel Edge') are set in the remote northern landscapes Auden loved, and *Paid on Both Sides* owes something to Gibson's settings and plots, and also to the slow pace of his rather grand if sometimes wooden dialect. The image of the buried engine-room (37–39) harks back to 'The Engine House', 'Dethroned', and 'The Evolution of the Dragon', and it is elucidated by a reference in the will that survives from Auden's lost 1930 play *The Fronny* (see note to 'The Evolution of the Dragon'). Auden described the scene yet again in ll. 330–51 of his unfinished epic 'In the year of my youth when yoyos came in' (see notes to 'The Engine House' and 'The Evolution of the Dragon'). Saint Martin's summer (54) is a period of fine weather expected between 18 October and 11 November (St Martin's Day).

When Auden sent the poem to Isherwood he mentioned in his accompanying letter 'Hodge is scrapped'. 'I chose this lean country' takes many lines from 'Hodge Looks toward London' (16–17, 38–39, 52, 55–58), but it marks a new strength and simplicity of style influenced by Yeats and by Robert Graves. Day-Lewis was under the spell of Yeats during this period, as evidenced by his 'Transitional Poem' (part 2) published in *Oxford Poetry 1927*, and it was he who fixed Auden's attention on Yeats's more recent work. Auden greatly admired 'The Tower', which he read in *The Criterion* that June, and both Stephen Spender and Richard Ellmann have observed that 'I chose this lean country' is closely modelled on the third part of 'The Tower'; see Spender, 'The Influence of Yeats on Later English Poets', *Tri-Quarterly* 4, nos. 84–85; Ellmann, *Eminent Domain: Yeats among Wilde, Joyce, Pound, Eliot, and Auden* (New York, 1967), 102–3. Ellmann also noted that ll. 5–6 echo 'In Memory of Major Robert Gregory' (ll. 67–68), though they also recall ll. 3–4 from Auden's own earlier composition 'Alston Moor'; see Fuller, 263 n. 2, and E. R. Dodds, 'Background to a Poet', *Shenandoah* 18 (Winter 1967): 9. Ll. 25ff. are reminiscent of Yeats's 'Adam's Curse'. Auden apparently also had in mind Graves's early poem 'Rocky Acres'. But in Berlin in January 1929, Auden wrote a new version of the poem, beginning 'From scars where kestrels hover'; he combined it with material from another 1927 poem beginning 'The weeks of blizzard over' and eliminated the most obvious influence of Yeats and Graves. One line he abandoned at this time (52) reappeared in 1936 as the opening of a song, 'Underneath the abject willow' (*EA*, 160; slightly revised in *CP*, 140), that he wrote for Benjamin Britten. In the same song for Britten were other images probably derived from the transitional 1927 period: ll. 17ff. perhaps recall 'Cold Night', a poem by a little-known American, Raymond Holden, which Auden copied out for Isherwood in the letter he sent enclosing 'I chose this lean country', and ll. 7–8 echo Emily Dickinson's 'Power', from which in the same 1927 letter Auden quoted the following two lines: 'You cannot fold a flood / And put it in a drawer.' Isherwood may have showed Auden these 1927 materials in March 1936 when Auden visited him in Portugal to work on *The Ascent of F6*; possibly because Isherwood himself may already have been at work on his essay 'Some Notes on Auden's Early Poetry', which appeared in *New Verse* in November 1937. He began writing *Lions and Shadows* the following October (1936); see Textual Note, p. lviii.

□   □   □

On the frontier at dawn getting down,
Hot eyes were soothed with swallows: ploughs began
Upon the stunted ridge behind the town,
And bridles flashed. In the dog days she ran
Indoors to read her letter. He in love,
Too curious for the East stiffens to a tower;
The jaw-bone juts from the ice; wisdom of
The cooled brain in an irreverent hour.

At the half-close the muted violin
Put cloth and glasses by; the hour deferred   10
Peculiar idols nodded. Miles away
A horse neighed in the half-light, and a bird
Cried loudly over and over again
Upon the natural ending of a day.

July 1927

P(28), poem 5, 15; DL, ink autograph on 'H. P. Pope / Stationers Printers / Birming-
ham', numbered '1)' and with 'Zagreb. July' added at foot in Auden's autograph; CI,
ink autograph with 'Zagreb' at foot in Auden's autograph. Variants: CI is entitled 'Love
in Absence'. 5. He in love] Cupboard love *DL, CI*. 6. stiffens] hardens *DL, CI.*
   In the summer of 1927 Auden travelled in Yugoslavia for some weeks with his father,
departing about 21 July and returning by 19 August. A version of ll. 4–5 had appeared
previously in ll. 4–5 of 'Hodge Looks toward London', although the new phrase, 'dog
days', and all of l. 8 are borrowed from a letter to Isherwood describing Auden's where-
abouts and what he called his 'spiritual progress' (ALS, Hotel Elephant, Ljubljana,
Croatia, [July 1927], private American collection). L. 8 also echoes the conclusion of
Eliot's 'Gerontion': 'Thoughts of a dry brain in a dry season'. Apparently Auden
changed 'cupboard love' at Isherwood's suggestion, although first he tried to defend
the phrase: 'hungry would do I think, but cupboard love really can't be personified and
the contrast of sex is an added point' (AL, possibly January 1928). The phrase 'the hour
deferred' (10) is borrowed from the penultimate line of the first stanza of Isherwood's
long Mortmere poem, 'The Recessional from Cambridge', which also uses the theme of
a train journey. This unpublished typescript (Upward Papers, British Library) was writ-
ten probably between 1924 and 1926 and typed by Upward in the late 1980s; a few
stanzas of 'The Recessional from Cambridge', though not the relevant ones, were
printed in Graham Chainey, *A Literary History of Cambridge* (Cambridge, 1985), 206. The
opening line of 'On the frontier at dawn getting down' and the image of the swallows
were reused in a prose passage in *The Orators* (*EA*, 65). Auden reused l. 7 in one of
Quant's speeches in part 2 of *The Age of Anxiety* (*CP*, 479).

□   □   □

No trenchant parting this
Of future from the past,
No idol fractured is,
Nor bogey scared at last.
But still the mind would tease
In local irritation,
And difficult images
Demand an explanation.
Across this finite space,
Buttressed expensively,   10
The pointed hand would place
Error in you, in me;
Eye squiny for a way
To mitigate the stare,
When shadow turns on day
Find argument too bare,
Till pendulum again
Restore the gravamen.

But standing now I see
The diver's brilliant bow,   20
His quiet break from the sea,
With one trained movement throw
The hair from his forehead.
And I, stung by the sun,
Think, semi-satisfied,
That ere the smile is done
The eye deliberate
May qualify the joy,
And that which we create
We also may destroy.   30

August 1927

P(28), poem 3, 12–13; DL, ink autograph on 'H. P. Pope / Printers Stationers / Bir-
mingham' numbered '2)' and with 'Dubrovnik. August.' at foot in Auden's hand; AA,
33, ink autograph with 'Dubrovnik. August 1927' at foot in Auden's hand. Variants: 5.
But . . . would] Yet . . . would *DL*; Yet . . . will *AA*. 10. Buttressed expensively] Buttressed

expansively *uncorrected copies of P(28)*; Nourished expensively *CI*.   13. squiny] squint *uncorrected copies of P(28)*. 23. hair from] hair back from *uncorrected copies of P(28)*. Reprinted in *P(30)*.

For Auden's trip to Yugoslavia, see note to 'On the frontier at dawn getting down'. Auden used the image of 'The diver's brilliant bow' (20) again in his 1937 ballad beginning 'As I walked out one evening' (*EA*, 228; *CP*, 134). Spender recalls the image may 'come from the Yugoslav trip' (AN, 30 March 1992, to Katherine Bucknell), but it may refer to Robert Medley, who, at Gresham's, spent 'as much time as possible at the swimming pool' during summer term and who was a skilled diver. Medley recalls that Auden once attempted a double dive on his shoulders, but Auden's poor co-ordination, in a feat easily achieved by other boys, gave Auden a bloody nose (Medley, 39). In 1923 Auden had written a poem about the swimming pool at Gresham's which was erotic enough to bring about an embarrassing confrontation with his parents over his friendship with Medley (see note to 'Early Morning Bathing'); this may be the source of the close association in 'No trenchant parting this' between the sense of personal guilt and the diver's vivid, ephemeral perfection.

□   □   □

Truly our fathers had the gout
    And we were born
On the wrong side of the line:
The eagle strangles in the snare
    The tide is out
    And the ash-pit bare

Over a crooked steeple geese
    Incurious pass
The spoon tinkles in the glass
A dry face mutters to the wall   10
      Till lightning loose
      The frantic skull

August 1927

DL, ink autograph on 'H. P. Pope / Printers Stationers / Birmingham' numbered '3.)' and with 'Split. August.' at foot in Auden's hand; Catullus (HRHRC), ink autograph on the recto of the rear free endpaper of Auden's copy of the Loeb edition of *Catullus Tibullus and Pervigilium Veneris*, trans. F. W. Cornish, J. P. Postgate, and J. W. MacKail (London and New York, 1925). The Catullus version may have been written before August, but the only certain date for the poem is Auden's own. Variants: 1–4. Truly . . . / And . . . / On . . . / . . . snare] Hanged men swing in the air / Truly our fathers had the gout / And we were born / On the wrong side of the line *Catullus*. 6. pit] heap *Catullus*. 7–10. Over . . . / Incurious . . . / The . . . / . . . wall] Turn the face to the wall

/ The houses [?tumble down] and the [?goose] / Will brave its [?stare] / And [?trams
bray] in the ear *Catullus*. Printed in *Oxford Poetry* 1, no. 3 (Spring 1984): 89.

For a time Auden included this poem in one of the transitional versions of 'The
Megalopsych'; then in a long list of revisions sent to Isherwood apparently in November
1927 he mentioned, 'I have cut Truly our fathers had the gout' (ALS, Christ Church
letterhead; for the difficulty of dating this letter, see note to 'The colonel to be shot at
dawn'). Auden reused ll. 11–12 in 'The mind to body spoke the whole night through',
printed in *P(28)*.

□ □ □

We, knowing the family history
The lethal factors there were in the stock
Were scarcely surprised at the way he took
If at first the danger were hard to see,
And collapse no sooner suspect than known,
What was laudable once. There must have been
An indolent ulcer beneath the skin
Which burrowed until it attacked the bone.

A moment there was between certainties
When a thought decided it less or more   10
For the case which proceded the way we saw
As to how and when, or questions like these
The story was never more reticent
Always afraid to say more than it meant.

August 1927

DL, ink autograph on 'H. P. Pope / Stationers Printers / Birmingham', numbered '4.'
and with 'Harborne. August' at foot in Auden's hand. The poem has a cancelled title
'Family Likeness'. Printed in *Oxford Poetry* 1, no. 3 (Spring 1984): 89–90.

Auden reused the image of the 'indolent ulcer' (7) in the poem beginning 'Because
sap fell away', printed in *P(28)*, and again in one of Quant's speeches in part 2 of *The Age
of Anxiety* (*CP*, 470). The last two lines became the conclusion to the poem beginning
'From the very first coming down', also printed in *P(28)*.

□ □ □

Who stands, the crux left of the watershed,
On the wet road between the chafing grass,
Below him sees dismantled washing-floors,
Snatches of tramline running to the wood,
An industry already comatose,
Yet sparsely living. A ramshackle engine
At Cashwell raises water; for ten years
It lay in flooded workings until this,
Its latter office, grudgingly performed.
And further here and there, though many dead   10
Lie under the poor soil, some acts are chosen,
Taken from recent winters. Two there were,
Cleaned out a damaged shaft by hand, clutching
The winch the gale would tear them from; one died
During a storm, the fells impassable,
Not at his village; in his wooden shape
Through long abandoned levels nosed his way,
And in a final valley went to ground.

Go home now, stranger, proud of your young stock;
Stranger, turn back again, frustrate and vexed.   20
This land, cut off, will not communicate,
Be no accessory content to one
Aimless for faces rather there than here.
Beams from your car may cross a bedroom wall,
They wake no sleeper; you may hear the wind
Arriving, driven from the ignorant sea
To hurt itself on pane, on bark of elm
Where sap unbaffled rises, being spring.
But seldom this. Near you, taller than grass,
Ears poise before decision, scenting danger.   30

August 1927

P(28), poem 6, 16–17; AA, 37, ink autograph with pencil autograph revisions and 'Harborne August 1927.' at foot in Auden's hand; DL, ink autograph on 'H. P. Pope / Stationers Printers / Birmingham', numbered '5).' with 'Harborne. August.' at foot in Auden's hand; CI, ink autograph on lined sheet watermarked 'H.P. Pope Ltd / Stationers Printers / Birmingham'. Variants: 4–5. running to the wood, / An industry already comatose,] banked up from the stream, / The signs of a declining industry *DL, CI*. 16. in . . . wooden] but in . . . new *DL*; and in . . . new *CI*. 18. a] his *DL*. 19. stock; *AA*] stock *uncorrected copies of P(28)*. 20. frustrate] non-plussed *DL, CI*. 27. To hurt . . . pane] Hurting . . . pane *DL*; Hurting . . . panes *CI*. Reprinted in *P(30)* and thereafter.

This poem draws imagery and narrative shape from several of Auden's earlier poems on mining subjects. In one letter to Isherwood, Auden calls the poem 'Rookhope' (ALI, Lordswood Road letterhead, probably 14 September 1927), a title that places it in the chain of lead-mine poems which culminates in Auden's account in 'New Year Letter' of the all-important discovery at Rookhope of himself as a civilizing, creating, and guilty human being; see 'Rookhope (Weardale, Summer 1922)', 'The Old Lead-mine', 'Alston Moor', 'Allendale', and notes, and *CP*, 227–28. 'Washing-floors' (3) are where stones are sorted and washed on first coming out of the mines. The tramline (4) is for transporting stones and ore. The 'ramshackle engine' (6) had previously been the subject of 'The Pumping Engine, Cashwell'. Cashwell is mentioned in 'Lead's the Best', which, like the earlier poem 'The Miner's Wife', also treats the theme of the accident at the mine. The stories of implied heroism and death in 'Who stands, the crux left of the watershed,' were probably suggested to Auden by lore gathered in conversation, or possibly from local history books, in the mining district. He may have been familiar with two stories still told decades later to visitors at the Killhope Lead-mining Museum near Alston by a curator, Sally Orrell. The first concerns the Corpse Road over Crossfell, which according to local tradition was used by the villagers from Garrigill to carry their dead to Kirkland for burial before they had their own church. One year a burial party was overtaken by a snowstorm and the coffin had to be abandoned for a fortnight on top of Crossfell. This story is also told by William Wallace, in *Alston Moor: Its Pastoral People, Its Mining, and Manors* (Newcastle-on-Tyne, 1890), 18–19. Wallace dates the events in the mid-sixteenth century, and suggests that the inhabitants of Garrigill had originally come from Kirkland and liked to be buried with their ancestors, even after they had a church. Possibly Auden knew this book. The second story is about a miner injured by a rock fall in one of the mines, who, again because of deep snow on the fells, had to be carried underground through the abandoned levels of old mines to Carrshield where there was a doctor; he caught pneumonia on the way and died a few days later; see *The W. H. Auden Society Newsletter* 2 (September 1988): 1–2. 'Levels' (17) are the main horizontal galleries in a mine, from which all minor tunnels and drives are worked; they are usually provided with tramlines. In another letter Auden explained to Isherwood 'I don't understand your perplexity over the funeral. In his new shape means of course, his coffin. The shape of the coffin should justify nosed. The deliberate association of the process with animals is obvious' (ALI, probably early September 1927).

The diction and phrasing of the poem are intermittently Hardyesque; the telling word 'frustrate', for instance, may be found several times in *The Dynasts*; see 3.4.8 and 3.5.1. Ll. 23 and 25–28 are borrowed from the last stanza of 'Quique Amavit', written for McElwee. The fragmentary image of the frightened animal in the poem's final lines recalls Auden's much earlier 'To a Field-mouse', and may owe something to Robert Graves's 'Rocky Acres', a poem with similar atmosphere.

After 'Aware', this is the earliest of Auden's poems that he preserved in his published work beyond *P(28)*, and it is the earliest to survive beyond *P(30)*; see *Early Auden*, 32.

□ □ □

Suppose they met, the inevitable procedure
Of hand to nape would drown the staling cry
Of cuckoos, filter off the day's detritus,
And breach in their continual history.

Yet, spite of this new heroism they feared
That doddering Jehovah whom they mocked;
Enough for him to show them to their rooms—
—They slept apart, though doors were never locked.

(The womb began its crucial expulsion.
The fishermen, aching, drenched to the skin,   10
The ledge cleared, dragged their boat upon the beach.
The survivor dropped, the bayonets closing in.)

In these, who saw and never rubbed an eye
A thousand dancers brought to sudden rest,
Transformed to tiger-lilies by the band,
It was no wonder they were not impressed

By certain curious carvings on the porch,
A generous designation of the fate
Of those shut altogether from salvation.
Down they fell. Sorrow they had after that.   20

September 1927

P(28), poem 4, 14–15; S, TS (carbon) on 'Croxley Extra Strong' with ink autograph revisions, apparently Spender's printer's copy; AA, 39, ink autograph with pencil autograph revisions and with 'Carr Bridge. September 1927.' at foot in Auden's hand; DL, ink autograph on 'H. P. Pope / Stationers Printers / Birmingham' numbered '6.)' and with 'Dalbuich. September.' at foot in Auden's hand; CI, ink autograph. Variants: 2. to nape] and lip *DL, CI*. 5. this *S, AA, DL, CI*] thir *P(28)*; in the Upward copy of *P(28)* 'thir' is emended to 'their' by an unidentified hand, but other copies of *P(28)* that I have seen are uncorrected, so I have followed the fair copies. 7. show] lead *CI*. 8. locked. *S, AA, DL, CI*] locked *P(28)*. 10. skin, *S, AA, DL, CI*] skin *P(28)*. 14. thousand] hundred *DL, CI*. 17. carvings on] carving in *S, AA, DL, CI*. 19. shut altogether from] never involved in a *DL, CI*. 20. had they] they had *S, AA, DL, CI*. Reprinted in *P(30)*.

When he sent this poem to Isherwood, Auden told him: 'you will see the influence of the Virgin Wolf, the proper place as I think for such technique' (ALI; Dalbuich, Carr Bridge, Aviemore, Invernesshire, N.B.; September 1927). He was apparently referring to the parentheses around the poem's middle stanza. In an earlier letter to Isherwood, Auden had mentioned reading Virginia Woolf's *Mrs Dalloway*, but he is probably referring here to *To the Lighthouse*, published in May 1927. In *To the Lighthouse* Woolf uses parentheses several times in the novel's middle section, 'Time Passes', to downplay the conventionally significant narrative events of birth, marriage, and death. In a later letter to Isherwood, Auden added these details: 'Womb—epic birth—Fishermen—The epic life—Bayonets the epic death, a vision of the life cycle, outside the two pathics, who consider themselves living the free, the true life' (ALI, September 1927, before 14 September). This gloss reveals the poem's cynicism; by calling both lovers pathics, Auden suggests their mutual passivity. And thus the epic life cycle at the heart of the poem does not highlight their self-conscious psychological heroism (as two homosexuals striving to find an acceptable way of loving), but helps expose it as false; their fear of a Christian morality that they know to be outdated ('doddering Jehovah', l. 6) prevents them from consummating their love until the last line of the poem, and when they do, the poem describes this consummation as a fall which brings them sorrow. In another letter to Isherwood, Auden said that the phrase 'Sorrow they had after that' in the poem's closing line, 'is not as far as I can remember a direct quotation from OE verse, only a typical remark. I may be wrong though will write when parturition comes' (ALI, Lordswood Road letterhead, probably 14 September 1927). But the line is given in the voice of the poetic persona, and hints that the poem may be a rather harsh self-criticism in so far as it refers to some aspects of Auden's relationship with McElwee, a publicly avowed heterosexual who nevertheless accepted Auden's intense Platonic affections and for love of whom Auden practised celibacy for over a year.

□ □ □

The crowing of the cock
Though it may scare the dead
Call on the fire to strike
Sever the yawing cloud,
Shall also summon up
The pointed crocus-top
Which, smelling of the mould,
Breathes of the underworld.

A god was slain for love,
A god was brought to birth   10
There in the sunless grove
Not pierceable by star
Nor spidery moonlight, where
The crow may startle us
Back from her foul nest with
A solitary curse.

The chosen in a cave
Forgot old whiffs, alive

Suffered the dizzy calm,
Waited the rising storm,   20
Prayed through the scorching season
And saw 'ere daylight set
Blocked conduits in spate,
Delectable horizon.

Such kept back since, done with,
The tired ears prick and beg
An altered pressure, eyes
Look in the glass, confess
The tightening of the mouth;
Know the receding face   30
A blemished psychogogue;
But symmetry will please,

Now straightly swallowed up
In memory, like these
Its tilting planes disclose
—The snowstorm on the marsh,
The champagne at the lip—
Swung into vision, fresh
By fleeting contact; mind
Sees faculty confined   40

To breast the final hill
Θάλασσα on the tongue,
Snap at the dragon's tail
To find the yelp its own;
Or sit, the doors being shut,
'Twixt coffee and the fruit,
Touching, decline to hear
Sounds of conclusive war.

September 1927

P(28), poem 8, 19–21; *AA*, 41–43, ink autograph headed by the encircled numeral '2' and with 'Carr Bridge. September. 1927' at the foot in Auden's hand; DL, ink autograph on 'Devon Valley Parchment', letterhead of L.N.U. [London Nurses Union] /Harborne Branch, with Mrs Auden named as Secretary and her Lordswood Road address. Variants: 8. underworld. *AA, DL*] underworld *P(28)*. 9. A] The *AA, DL*. 10. A] The *AA, DL*. 36. on] in *AA, DL*. Reprinted with slight revisions in *P(30)*.

Auden recorded a number of his sources for this poem in the Ansen notebook. Opposite the first four lines he wrote out in Latin, with a precise reference, the first four lines of Prudentius's 'Hymnus Matutinus' ('Morning Hymn'), from his fourth-century *Liber Cathemerinon* (*The Daily Round*):

> Nox et tenebrae et nubila,
> confusa mundi et turbida,
> lux intrat, albescit polus,
> Christus venit, discedite.

The Loeb edition gives H. J. Thomson's translation: 'Night and darkness and clouds, all the world's perplexed disorder, get ye gone! The dawn comes in, the sky is lightening, Christ is coming' (London, 1949), 1:12–13. As Lawlor points out in the facsimile edition of the Ansen notebook (129), the hymn preceding this one in the *Liber Cathemerinon* is the 'Hymnus ad Galli Cantum' ('A Hymn for Cock-crow'), which mentions, among other things, the belief that Christ rose from the dead at the hour of cock-crow. This is alluded to in the 'Hymnus Matutinus', which emphasises the way in which the spreading light of dawn clears the darkness in the soul, and makes sin impossible: 'fur ante lucem squalido / inpune peccat tempore' (sin belongs to 'the murky time before the light comes,' 12–13). With the sun come regret and shame and sorrow, and 'nec teste quisquam lumine / peccare constanter potest' ('no man can sin cooly under the eye of light,' 14–15).

Facing l. 12 in the Ansen notebook, Auden wrote 'c.f. Spenser. Faery Queen "Not pierceable by anie starre . . . "', a slight misquotation from book 1, 1.7.6, 'Not perceable with power of any starr', which refers to the grove where, at the opening of *The Faerie Queene*, Redcrosse knight and the veiled lady shelter from a rainstorm and become lost among the trees 'that heavens light did hide' (1.7.5). The imagery of death and rebirth in stanzas 1 and 2 refers again to the mythology of the vegetation gods such as Adonis, Attis, and Osiris described in Frazer's *The Golden Bough* and linked by Frazer to the story of Christ. Auden had drawn on this material for 'Easter Monday'; and combined here with the allusions to Prudentius and Spenser, it once again underlines his obsession with the possibility of spiritual or psychological enlightenment and renewal.

Auden often used 'the whiff' (cp. 18) in his letters to Isherwood and to his brother John to suggest sexual attractiveness arousing lust; usually, though not always, he applied it to young boys, as in a letter to William McElwee's fiancée, Patience, 'Its whiff of clean English Boyhood nearly gave me a stroke and for nights I shant be able to sleep without three orgasms' (TLS; Bei Muthesius / Berlin / Nikolassee / Potsdamer Chausee 49 / [31.12.28]; with M, British Library).

Across from l. 31 Auden noted in the Ansen notebook '. . . . . "der liebende psychogogue." Thomas Mann. Tod und Venedig', a near misquotation from the penultimate paragraph of *Der Tod in Venedig*, where Mann wrote, in a slightly longer phrase, 'der bleiche und liebliche Psychagog' (Munich, 1912), 97. In the first English translation of *Death in Venice* (London, 1928), H. T. Lowe-Porter rendered this as 'the pale and lovely Summoner' (117), but working directly from the German text, Auden stayed closer to the Greek root; *The Oxford English Dictionary*, 2nd edn, credits him among the first users of the word in English in the sense of one who calls up departed spirits, a necromancer, but this does not fully capture the association of the word with Hermes as the leader of dead souls to Hades.

Opposite l. 42 in the Ansen notebook, Auden wrote 'Xenophon. Anabasis', referring to the cry of Xenophon's soldiers on first catching sight of the sea on their return from Persia (*Anabasis*, 4.7); 'Thalassa' had appeared previously with the last four lines of the poem as the conclusion to 'Quique Amavit', written for William McElwee. In a 1930 letter to Naomi Mitchison, Auden glossed the first pair of these lines: 'Our asymptotic movement towards emotional satisfaction' and the second pair: 'The result of repression The divided self Puritan right and wrong' (ALS, Larchfield Academy / Helensburgh / Dumbartonshire / N.B., 28/10/30).

Opposite l. 45 in the Ansen notebook, Auden wrote '"When the doors were shut. . . . for fear of the Jews." S John XX v 19.'

□   □   □

Nor was that final, for about that time
Gannets, blown over northward, going home,
Surprised the secrecy beneath the skin.

'Wonderful was that cross, and I full of sin.'
'Approaching, utterly generous, came one,
For years expected, born only for me.'

Returned from that dishonest country, we
Awake, yet tasting the delicious lie;
And boys and girls, equal to be, are different still.

No, these bones shall live, while daffodil   10
And saxophone have something to recall
Of Adam's brow and of the wounded heel.

October 1927

P(28), poem 7, 18; S, TS (carbon) on 'Croxley Extra Strong', Spender's printer's copy; AA, 45, ink autograph with 'Harborne. October 1927.' at foot in Auden's hand; CI, ink autograph on the verso of an ALS on Lordswood Road letterhead. Variants: 1. was that] was it *CI.* 3. Surprised . . . beneath] Startled . . . below *CI.* 4. 'Wonderful was *S, CI*] Wonderful, was *P(28).* Following l. 4, CI has an asterisk and at the foot of the poem Auden's note of the Old English original '"Sillig waes þet sigeraed, and ic wið sinnum fah." The dream of the Rood.' 8. yet] still *CI.* 9. And] All *uncorrected copies of P(28).* Reprinted in *P(30).*

In the Ansen notebook, Auden recorded some of his sources for the poem. Facing the first stanza is:

ðonne onwæcneð eft   winelēas guma
gesihð him biforan   fealwe wǣgas
baþian brimfuglas
                                            ('The Wanderer', 45–47)

Israel Gollancz renders this as: 'Then wakes again the friendless wight, / sees before him the fallow ways, / sea-birds bathing'; *The Exeter Book: An Anthology of Anglo-Saxon Poetry* (London, 1895), part 1, p. 288. But the gannets (2) are probably recalled from

The Seafarer (20). Opposite the second stanza is a more accurate transcription than Auden sent to Isherwood of the source for the first line of this stanza, '"Syllic wæs se sigebēam, and ic synnum fáh" Dream of the Rood l. 13.' Ll. 5–6, spoken by the cross, also echo *The Dream of the Rood*; see ll. 33–34, 57–58. Opposite stanza 3 is '"Boys and girls are level now with men" Antony and Cleopatra IV 13 [for 15]'. At first Auden quoted wrongly and wrote 'equal', then crossed it out and corrected it to 'level'; he did the same in his draft of the poem, but changed his mind yet again, crossed out 'level' and returned to his first thought, 'equal'. Facing the last stanza in the Ansen notebook Auden noted 'cf. Ezekiel XXXVII v. 3.'; he had already drawn on this verse of Ezekiel in 'Cinders': 'And he said unto me, Son of man, can these bones live? And I answered, O Lord God, thou knowest' (see note to 'Cinders').

□   □   □

Deemed this an outpost, I
The exiled governor,
Myself a photograph
In mittens on the snow,
To write home once a year
Watching the last leaf fall.

At vigil heard approach
The old and twilight foe,
Experienced, for this
Deliberately come: 10
But 'neath my supple grip
There was no contrite roar;

Scales wriggled into flesh
Of a more yielding neck;
Glare fading from the eye
Left limp within the arms
Your new and sensible
Assertive innocence.

Then at the Hall all night
The babble of the flute   20
And inarticulate 'cello
Held insolent revel
To testify at last
The destined regimen.

Dawn leans across the sea
Though dark is scarcely dry:
And rising from the feast,
This felt unusual
And satisfactory,
Palm pressed to palm, we walk   30

Out into chattering lanes.
The dead Spell carried past
Cries backward no reproach,
Nor loutish villagers
Staring or praise, who know
Sufficient any cause.

[*October or November 1927*]

CI, ink autograph on Christ Church letterhead watermarked 'Alexander'; AA, 46, ink autograph. As in most poems from this period, AA shows revisions that clearly postdate the CI copy; however, AA has only four stanzas, followed by a gap where folios are excised from the notebook, and it is entirely cancelled. Therefore, I have incorporated the AA variants and punctuation into the longer CI text. The poem is not dated, but its position in the sequence in AA makes composition in October or November fairly certain. Variants: 9. for] to *CI.* 11. But 'neath] Beneath *CI.* 16. limp within] hung upon *CI.* 24. The] Such *CI.* Printed in *Oxford Poetry* 1, no. 3 (Spring 1984): 90–91.

This poem was originally among the poems given to Spender for *P(28)*, but Spender dropped it according to instructions in a letter from Auden in the late summer or early autumn of 1928: 'If you must leave anything out they may be omitted in this order of choice 1) "Deemed this an outpost, I" 2) "The houses rolled into the sun" 3) "The weeks of blizzard over' " (ALS, on watermark 'H. P. Pope / Stationers Printers / Birmingham' possibly sent from the home of Auden's parents, unless he carried the paper with him to Spa or elsewhere; the verso has the poem beginning 'Out of sight assuredly, not out of mind', see the note to this poem, and see 'Textual Note', p. lxix).

At the foot of the Isherwood copy, Auden wrote 'If obscure try "The Laily Worm" as a subtitle'. 'The Laily Worm' was a Mortmere figure invented by Isherwood and Upward. Isherwood explains in *Lions and Shadows* that they took the name from 'The Ballad of the Laily Worm' in *The Oxford Book of Ballads*; this would be 'The Laily Worm and the Machrel of the Sea' in Arthur Quiller-Couch's 1910 edition, which glosses 'Laily' as 'Loathely' (59). In the early to middle 1920s Upward wrote a long, unfinished poem about Laily, somewhat influenced by T. S. Eliot and entitled 'Tale of a Scholar', which he later printed in *No Home But the Struggle*, the third and final volume of his autobiographical novel *The Spiral Ascent* (London, 1977), 672–77. When Upward had already gone up to Cambridge and Isherwood was still at Repton where they had been at school together, they used Laily in their letters as a term for the enemy. He was 'the symbol of the Public School social-team spirit'. By the time they were both at university, Laily changed. They made him into 'a mere sycophant who consorted with the social majority only to further his private academic ambitions'; he was 'a self-seeking scholarship number' (see Isherwood, 'Mortmere "Introductory Dialogue"', written late 1925 or 1926, unpublished TS in Upward Papers, British Library). In *Lions and Shadows* Isherwood wrote that he and 'Chalmers', the Upward figure in the novel, had invented Laily as 'an ideal, imaginary don, the representative of all his kind, to be our special enemy and butt.' He was 'the typical swotter, the book-worm, the academic pot-hunter; but, at the same time, being eager to succeed with and be accepted by the Poshocracy, he was careful to pretend an enthusiasm for athletics and the team spirit' (66–67). Years later, in *The Spiral Ascent*, Upward said Laily came to represent 'the spirit of Historical studies at Cambridge' (674), which in his view 'had no heart, were devoid of any feeling for the sufferings of the human race' (676). All this tends to characterize the 'exiled governor' of l. 2 as a despicably self-advancing upper-middle-class hypocrite.

☐ ☐ ☐

Because sap fell away
Before cold's night attack, we see
A harried vegetation.
Upon our failure come
Down to the lower changing-room,
Honours on pegs, cast humours, we sit lax,
In close ungenerous intimacy,
Remember
Falling in slush, shaking hands
With a snub-nosed winner;   10
Open a random locker, sniff with distaste
At a mouldy passion.

Love, is this love, that notable forked-one,
Riding away from the farm, the ill word said,
Fought at the frozen dam? Who prophesied
Such lethal factors, understood
The indolent ulcer? Brought in now,
Love lies at surgical extremity;
Gauze pressed over the mouth, a breathed surrender.

November 1927

P(28), poem 9, 22; AA, 51, ink autograph with pencil autograph revisions and with 'Oxford. November 1927.' at foot in Auden's hand; CI, ink autograph on Christ Church letterhead. Variants: AA has a dedication '(For G.C)'.   5. Down to the lower] To the perpetual *CI*.   7–9. intimacy, / Remember / Falling] intimacy; remember / Falling *CI*. 18–19. extremity; / Gauze] extremity, / The bowls prepared, the rubber-gloves assumed, / Gauze *CI*. AA is probably the earliest draft of this poem to survive, but it also shows revisions that postdate CI, suggesting that Auden returned to the notebook and altered the poem after sending a copy to Isherwood; this apparently was his practice with many of the poems of this period (see note to 'Deemed this an outpost, I').

The dedication in the Ansen notebook is to Gabriel Carritt, the 'snub-nosed winner' (10) whom Auden met for the first time in November 1927. Carritt recalls that this occurred at the College Essay Club (*Tribute*, 46), but the poem refers to a meeting that was apparently more vivid for Auden, which occurred probably after a rugby match played in Oxford on 21 November 1927 between Oxford and Cambridge Old Sedberghians. According to the Oxford correspondent for *The Sedberghian*, 'It was a real Sedber' day—cold with a nasty drizzle falling'. This would have produced the 'slush' referred to in the poem. The Oxford side was reduced by illness to thirteen players, but still succeeded in beating the Cambridge fifteen by eight points to three. 'Carritt junr.', a newly arrived freshman, was prominent that day for Oxford. The 'junr.' suggests that his elder brother Michael, a Greek scholar at Queen's, was also among the thirteen; see *The Sedberghian* 68.6 (December 1927), 272. Auden was already interested in Sedbergh because of his friendship with William McElwee and with McElwee's younger brother, Patrick, still at the school. Much later Auden planned, for a time, to take a job there as a master. A letter to John Auden apparently written during summer term 1927 shows that Auden first planned to visit the school in June 1927: 'I am going down a day early in order to go to Sedbergh to visit a boy to whom I have appointed myself as spiritual guide' (ALS, from Christ Church). The boy was almost certainly Patrick McElwee, but the visit may never have occurred; Auden went to Appletreewick with Day-Lewis at the end of the summer term in 1927. The 'frozen dam' (15) alludes to Burke's Dam at Sedbergh. Although his letters to Isherwood and McElwee make fairly clear that Auden did *not* visit the school for the first time until 9 December 1927 (after he had written this poem), someone (probably McElwee or maybe Carritt) must have told him about the dam before this. Isherwood knew about it, too, as Auden wrote to him on returning from the 9 December visit: 'I was shown the frozen dam in moonlight by a nut-hatcher' (ALI, Lordswood Road letterhead, 13 or 14 December 1927). Apparently this comment amounted to a romantic boast, as the dam was probably a trysting place. (In another letter to McElwee Auden used the term 'nut-hatcher' to describe a girl—at Sedbergh, he must have meant a boy—at the pub in Appletreewick: 'The chauffeur at our pub is an Adonis, and there is a girl like a nut-hatcher'; ALS, pencil, the New Inn Appletreewick, late June 1927). One thing Auden had not been told before visiting the school was that Lupton House, where he stayed, had its changing-room underground; this appealed enormously to his love of subterranean places. He wrote to McElwee, 'Why did you never tell me that Lupton House changing-room was underground? I was so delighted I fell into a bath' (ALS, Lordswood Road letterhead, mid-December 1927). He also mentioned the underground changing-room in his mid-December letter to Isherwood, but in the poem he refers only to a 'lower-changing room' (5) because, apparently, he had not yet found out about it.

The epithet 'snub-nosed' (10) may be Auden's translation of Thomas Mann's 'stumpfnäsiges' in Mann's description in *Der Tod in Venedig* of the lascivious entertainer at the hotel who smells suspicious to Aschenbach but refuses to answer questions about the possibility of plague in Venice (Munich, 1912), 77; the bullying gondolier who first conveys Aschenbach to the Lido also has a 'kurz aufgeworfenen Nase' (26–27). Auden was reading Mann during the second half of 1927 (see note to 'The crowing of the cock'), and Carritt recalls that Auden gave him copies of *Death in Venice* and *Tonio Kröger* early in their friendship. The epithet suggests a parallel between Auden's 'falling in slush' (9) for Carritt and Aschenbach's falling for Tadzio. For nearly a year before meeting Carritt, Auden had kept to a vow of celibacy sworn partly for love of McElwee and partly for purposes of spiritual purification and greater artistic devotion. The figure of the artist as a priest or initiate sacrificing life and love for his work was continually in Auden's mind during this period; writing to his brother John that year, he twice cited a passage from Flaubert's letters to support the notion that asceticism was the only suitable condition for an artist: 'You shall paint wine, women and glory on condition my good man that you are none of these, neither husband nor lover, drunkard nor cuckold' (2 ALS, Christ Church, possibly both June or June and December 1927). The Flaubert is slightly mistranslated; see *Oeuvres complètes de Gustave Flaubert* (Paris, 1926), *Correspondance*, 2.268–69. Fisher noted that Auden used to tease Carritt that his nose was syphilitic, as if it were physical evidence of a fatal disease like the one carried by the snub-nosed entertainer who infected Aschenbach, but Carritt was also handsome in the classical style of Mann's Tadzio. Auden reworked the lines about the snub-nosed winner for his 1930 poem beginning 'Between attention and attention':

> Falling in slush,
> Before a friend's friends
> Or shaking hands
> With a snub-nosed winner.
>
> (*EA*, 53; 'Easy Knowledge' in *CP*, 37)

He used ll. 13–15 in a prose passage in *The Orators* (*EA*, 68). The 'indolent ulcer' (17) previously appeared in 'We, knowing the family history', and reappeared in *The Age of Anxiety* (*CP*, 470).

□ □ □

The mind to body spoke the whole night through:
'Often, equipped and early, you
Traced figures in the dust, eager
To start, but on the edge of snow
As often then refused me further;
Proffered a real object, fresh,
Constant to every loyal wish.

Never to the Dark Tower we rode,
But, turning on the hill crest, heard,
Catching the breath for the applause,   10
A tolling disillusioned bell
The leaking of an hour-glass,
Till lightning loosed the frantic skull.

Granted that in a garden once
And a wind blowing, a voice,

Beyond the wall, unbroken, hid
The jabber of the blood, and bred
No fever.'

Cocks crew, and sleeping men turned over.
Rain fell for miles; ghosts went away.   20
The jaw, long dropped, stopped at reply.

[*November or December 1927*]

P(28), poem 10, 23–24; AA, 54, ink autograph with pencil autograph revisions; CI(1), ink autograph, on same folio with 'From the very first coming down'; CI(2), ink autograph. The Ansen notebook also contains an earlier unfinished draft of the poem, which is cancelled and not recorded in this edition (53). Variants: 1. The mind to body spoke the . . . through: / 'Often] Mind spoke with flesh the . . . through. / 'Often *AA*; This is the address of the lost soul / To the lost body./ / That was ill / Cancelled original light, secured / A sour union, not preferred. / Death's insulation now between, / Sorry that you no longer please, / Love, trespassing apart enjoys / The luxury of cooling bone/ / Often *CI(1)*; This is the address of the lost soul / To the lost body—/ 'That was ill / 'Cancelled original light, secured / 'A sour union, not preferred.// 'Often *CI(2)*. 5–8. further; / Proffered a real object, fresh, / Constant . . . wish./ / Never . . . rode,] further; Preferred a real image, fresh, / Constant . . . wish./ / Never . . . rode *AA*; further, Preferred a real image, fresh, / Constant . . . wish./ / Never . . . rode *CI(1)*; further/ / 'Disarming me with the concussion / 'Of lamp and violin and passion, /'Offered a real image, fresh, / 'Constant . . . wish./ / 'Denied the straining hawk the wood / 'Though little quarry vexing him. / 'Never came, *CI(2)*. 9–10. turning . . . heard, / Catching] standing . . . catching *AA, CI(1)*; turning . . . heard,/ / 'Catching *CI(2)*. 13–14. skull./ / Granted] skull./ / 'Death's insulation put between, / 'Sorry that you no longer please, / 'Love trespassing apart enjoys / 'The luxury of cooling bone./ /'Granted *CI(2)*. 19. crew] crow *uncorrected copies of P(28)*. The CI(1) version was printed in *Oxford Poetry* 1, no. 3 (Spring 1984): 91–92.

Unlike most of the other drafts in the Ansen notebook, this one bears no date. In a letter to Isherwood sent around 1 December, Auden describes almost all the revisions incorporated into AA (the revisions in the notebook show that the cancelled Ansen version was very similar to the versions Auden sent Isherwood), making clear that apart from the opening line the poem was complete by this time (ALS, probably from Christ Church).

The idea of a conversation between opposites, which Auden had taken from the Middle English poem *The Owl and the Nightingale* and tried in the early, abandoned version of the poem beginning 'Out of sight assuredly, not out of mind', gives way in this poem to a monologue; now the mind does the talking and the body is silent, its talk referred to only as 'The jabber of the blood' (17), a phrase which, along with the rest of ll. 17–18, had previously appeared in the abandoned version of 'Out of sight assuredly, not out of mind'. The poem may also owe something to the Old English 'The Soul's Address to the Body', in *The Exeter Book*, in which the soul reviles the body for oppressing it with worldly appetites and warns it of the coming horrors of grave and worm. Auden's final stanza, in which 'ghosts went away' at cock-crow, recalls from the same Old English poem the soul's account of how it was compelled to leave the body at cock-crow every morning (ll. 62–63), and his line 'The jaw, long dropped, stopped at reply,' perhaps echoes the conclusion, which tells how the body cannot answer the soul as it is split, dismembered, and 'geaflas toginene' (l. 104), or 'the jaws made to gape'; Early English Text Society, No. 194, trans. and ed. W. S. Mackie (London, 1934), part 2, p. 81.

Auden had previously alluded to the enigmatic climax of Browning's 'Childe Roland to the Dark Tower Came' (8) in 'Cinders' and in 'Hodge Looks toward London'. The 'tolling disillusioned bell' (11) which echoes the 'Tolling reminiscent bells' in section 5 of *The Waste Land* (384), had previously appeared in 'Day-dreams of a Tourist' (12). L. 13 had served as the conclusion to the pair of stanzas beginning 'Truly our fathers had the gout' which Auden dropped from 'The Megalopsych', probably in November 1927, just before he used the lines in their new position here. He recycled l. 20 from the first stanza of 'Encounter' and the last stanza of 'After'; in the second instance, he had also used the line, as here, together with an image of cock-crow.

☐ ☐ ☐

From the very first coming down
Into a new valley with a frown
Because of the sun and a lost way
You certainly remain. To-day
I, crouching behind a sheep-pen, heard
Travel across a sudden bird,
Cry out against the storm, and found
The year's arc a completed round
And love's worn circuit rebegun
Endless with no dissenting turn.   10
Shall see, shall pass, as we have seen
The swallow on the tiles, Spring's green
Preliminary shiver, passed
A solitary truck, the last
Of shunting in the Autumn; but now,
To interrupt the homely brow,
Thought warmed to evening through and through,
Your letter comes, speaking as you
Speaking of much but not to come.

Nor speech is close, nor fingers numb   20
If love not seldom has received
An unjust answer, was deceived;
I, decent with the seasons, move
Different or with a different love,

Nor question overmuch the nod,
The stone smile of this country god,
That never was more reticent,
Always afraid to say more than it meant.

December 1927

P(28), poem 11, 25–26; AA, 57, ink autograph with 'Oxford Dec 1927.' at foot in Auden's hand; CI, ink autograph on same folio with draft beginning 'This is the address of the lost soul to the lost body', which became 'The mind to body spoke the whole night through'. Variants: 12. tiles] tile *AA, CI.* 13. shiver] giggle *CI.* 14. truck] waggon *CI.* 20. Nor speech is] Speech is not *CI.*

This poem was inspired by William McElwee; Auden wrote 'W.M.' beside it in Peter Salus's copy of *Poems* (the 1934 American edition; see Carpenter, 76, where Carpenter mistakenly says the copy belonged to Chester Kallman). The second stanza, however, hints that a new love, possibly Gabriel Carritt, has changed the poet. L. 13 (more exactly in the CI version) and l. 15 appeared previously in the abandoned middle section of the poem beginning 'Out of sight assuredly, not out of mind'. The slant rhyme in ll. 23–24 echoes a slant-rhymed couplet from W. H. Davies' 'Bird and Brook': 'And in my season I am moved / No more nor less from being loved'; *The Song of Life*, reprinted in *Collected Poems: Second Series* (London, 1923). L. 25 recalls the second line in Donne's 'The Funerall': 'Nor question much'. Auden had used a version of ll. 25–26 in 'Easter Monday', but here changes the 'garden god' to a 'country god', perhaps with the intention of substituting the amorous power of the rustic Pan for the castrated Attis (see note to 'Easter Monday'). The last two lines of 'From the very first coming down' are slightly revised from the conclusion to Auden's earlier poem beginning 'We, knowing the family history'.

□   □   □

The four sat on in the bare room
Together and the fire unlighted,
And One was speaking;—'she turned the page,
More quavers on the other side.'

'We parted in the waiting-room,
Scraping back chairs for the wrong train.'
Said Two, and Three,—'All kinds of love
Are obsolete or extremely rare.'

'Yesterday,' Four said, 'falling on me
Through the glass pavement overhead   10
The shadow of returning girls
Proclaimed an insolent new Spring.'

They said, the four distinguished men
Who sat waiting the enemy,
Saw closing upon the bare room
The weight of a whole winter night,
Beyond the reef high-breaking surf.

December 1927

P(28), poem 12, 27; AA(1), 58, ink autograph with pencil autograph revisions; Carritt (Houghton Library, Harvard University), ink autograph on Lordswood Road letterhead; CI, ink autograph on Lordswood Road letterhead; AA(2), 59, ink autograph with 'Harborne. Dec 1927' at foot. Variants: 3. And One was speaking;—'she turned the page,] One said, 'We played duets;—she turned the page *AA(1)*; And One was speaking; 'The page turned over, *Carritt, CI.* 5. We . . . the] And . . . a *AA(2)*. 7. Said Two, and Three,] Another then *AA(2)*. 9. Four said, 'falling on me] said the last to me *AA(2)*. 10–12. Through the glass pavement overhead / The shadow of returning girls / Proclaimed an insolent new Spring.'] The shadows of returning girls / Proclaimed an insolent new spring, / Coming, and eagles above the pools.' *Carritt*; The shadows of returning girls / Proclaimed an insolent new Spring, / New Law, and eagles above the pools' *CI*; 'The shadow of returning girls / Proclaimed an insolent new day / New Law, And eagles above the pools.' *AA(2)*. 13. They] Thus *AA(1), AA(2)*. 16. Beyond] And beyond *CI, AA(2)*. CI appears to be a revised fair copy of AA(2), and Carritt a slightly revised version, though it is difficult to say for certain whether the Carritt version is later than CI. AA(1) appears to be a still later revision, postdating the date of composition recorded for AA(2), and possibly also postdating the text for *P(28)*, since the revision to l. 3 first appears in the early version of *Paid on Both Sides*, which was completed in July or August 1928 (*EA*, 412–13; *Plays*, 8–9). I have followed the *P(28)* text, rather than AA(1), since Auden did not make the revision in Isherwood's or Upward's copies of *P(28)*; see Textual Note, p. lxxi.

Ll. 3–4 probably refer to Auden's childhood practice of playing duets at the piano with his mother; see the third stanza of 'The Happy Tree', where he previously used these lines, and note, p. 168. Ll. 5–6 appeared in 'The Evolution of the Dragon' (38–39), and l. 6 reappeared as ll. 16–17 of the 1930 poem 'Between attention and attention' (*EA*, 153; *CP*, 37). Ll. 7–8 are partly borrowed from an obscure joke Auden made in an autograph postcard to McElwee, 'All kinds of sciofacias are now either obsolete or extremely rare' (from Christ Church, 7 December 1927); 'sciofacias' may refer to an old requirement at Oxford for a minimum number of 'scios' to get a degree, or it may refer to *scire facias*, a mostly obsolete judicial writ requiring someone to show cause why the applicant should not have advantage of some matter of record, or, in certain circumstances, why the record should not be annulled and vacated. Auden had first tried a version of ll. 10–11 in 'Before' ('Unkempt and furtive the wind crawls'). The abandoned l. 12 from the Carritt, CI, and AA(2) versions was later revised as the final line for the lyric beginning 'Light strives with darkness, right with wrong' printed in *P(28)*.

The poem traces a progression through three different kinds of love: the first two stanzas obliquely recall moments of charged intimacy, first in childhood with Auden's mother, later in adolescence, probably with McElwee. The third stanza predicts a further evolution of love towards love of women, but the fourth stanza makes clear that the poet regards this new epoch with a sense of doom. The pattern overall prefigures the shape and preoccupations of later works taking love as a central theme, such as the the 1929 poem beginning 'It was Easter as I walked in the public garden', and *The Orators*.

□ □ □

The houses rolled into the sun,
The pigeons falling for their food
Down from the tower's intense stone
Expect, receive a present good.
Mind loves or hates, and not desires
A genuine voice deliver from
One mischief. So it is with us.

Last night, because, leaving the room
Wind from the snows had cooled the brow,
We sighed for peace. These hills, prized now   10
Since Fagge and Clotters tired, too late
In getting up, may prove to be
Stumps of old systems that await
The last transgression of the sea.

[*Autumn 1927 or early 1928*]

S, TS (carbon) on 'Croxley Extra Strong', apparently Spender's printer's copy. Printed in *Oxford Poetry* 1, no. 3 (Spring 1984): 86.

This poem was originally among those Spender was to print in *P(28)*, but it was the second of the three Auden told him to drop if necessary (see note to 'Deemed this an outpost, I'). The opening line is revised from the opening of the 1926 poem 'Early Morning' ('Earth rolls these houses out into the sun'). The name Fagge (11) may be recalled from Auden's prep school days, as are several other names used in his poems of this period; Charles Hieton Fagge arrived at St Edmund's a year after Auden, and eventually went on to Charterhouse. Rosamira Bulley, daughter of the headmaster at St Edmund's, later recalled that in a variety entertainment put on in October 1919, Fagge and two other boys performed a country dance to Auden's piano accompaniment, but Auden ruined the performance by playing too quickly (*Tribute*, 32). The last two lines of this poem appeared first in 'Consequences' (19–20), and later reappeared in *Paid on Both Sides* (*EA*, 3; *Plays*, 16). 'Stumps of old systems' is probably intended in the geological sense.

□ □ □

The colonel to be shot at dawn
Plays a harmonium on the lawn.
Though stimulated by the tune
The subalterns will die in June.

December 1927

AA, 60, ink autograph with 'Harborne Xmas Day 1927' at foot in Auden's hand. Printed in *Oxford Poetry* 1, no. 3 (Spring 1984): 93.

Auden's date for this quatrain presents a crux best resolved by supposing that this is a revised version of an earlier piece now lost. At one time, Auden planned to include this quatrain or, more likely, the supposed earlier version of it, in 'The Megalopsych'. A letter to Isherwood detailing a number of changes to 'The Megalopsych' and other poems lists 'h) Between v[erses] 2 and 3 insert the Colonel to be shot etc' (ALS, Christ Church letterhead). *Possibly* this letter was written after Christmas 1927, but it seems more likely that it was written in November because it is on the same sheet as the November poem beginning 'Because sap fell away', and because it mentions dropping 'Truly our fathers had the gout' from 'The Megalopsych'—a telling detail, as Auden used two lines from 'Truly our fathers had the gout' in the poem beginning 'The mind to body spoke the whole night through', also written in November. Furthermore, the letter reminds Isherwood: 'Remember to write to G. B. Smith in about a fortnight', probably to prepare the headmaster of Sedbergh for Auden's four-day visit starting 9 December. The letter also refers to Auden's winning the Slade Exhibition, an under-graduate scholarship. This scholarship is now open to members of Christ Church tak-ing schools in the year of their election and is normally announced in Hilary Term, which starts in mid-January; thus Auden might not have known about the Slade until the beginning of 1928, but it is not clear that the Exhibition was administered in the same way in the 1920s; the *Oxford University Calendar* for 1927 describes it as tenable for one year (rather than just the two terms that would remain to a finalist winning the exhibition in Hilary), suggesting that Auden may have heard during Michaelmas Term (October–December) that he had won it.

□ □ □

To-night when a full storm surrounds the house
And the fire creaks, the many come to mind,
Sent forward in the thaw with anxious marrow;
For such might now return with a bleak face,
An image pause, half-lighted at the door,
A greater but not fortunate in all,
Come home deprived of an astonishing end,
—Morgan's who took a clean death in the North,
Shouting against the gale, or cousin Dodds',
Passed out, asleep in her chair, the snow falling.   10
The too-loved clays, born over by diverse drifts,
Fallen upon the far side of all enjoyment,
Unable to move closer, shall not speak
Out of that grave, stern on no capital fault.
—Enough to have lightly touched the unworthy thing.

January 1928

P(28), poem 13, 28; AA, 65, ink autograph with pencil autograph revisions and with 'Harborne January 1928' at foot in Auden's hand. Variants: 4–5. face, / An image pause] face / His hair cut off, and other messages / That action has a rudimentary eye; / What's felt at all, felt to extravagance, / For a poor stimulant/ / So, Almost seen / The image turns *AA*. 7. home] back *AA*. 9. Dodds' *AA*] Dodd's *P(28)*. Auden used a slightly altered version of the poem in *Paid on Both Sides* (*EA*, 15; *Plays*, 30).

It is of some slight significance whether in l. 9 Auden intended Dodd's or Dodds', because he probably took the name from his friends, Professor and Mrs E. R. Dodds. Dodds was Professor of Greek at Birmingham University, and Auden was introduced to him in the late 1920s by his father, who was a longtime member and past secretary of the Classical Association. In the Ansen notebook, Auden wrote Dodds', but in *P(28)* and *P(30)* Dodd's was printed without any correction; probably he never noticed, for throughout his early work he frequently made the error of forming plural possessives in exactly this way. I have followed the Ansen notebook. 'Morgan' may have been borrowed from E[dward] M[organ] Forster, a literary hero of Upward, Isherwood, and Auden (in an ALS from Allenheads, Northumberland, probably written in 1926, Auden told Isherwood that he had 'just read *Howards End*').

The poem is notably influenced by Yeats's 'In Memory of Major Robert Gregory', also a meditation on the fate of dead friends. Auden's poem begins at fireside in a house, just like Yeats's:

> Now that we're almost settled in our house
> I'll name the friends that cannot sup with us
> Beside a fire of turf in th'ancient tower . . . (1–3)

And Auden's turn of phrase 'the many come to mind' (2) is one that Yeats uses twice in his first few stanzas: 'For all that come into my mind are dead' (16) and 'Lionel Johnson comes the first to mind' (17). There are other similarities of theme, imagery, and phrasing throughout the two poems.

☐ ☐ ☐

The weeks of blizzard over
The sunlight enters now
The dale, and every bone
Sits well in its socket:
And Molly with her boy,
Her first since winter, walk
Along the path below
The kestrel on the scar

I, trespassing alone
About the village, read   10
The written names of three
Whose voices in the rock

Are now perpetual;
Foot, Cockshute, Tesser-Coop,
Who died beyond the border
Sent to a recent war.

Or leaning on the bridge
According to the wind
In shadow or in sun,
I stand, too drowsed to hear   20
The anger of the stream,
Supposing I shall meet
A hero in the wood,
Far from the capital

Where all is set in order
To greet the noted guest
Candles and wine are there
For supper on the lawn;
But prophets must migrate—
'Leave for Cape Wrath to-night.   30
Shall not arrive this week
Nor any week.
                          Writing.'

                                    [*January 1928*]

CI, ink autograph on the reverse of an autograph list of revisions to earlier poems. The latest of these poems is the one beginning 'To-night when a full storm surrounds the house', written in January 1928, which helps date this poem during the same month. Printed in *Oxford Poetry* 1, no. 3 (Spring 1984): 92–93.

This is the third of the three poems Auden told Spender he could cut from *P(28)* if necessary (see note to 'Deemed this an outpost, I'). The names in l. 14 reappeared in Auden's 1929 play *The Enemies of a Bishop* (see *Plays*, 74ff.), although Tesser-Coop was revised to Jesser-Coop. Possibly it was Isherwood who, when they worked on the play together, recalled the exact name of two brothers at St Edmund's, William Anthony Jesser Coope, who arrived in January 1916, and Edmund Charles David Jesser Coope, who arrived in May 1918; both went on to Lancing. Auden quarried this poem intensively for his January 1929 poem beginning 'From scars where kestrels hover'; ll. 8, 12–13, 15, 23–24, 25, and 27–30 are reworked and combined there with material from the poem beginning 'I chose this lean country' (see *EA*, 28; titled 'Missing' in *CP*, 30–31).

□ □ □

Light strives with darkness, right with wrong,
Man thinks to be called the fortunate,
To bring home a wife, to live long.

But he is defeated; let the son
Sell the farm lest the mountain fall:
His mother and her mother won.

His fields are used up where the moles visit,
The contours worn flat; if there show
Passage for water he will miss it.

Give up his breath, his woman, his team: 10
No life to touch, though later there be
Big fruit, eagles above the stream.

January 1928

P(28), poem 14, 29; AA(1), 66, ink autograph; CI, ink autograph on verso of an ALI;
AA(2), 67, ink autograph with 'London Jan. 1928.' at foot in Auden's hand, entirely
cancelled in ink and pencil. Variants: 1. Light *this edn*] Night *P(28)*. 7. fields *this edn*]
field *P(28)*. Both variants were misprinted and uncorrected in *P(28)*; I have followed the
text in the first version of *Paid on Both Sides* (*EA*, 416). The manuscript versions of this
poem do not include the opening stanza that appears in *P(28)*. They begin with the
second stanza; consequently, AA(1) has only three stanzas, while CI has five stanzas, of
which the first, third, and fifth stanzas correspond to the last three stanzas of *P(28)*, and
the second and the fourth stanzas run as follows:

> Yes, he will come when the girls call—
> —He has tasted good, and what is it?—
> Out of the shadow of the wall.

> Confusion if the judge think so
> Becomes important; unless his seem
> A comfortable answer he must go

In the first line of stanza 5, CI has 'wooing' for 'woman', but with Auden's query against
the line: 'Wooing? or woman?' In the six-stanza AA(2) version, stanzas 1, 4, and 6 corre-
spond to the last three stanzas of *P(28)*; in stanza 6 of AA(2) Auden wrote 'wooing', then
changed it to 'woman'. Stanza 5 in AA(2) is the same as stanza 4 in CI, printed above.
Stanzas 2 and 3 became stanza 2 in CI; they read:

> Yes, he will come when the girls call
> From the wood; he will step forward then
> Out of the shadow of the wall.

> Haemophilia is found in men.
> He has tasted good, and what is it?
> The white wyandot is a fine hen.

Auden later incorporated this poem, with a slightly altered opening stanza, into *Paid on Both Sides* (*EA*, 17; *Plays*, 33–34).

As Spender long ago pointed out, l. 2 echoes the penultimate line of Yeats's translation of Sophocles' *King Oedipus*: 'Call no man fortunate that is not dead'; *The Destructive Element* (London, 1935), 260–61. Yeats's version had been performed at the Abbey Theatre, Dublin, in 1926, but it was not published until March 1928, so Auden must have added the new first stanza soon after reading it. The poem's final line derives from an image Auden had first tried out in a draft of the poem beginning 'The four sat on in the bare room' (see note to same). The middle line of the abandoned second stanza of the CI version, which had orginated in the cancelled six-stanza AA(2) version, was eventually recycled as l. 7 of the poem beginning 'The spring will come', in *P(28)*.

□ □ □

Control of the Passes was, he saw, the key
To this new district, but who would get it?
He, the trained spy, had walked into the trap
For a bogus guide, seduced with the old tricks.

At Greenhearth was a fine site for a dam
And easy power, had they pushed the rail
Some stations nearer; they ignored his wires.
The bridges were unbuilt and trouble coming.

The street music seemed gracious now to one
For weeks up in the desert; woken by water   10
Running away in the dark, he often had
Reproached the night for a companion
Dreamed of already. They would shoot of course,
Parting easily who were never joined.

January 1928

P(28), poem 15, 30; AA(1), 68, ink autograph with pencil autograph revisions; CI, ink autograph; AA(2), 69, ink autograph, entirely cancelled, with 'Oxford. Jan 1928' at foot in Auden's hand; AA(3), 69, ink autograph, entirely cancelled. Variants: 2. new] fresh *AA(1), CI, AA(2), AA(3)*. 4–12. tricks./ / At . . . / And . . . / Some . . . / The . . . / / The . . . / For . . . desert; woken by water / Running . . . had / Reproached] tricks. / The business had its moments though it meant / Hard travelling for instance; woken by water / Running . . . had / Reproached *CI*; tricks. / The business had its moments though it meant / Rough travelling: for instance woken by water / Running . . . had /Reproached *AA(2)*; tricks, / The work had been exciting, though it meant / Continuous travel, sleeping in cottages / And he had often, woken by running water, / Reproached *AA(3)*. Reprinted in *P(30)* and thereafter.

Greenhearth (5) may be Greenhurth, the mine in Teesdale, north-west of Middleton and not far from Alston; see notes to 'The Engine House' and 'Lead's the Best'. As John

Fuller has pointed out, the poem's final line is taken from the Old English poem *Wulf and Eadwacer*, 'the monologue of a captive woman addressed to her lover' (Fuller, 34, and see *The Exeter Book*, 180). In W. S. Mackie's edition, the lines are 'þæt mon eaþe tosliteð þætte næfre gesomnad wæs', which he translates, less effectively than Auden, as 'What never was united is easily torn asunder'; *The Exeter Book: An Anthology of Anglo-Saxon Poetry*, Early English Text Society, No. 194 (London, 1934), part 2, pp. 86–87.

□　□　□

Taller to-day, we remember similar evenings,
Walking together in the windless orchard
Where the brook runs over the gravel, far from the glacier.

Again in the room with the sofa hiding the grate
Look down to the river when the rain is over,
See him turn in the window, hearing our last
Of Captain Ferguson.

It is seen how excellent hands have turned to commonness.
One, staring too long, went blind in a tower;
One sold all his manors to fight, broke through, and faltered.　10

Nights come bringing the snow; and the dead howl
Under the headlands in their windy dwelling,
Because the Adversary put too easy questions
On lonely roads.

But happy we, though no nearer each other,
See the farms lighted up the valley,
Down at the mill-shed the hammering stops
And men go home.

Noises at dawn will bring
Freedom to some, but not this peace　　　　　　　　　20
No bird can contradict, passing but is sufficient now
For something fulfilled this hour, loved or endured.

March 1928

P(28), poem 16, 31–32; AA, 89, ink autograph with 'Oxford March 1928.' at foot in Auden's hand. Variants: 10. manors . . . faltered] manor . . . trembled *AA*. 15. we] now *AA*. 16. up] all along *AA*. 20. to] for *AA*. Reprinted in *P(30)* and thereafter.

L. 8 was salvaged from 'Winter Afternoon', which Auden abandoned in late 1927 (see notes to 'Winter Afternoon' and the long poem beginning 'The sprinkler on the lawn'). The Yeatsian theme—of excellent hands turned to commonness—highlights echoes of Yeats throughout the stanza, notably from 'The Tower' and 'My House' (part 2 of 'Meditations in Time of Civil War'). Auden reused both the opening phrase, 'Taller to-day', and l. 8 in his 1928 epithalamium for Day-Lewis, 'This morning any touch is possible' (see note to 'Punchard').

Captain Ferguson (7) was a temporary master at Sedbergh who was looked down on by the other members of the staff. He admired Gabriel Carritt, and Carritt accepted, against the advice of his housemaster, his invitations to go out to meals. Ferguson later visited Carritt at Christ Church uninvited, and Carritt was rude to him in order to be rid of him. In fact, Carritt found him conceited and boring, and objected to his approaches. He never saw Ferguson again, and came to regret his unkindness, though he recalls that Auden enjoyed seeing this rival put down. Carritt recalls that to Auden, Ferguson represented the figure of the rejected homosexual, to be pitied, despised, and laughed at (conversation with Katherine Bucknell, 2 November 1992).

☐   ☐   ☐

> The spring will come,
> Not hesitate for an employer who,
> Though a fine day and every pulley running,
> Would quick lie down: nor save the wanted one
> That wounded in escaping swam the lake
> Safe to the reeds, collapsed in shallow water.
>
> You have tasted good and what is it? For you,
> Sick in the green plain, healed in the tundra, shall
> Turn westward back from your alone success
> Under a dwindling Alp to see your friends   10
> Cut down the wheat.
>
> For where are Basley who won the Ten,
> Dickon so tarted by the house,
> Thomas who kept a sparrow-hawk?
> The clock strikes; it is time to go
> The tongue ashamed, deceived by a shake of the hand.

[*Late March or early April 1928*]

P(28), poem 17, 33; AA, 90, ink autograph; S, ink autograph with pencil autograph revisions, possibly Spender's printer's copy; CI, ink autograph on Lordswood Road letterhead. Variants: 1. The] In your house came a voice—The *S*; In your house came a voice;— / The *CI*. 2. Not hesitate for an] Not hesitate for one *AA, S*; No tree stop short for one *CI.* 4. quick . . . one] all . . . man *CI.* 5. That . . . in escaping swam the lake] Who . . . in escaping swam the lake *S;* Who . . . swam across the river but *CI.* 6–7. to . . . water.// You] to . . . water. / You *S;* in . . . water. / You *CI.* 9. Turn] Come *CI.* 10. Under . . . to] Below . . . shall *CI.* 11–16. the wheat./ / For . . . / Dickon so tarted . . . / Thomas . . . /The . . . / The tongue ashamed] the wheat.//For . . . / Dickson so tasted . . . / Thomas . . . / The . . . / The tongue advanced *uncorrected copies of P(28)*; the everlasting wheat. /I wake, / Hearing you busy in the house, and sit, / The sunlight on my shoulders, unpursued. *S;* the everlasting wheat. / I woke / Hearing you busy in the house, and sat, / The sunlight on my shoulders, unpursued. *CI.* The poem was incorporated into both versions of *Paid on Both Sides* (*EA*, 414 and 15; *Plays*, 11 and 31), and reprinted thereafter.

AA appears on the verso of a folio that precedes a missing folio, and the stub of the missing folio shows the phrase 'Not hesitate', which Lawlor suggests is a marginal revision to an earlier draft of the poem (see his note in the facsimile edition, 134). The draft may have borne a date of March or April, as the poem was probably written during Easter vacation, after a visit to Auden's analyst, possibly Margaret Marshall. A note on the verso of the CI copy begins 'Had a most pleasant week with my analyst' (ALI, Lordswood Road letterhead; some unrelated correspondence shows that Auden was still in Oxford 12 March and reached Birmingham on 24 March, so this letter was probably sent after the 24th). Both the S and the CI versions are framed by lines that contextualize the contents of the poem as a dream; possibly the poem was partly inspired by Auden's analysis (see notes to 'I chose this lean country' ' "Grow thin by walking and go inland"', and 'To throw away the key and walk away'). L. 7 was first used in an early draft of 'Light strives with darkness, right with wrong' (see note to same; the cancelled Ansen version and the Isherwood fair copy both use the line). All of the poem's final stanza first appeared in 'Narcissus' (ll. 18–20, 26–27). See note to 'Narcissus' for 'the Ten', a cross-country race at Sedbergh. Auden went round the course in December 1927 with Gabriel Carritt and a boy named Wallace, but he had known about it before this.

□ □ □

The summer quickens grass
Scatters its promises
To you and me no less,
Though neither can compel.

The wish to last the year,
The longest look to live,
The urgent word survive
The movement of the air.

But loving now, let none
Think of divided days   10
When we shall choose from ways,
All of them evil, one.

Look on with stricter brows
The sacked and burning town,
The ice-sheet moving down,
The fall of an old house.

April 1928

P(28), poem 18, 34; AA, 93, ink autograph with substantial ink and and pencil auto-
graph revisions and with 'Harborne. April 1928.' at foot in Auden's hand; CI, ink auto-
graph on the verso of a letter with '42 Lordswood Rd.' at the top in Auden's hand.
Variants: In place of stanza 1, CI has two stanzas as follows:

There is a brilliant grass
A cover in the wood
And many seek the good
Promised to them and us

Day after day is well,
Hearing you speak; your eye
Meets mine, kind with a lie:
For neither can compel.

These stanzas are also among the cancelled attempts in the Ansen notebook. 7. word]
could *uncorrected copies of P(28)*. 9. loving] living *uncorrected copies of P(28)*. The poem was
incorporated, with a revised first line, into both versions of *Paid on Both Sides* (*EA*, 413–
14 and 14; *Plays*, 10 and 30) and reprinted thereafter.

□   □   □

'Grow thin by walking and go inland'
He told himself, as the unmended road
Climbed higher and he left the birds behind.
Rock-shadows lay unmoving and he crossed them,
His long stride brought him to the pass by noon
Where he found shelter from the wind until
The easy four o'clock descent he made
Following a growing stream and passing no one
Though one, nearer all day, turned suddenly
And left a clear path downhill to the station.   10
The line ran into cuttings either way,
Iron up valleys to a hidden village.
There were two trains. He could return, or go
Further, and learn some native ignorance,
No case from Belgium to explain it by.

'No need. Love is not there,' he said, for eyes
Looked outward only, and he chose his train.
Soon town lights welcomed him, and many people
To lie about the cost of a night's lodging:
Later he fell asleep, proud of his day.   20

April 1928

CI, ink autograph on Christ Church letterhead watermarked 'Crown Bond'; AA, 95, ink autograph, entirely cancelled, with 'Oxford. April 1928' at foot in Auden's hand. I have not recorded variants from the cancelled version, which can be seen in the published facsimile of the Ansen notebook. Printed in *Oxford Poetry* 1, no. 3 (Spring 1984): 93–94.

L. 15 may refer to a case history or anecdote recounted to Auden by his analyst, who possibly practiced in Spa, Belgium, during the summers; see notes to 'I chose this lean country', 'The spring will come', and 'To throw away the key and walk away'. Auden intensively quarried this piece for the poem beginning 'To throw away the key and walk away' printed in *P(28)*, and l. 6 reappeared in the 1929 poem beginning 'Under boughs between our tentative endearments' (*EA*, 29).

□   □   □

Some say that handsome raider still at large,
A terror to the Marches, in truth is love
And we must listen for such messengers
To tell us daily—'To-day a saint came blessing
The huts;'—'Seen lately in the provinces
Reading behind a tree and people passing.'
But love returns;
At once all heads are turned this way, and love
Calls order—silenced the angry sons—
Steps forward, greets, repeats what he has heard   10
And seen, feature for feature, word for word.

[April or May 1928]

P(28), poem 19, 35; AA, 96, ink autograph; Gavin Ewart, ink autograph; CI, ink autograph on Christ Church letterhead watermarked 'Crown Bond'. Variants: 2. love] you; *Ewart, CI*. 3–4. for such messengers / To tell us daily—'To-day] to what these allege, / Worried for all dreamt badly. Messages / Come daily in 'To day *Ewart*; to what these allege, / Snatch at, believe whatever may come through, / Worried, for all dreamt badly. Messages / Pour daily in—'To-day *CI*. 6–7. passing.' / But love returns;] passing.' / / But love returns *AA*; passing. / But now as uproar threatens, you return: *Ewart*; passing'—./ / So rumours tantalise, easy to prove, / But now as uproar threatens, love returns: *CI*. 8–9. and love / Calls] and you / Call *Ewart*. 10. Steps . . . , greets, repeats . . . he has] Step . . . , greet, repeat . . . you have *Ewart*. The poem was revised and incorporated into both versions of *Paid on Both Sides* (*EA*, 413 and 14; *Plays*, 9 and 29–30) and reprinted thereafter. The Ewart manuscript was reproduced in facsimile in *The Review*, nos. 11–12 [1964]: 82. Stephen Spender gave it to Ewart in 1933 or 1934; at present it is mislaid.

AA is written on the verso of the same folio as ' "Grow thin by walking and go inland"'; it faces a folio torn out from the notebook but whose stub bears the words 'At on'. Lawlor suggests this is a revision surviving from an earlier draft of the poem (cp. l. 8; see his note in the facsimile edition, p. 134). The draft would almost certainly have borne a date, probably April or May as suggested above. Apparently Auden wrote no poetry leading up to his final Honour School in June and for a time afterwards. There is a gap in the notebook until July.

□ □ □

Often the man, alone shut, shall consider
The killings in old winters, death of friends,
Sitting with stranger shall expect no good.

There was no food in the assaulted city
Men spoke at corners, asking for news, saw
Outside the watchfires of a stronger army.

Spring came urging to ships, a casting-off
But one would stay, vengeance not done; it seemed
Doubtful to them that they should meet again.

Fording in the cool of the day, they rode   10
To meet at crossroads when the year was over.
Dead is Brody. Such a man was Morl.

I will say this, not falsely: I have seen
The just and the unjust die in the day.
All, willing or not; and some were willing.

July 1928

AA, 101, ink autograph with 'Hampstead. July 1928.' at foot in Auden's hand. This poem was incorporated, with slight revisions, into the first version of *Paid on Both Sides* (*EA*, 411; *Plays*, 7), and later a four-stanza version, omitting stanza 2, was incorporated into the second version of *Paid on Both Sides* (*EA*, 5; *Plays*, 19) and reprinted thereafter.

John Fuller has suggested a comparison between the elegiac tone of this poem and poems in Old English, especially the opening of 'The Wanderer' (Fuller, 18). Also, see Patrick Lawlor's note (Lawlor, 135) for a comparison in a doctoral thesis by Robert Horace Boyer with *Beowulf* ('Anglo-Saxon and Middle English Influences in the Poetry of W. H. Auden', University of Pennsylvania, 1969).

□   □   □

To throw away the key and walk away
Not abrupt exile, the neighbours asking why
But following a line with left and right,
An altered gradient at another rate
Learns more than maps upon the whitewashed wall,
A hand put up to ask, and makes us well
Without confession of the ill. All pasts
Are single old past now although some posts
Are forwarded, held, looking on a new view.
The future shall fulfill a surer vow,   10
Not smiling at Queen over the glass rim,
Not making gunpowder in the top room,
Not swooping at the surface still like gulls,
But with prolonged drowning shall develop gills.

But these are still to tempt; areas not seen
Because of blizzards or an erring sign
When guessed-at wonders would be worth alleging,
And lies about the cost of a night's lodging
Travellers may meet at inns but not attach.
They sleep one night together, not asked to touch,   20
Receive no normal welcome, not the pressed lip,
Children to lift, not the assuaging lap;
Crossing the pass, descend the growing stream,
Too tired to hear except the pulse's strum,
Reach villages to ask for a bed in
Rocks shutting out the sky, the old life done.

August 1928

P(28), poem 20, 36–37; AA, 103, ink autograph with ink and pencil autograph revisions and with 'Spa. August 1928' at foot in Auden's hand. Variants: 6. A] The *AA*. 7. ill. All] ill. Base to wind / It may examine but cannot unwind / Bandage of flesh nor disguise the bane / Which has for some time now attacked the bone— / Without a set smile for the guest. All *AA*. 9. forwarded, held, looking] forwarded and reproduce the tang /Important once on the tip of the tongue, / Held in the hand and looking *AA*. 12–13. Not . . . top room / Not swooping] Nor . . . top-room / Not promised to this, not to that. [illegible] shall increase, / Travelling up local lines shall come across / A variation on the Dancing Boy / No case from Belgium to explain it by: Not swooping *AA*. 15. these] there *AA*. 17. When] Whose *AA*. 19. attach] attack *uncorrected copies of P(28)*. The poem was incorporated into *Paid on Both Sides* with slight changes and reprinted thereafter (*EA*, 12; *Plays*, 27–28).

In a letter written apparently in August 1928 to his Oxford friend David Ayerst, Auden mentioned spending three weeks in Spa, Belgium, 'staying with a psychologist' (quoted in Carpenter, 82, and *Early Auden*, 54); some unrelated correspondence suggests he returned from Spa about 17 August, so he must have begun his visit there during the third week of July. This poem draws heavily on the abandoned April poem beginning "Grow thin by walking and go inland", which mentions Belgium, perhaps alluding to a story his analyst told him about Belgium (see notes to 'The spring will come' ' "Grow thin by walking and go inland" ', and 'I chose this lean country'). Auden may have been undergoing further analysis, perhaps with Margaret Marshall, or with someone else. Margaret Marshall may have been a follower of Emile Coué (1857–1926); Coué was not a psychoanalyst at all, but a French chemist with a charismatic personality who promoted, as the title of one of his books makes clear, *Self-mastery Through Conscious Auto-suggestion* (London, 1922). The subject could cure himself or herself by surrendering the will to conscious positive suggestions; one regime was to repeat twenty times every morning and every night, 'Every day, in every way, I am getting better and better.' The testimony of his disciples suggests that Coué's work might be compared to that of Dale Carnegie or est; his method could improve the speaking voice, help with stammers, improve muscle control, and generally increase self-confidence. It gave the benefits of hypnosis, but self-administered and without the trance. Isherwood mentions auto-suggestion in *All the Conspirators* (London, 1928); his character Victor Page recalls in a passage of internal monologue: 'I once had to go to a lecture in the Parish Hall. Some worthy on Auto-Suggestion. There's a good deal in it. Useful when you're listening to Sermons' (117). Perhaps Margaret Marshall counselled Auden simply to give up the past and to imagine the future more successfully in order to achieve the self-change he desired. This is precisely the argument the poem is making; indeed, the poem may be in part a rejection of the conventional analytic method, since it proposes in its opening lines something like a change of course rather than 'confession of the ill' (7). However, it does not indicate that Auden had given up hope of self-change through psychological means, and he continued to search for a psychological cure for his personal unhappiness. The poem's resigned tone may also derive from the likelihood that Auden would by now have received the rather disappointing results of a third-class degree in his final Honour School.

John Fuller has compared l. 3 to 'But left and right alternately / Is consonant with History' in Auden's 1940 poem beginning 'Anthropos apteros for days' (see the notes to *New Year Letter*, 155; this poem was later published as 'The Maze', *CP*, 303; Fuller, 262); the poems share similar concerns. Monroe Spears has suggested that ll. 13–14 refer to the passage in Conrad's *Lord Jim* describing immersion in 'the destructive element' *The Poetry of W. H. Auden: The Disenchanted Island* (New York, 1963), 17.

□ □ □

The Spring unsettles sleeping partnerships:
Foundries improve upon their process, and shops
Open a further wing, on credit till
The winter. In summer boys grow tall
With running races on the frothwet sand;
War is declared there, here a treaty signed,
Here a scrum breaks up like a bomb, there troops
Deploy like birds. But coming Autumn trips
Proudest: those gears which ran in oil for week
By week, needing no look, now will not work,   10
Those manors mortgaged twice to pay for love
Go to another.
                          O how shall man live
Whose thought is born, child of one farcical night,
To find him old? The body warm but not
By choice, he dreams of folk in dancing bunches
And tart wine spilt on home-made benches
Where learns—one drawn apart—a secret will
Restore the dead, but comes thence to a wall;
Outside on frozen soil lie armies killed   20
Who seem familiar but they are cold.
Now the most solid wish he tries to keep
His hands show through; he never will look up,
Say 'I am good'. On him misfortune falls
More than enough: better to be where fools
And wise are unmarked, where none stand or sit,
The out-of-sight, too deep for shafts.

August 1928

CI, ink autograph on 'H. P. Pope / Stationers Printers / Birmingham'; AA, 117, ink autograph with 'Harborne August 1928' at foot in Auden's hand. Variants: 5. frothwet] wetted *AA*. 14. Whose thought is] His thought *AA*. 15. The body warm] He always breathes *AA*. 16. in dancing] dancing in *AA*. 17. And] Of *AA*. 18. learns . . . apart] hears . . . aside *AA*. 19. thence] then *AA*. 24. Say 'I am good'] Now feeling good *AA*. The poem was later revised and incorporated into *Paid on Both Sides* (*EA*, 7–8; *Plays*, 21–22).
    On the verso of the Isherwood manuscript is a letter telling Isherwood that *Paid on Both Sides* will not be performed at McElwee's house: 'They refuse to do the play, as they

say the village wont stand it.' Nonetheless Auden planned to spend the first two weeks of September with McElwee at Tapscott, and invited Isherwood to join him there (ALS, probably from Harborne, August 1928).

The slant rhymes and military theme of this poem are borrowed from Wilfred Owen's 'Strange Meeting', and Auden's final line echoes a line in Owen's poem: 'Even with truths that lie too deep for taint'. (Owen was echoing the final line of Wordsworth's Immortality Ode, 'Thoughts that do often lie too deep for tears.')

□   □   □

No, not from this life, not from this life is any
To keep; sleep, day and play would not help there,
Dangerous to new ghost; new ghost learns from many,
Learns from old termers what death is, where.

Who's jealous of his latest company,
Or kept back stammering at the word death,
Scared as by summer lightning, now that he,
Life's painful romping over, is out of breath?

Receive one, earth, who comes to death from life
Grateful as ever girl looks from ship-rails,   10
Rescued in Africa returns a wife
To his ancestral property in Wales.

September 1928

CI, ink autograph; AA, 119, ink autograph, with 'Tapscott Sept 1928' at foot in Auden's hand. In AA the third stanza is cancelled and a revised version of the whole poem is written out underneath, with 'Revised Dec 1928 Berlin' at the foot, again in Auden's hand. (The Berlin version may be found in the published facsimile of the Ansen notebook.) Auden revised the poem further before incorporating it into *Paid on Both Sides* (*EA*, 2; *Plays*, 15).

The early version appears to be the last poem Auden wrote before leaving England for Berlin in October 1928. He was staying with William McElwee's family at their home in Tapscott, Somerset, during the first two weeks of September. The third stanza, cancelled in AA, was resurrected in part 2 of the 1929 sequence beginning 'It was Easter as I walked in the public gardens' (*EA*, 38; *CP*, 47).

APPENDIX

Rotation

BY MYSTAN BAUDOM

In effect, the planets
Continually satirize themselves.

Fronted like Mozart;
They put it on logs and it rolled
At once he was a god.
When I was young, I found Hooke's Law
Apotheosis was childish then, now more sublime.

We walked together to the pithead.
Unhastily up and over
As the cage dropped: 10
'Darling, I'm so giddy;' she grasped my hand.
The page turned over, more crotchets on the
    other side.

He drew in sand, but forced the sky to answer—
Stupidly the hour glass leaked.
Still on, div I, rot I, curl I*
Between the thumb and forefinger
Making kinks in space.

The martyr, butterfly-broken;
Now the sparks fly outward:
'This isn't real.' I hugged her   20
Lacking love. All my love a twist in the mind,
Doubling infinity.

*—The contracted form of three differential functions.

[*November? 1926*]

The Oxford University Review 2, no. 6 (25 November 1926): 210.

This parody was written by someone intimately familiar with Auden's work in the autumn of 1926; it borrows from both published and unpublished poems. The author may have been Isherwood. In a letter sent to Isherwood, probably in January 1927, Auden wrote, 'Thank you for your letter and the Parody which is now an important part of my world picture' (ALS, Lordswood Road letterhead). Possibly this refers to 'Rotation', although Auden might have been expected to have commented sooner to Isherwood on the poem. Another, perhaps more likely, author for 'Rotation' is Tom Driberg.

Intriguingly, l. 7 appears in an abandoned draft of the poem beginning 'Out of sight assuredly, not out of mind', which Auden wrote in late May or June 1927, six to seven months after the parody was published; see p. 196. Thus, either the author of 'Rotation' was privy to another earlier poem or draft, now lost, in which Auden had previously used this line, or Auden liked the line enough to borrow it from his parodist. (If his letter to Isherwood *does* refer to 'Rotation', it may confirm the latter possibility, as Auden says the parody has become part of his 'world picture'.) The other poems to which 'Rotation' explicitly refers were probably written in the autumn of 1926 or earlier. L. 12 draws on 'The Happy Tree' (23–24), though the actual phrase used in the parody, 'The page turned over', does not appear in any surviving copy of that poem, but only in an abandoned draft of the 1927 poem 'The four sat on in the bare room', in which Auden reused in an altered form the line from 'The Happy Tree'. Again, Auden may already have been circulating this version of the line in the autumn of 1926, even though no evidence survives to confirm this, or possibly he tried out the parodist's phrasing in his own later poem.

Ll 13–15 are taken from 'The Megalopsych', part 4, stanza 1, suggesting that this part of 'The Megalopsych', or at least some version of it, had been written before 25 November 1926—unless Auden borrowed these lines as well from the parody, an idea that begins to stretch credulity. Ll. 8–10 are perhaps meant to reflect the tone and setting of stanza 2 in 'The Evolution of the Dragon', or perhaps of 'Consequences'. The dialogue of the final stanza and the pedantic footnote also seem to refer to 'Consequences'.

Possibly 'Rotation' is by Auden himself. As a prank it has perhaps too much sting for this to make sense, unless Auden wrote and submitted the poem to *The Oxford University Review* in full seriousness, only to have the editors make a joke of him and his work by parodying his name. It is in any case remarkable that after only a year in Oxford, Auden's poetic reputation was both high enough and distinctive enough to inspire such a piece and to make it worth publishing.

INDEX

This index lists poem titles (in large and small capitals), first lines, and selected people and places mentioned in the poems, notes, and introductory material. For poems by Auden printed in this edition, page numbers indicate the page on which the poem begins; where more than one page number occurs, bold numerals point to the text of the poem.